A LANTE... ...N
THE STERN

LIVERPOOL'S SEAFARING HERITAGE

THE LIVERPOOL MASTER MARINERS' CLUB

Volume One
The Early Years

Edited by

Bob Evans

This book is dedicated to my comrades in the
Liverpool Master Mariners' Club
For friendship over half a century.

Previous books by Bob Evans:

A Dog Collar in the Docks
Mersey Mariners
The Way to Liverpool
The Training Ships of Liverpool
H.M.S. Eaglet
The Indefatigable
The Mersey Mission to Seamen

First Published 2007 by Countyvise Limited,
14 Appin Road, Birkenhead, Wirral CH41 9HH.

British Library Cataloguing in Publication Data.
A catalogue record for this book is available from the British Library.

ISBN 978 1 901231 96 0

The first thought about a title for this book was 'The Seadogs of Liverpool', but sense prevailed as these anthologies stretch across the world and a wider title was required. As ever, Captain Graeme Cubbin produced what was necessary. If seafarers can produce a 'wake', the 'light on the stern' will uncover their stories ... convoluted, but apt!

If men could learn from history, what
lessons it might teach us!
But passion and party blind our eyes,
and the light, which experience gives
Is a Lantern on the Stern
Which shines only on the waves behind us.

Samuel Taylor Coleridge

INTERNATIONAL REGULATIONS
FOR PREVENTING COLLISION AT SEA
(1938 Edition)

Article 10.
STERN LIGHTS

The white light required to be shown by this Article may be fixed and carried in a lantern, but in such case the lantern should be so constructed, fitted and screened that it shall throw an unbroken light over an arc of the horizon of 12 points of the compass, viz., for 6 points from right aft on each side of the vessel so as to be visible at distance of at least a mile. Such light to be carried as nearly practicable on the same level as the side lights.

Barrie Youde was a serving Liverpool Pilot from 1966 to 1988 and retired on health grounds. He at once changed careers and read law. Barrie was called to the (legal) Bar in 1990. He remains in legal practice with R. A. Wilkinson & Co., from which firm his services are retained by the United Kingdom Maritime Pilots' Association. He has published a number of books ... 'Beyond the Bar', 'Sitting on a Bollard' and 'Sitting on Another Bollard'. We happily print his poem ... 'The Light at the Stern'... with his warmest good wishes, in the hope of conveying the spirit in which it was written

THE LIGHT AT THE STERN

Attend at the stern, Mr Lamptrimmer,
Replenish and polish the light,
The followers-on, Mr Lamptrimmer,
Will all wish to have us in sight.
Attend to the light, Mr Lamptrimmer,
The weather is closing-in thick,
Attend to the light, Mr Lamptrimmer,
Be sure that you turn-up the wick.
We're a Liverpool ship, Mr Lamptrimmer,
We're one of a privileged breed.
Our fathers before, Mr Lamptrimmer,
Were looked-to by others in need.
So let us be right, Mr Lamptrimmer,
Our ancestors all taught us how;
And let it be bright, Mr Lamptrimmer,
As others may look to us now.
We'll weather the storm, Mr Lamptrimmer,
As long as we're willing to learn.
We're on watch tonight, Mr Lamptrimmer,
Please look to the Light at the Stern.
God has us in sight, Mr Lamptrimmer,
Expecting no more than our best:
And Such, in due course, Mr Lamptrimmer,
Determines our ultimate rest.

Barrie Youde

Foreword

Colin Jones
President of the Merseyside Master Mariners' Club

The membership of the Club, now approaching its Diamond Jubilee, represents a broad spectrum of maritime experience. Ship Masters and Pilots, Marine Engineers and Shipping Company executives, not to mention many like myself, who left the sea to pursue careers ashore ... a diverse crew with a common bond which stems from shared experience within an industry which was not just a job, but a complete way of life.

The relentless decline of the British Merchant Fleet, which started in the sixties, means that most of the companies which formed the backbone of Liverpool shipping such as Blue Funnel, T & J Harrison, Elder Dempster, etc., are now distant memories, but the flag loyalties and memories of the men who served in these fleets and others, are still strong. Certainly there has been no shortage of material submitted by members for inclusion in this book ... incidents and accidents in war and peace, some humorous, some dramatic, but all written by men who made their business in great waters.

Who better to act as compiler and editor, than Bob Evans, an Honorary Life Member of the Club, whose name has been synonymous with the welfare of seafarers in the Mersey ports for almost half a Century.

Captain Roland Owens
Master of the Merseyside Master Mariners' Club

It is my honour to be the Master of the Merseyside Master Mariners' Club in this its 59th year and my pleasure to be able to write the Foreword to this book. Our members enjoy meeting to keep in touch with old shipmates and acquaintances and to make new friends and, of course, to 'swing the lamp'. It was felt that the experiences of the members represented a way of life that is fast disappearing with the decline of the Merchant Navy as we knew it and that it would be a great pity if this was allowed to go unrecorded. Canon Bob Evans, an Honorary Member, volunteered his expertise to compile, type and organise these yarns into a book of two volumes and the subsequent publication is a tribute to his experience and heroic endeavours. Here are the stories of the seafarers, some of whom have had remarkable careers and others who have had extraordinary experiences. They make a very good read.

The Master, the Chaplain and the President

Preface

For almost half a century I have been in contact with the Master Mariners' Club as Chaplain. My first connection in 1960 was with the Club-ship LANDFALL, which sat in Canning Dock opposite Kingston House, the headquarters of the Mersey Mission to Seamen. In those long past years, there were Masters who had survived the bitter experiences of the Battle of the Atlantic, the Russian Convoys and all the dangers of war at sea. They had always been in peril and their daily courage kept our nation alive. Without them we would not have survived.

My happy task was to be the Chaplain-Superintendent of the Mersey Mission to Seamen and for some years I was also the Chaplain to H.M.S. EAGLET, the Royal Navy Reserves. Even in retirement I have never lost contact. The real work of the Padre is to listen ... if only I had taken notes at the time! Seafarers are great talkers ... they call it 'swinging the lamp'.

Casually over yet another lunch I suggested to the Master Mariners that their tales ought to be recorded and that I was happy to undertake the task. The response was slow so I wrote an urgent plea ... it really worked! The intention was to produce a book of some three hundred pages. In the end there were over five hundred pages and the end-product was two volumes. I suspect that there could be another two volumes!

This is an anthology of seafaring memories. Very little editing was needed as the stories speak for themselves. In many cases I had to condense and even omit sections and for that I apologise to the contributors.

Many good folk have helped in the formation of the anthology and nothing would have been achieved without them. I did start on a list, but the books themselves must be their thanks. You are many and I thank you all. Perhaps, there could have been many more photographs ... but space was at a premium. Captain Colin Lee has 'doodled' to good effect and we had much fun uncovering designs of stern lights. The painting of the tug, BROCKLEBANK, on the back cover is one of my efforts! My sternest critics are my family ... the proof readers, coffee providers, computer buffs and tolerant listeners to my enthusiastic burblings. John and Jean Emmerson of Countyvise are understanding with their printing expertise and are good friends over many years. However, I am aware that there will ever be blemishes, mistakes, misjudgements and omissions and they can only be attributed to me with apologies.

People are unbelieving when I tell them that 95% of our trade goes by sea. We chance to live on an island! We need the seafarer.

My greatest joy is that I have shared my life with seafarers and through them I find my vision and understanding of mankind.

To them I dedicate these books.

Bob Evans,
November 2007.

THE TITLE THAT MIGHT HAVE BEEN
THE SEA-DOGS OF LIVERPOOL

The Sea-Dogs of Liverpool: Tell me about them.
Just look at a ship and let nobody doubt them,
Whose ships drew the world rather closer in thought,
Who traded in every approachable port,
Archangel to Adelaide, East unto West,
Built Liverpool into the biggest and best
In the world, for a while, not so far long ago,
Through trade, (nothing more, no great glamorous show,)
Who looked to the world and the world would look back,
And a deal would be done, trading barrel and sack:
Who smiled in the face of the poor xenophobe
And profited Liverpool, London & Globe.

The Sea-Dogs of Liverpool: Tell me about them.
Their merits are many. None ever did shout them.
Each learned as a boy in a cockleshell boat,
From his father, the paramount, "Keep it afloat."
Each grew with the basics of, "Hand, reef and steer"
As he rose to maturity, year after year,
Until he showed fitness, by trust and by laws,
And a ship would commission him: "Sir, this is yours,
To navigate, ministrate, keep it, protect it,
And run it for profit, that's why we have decked it.
Now sail it, and honour each promissory note;
And come back to Liverpool. Keep it afloat."

The Sea-Dogs of Liverpool: Tell me about them.
I've grown with them, own with them, so much about them.
Honour is mine to have sailed in their fleet:
For a pilot, a Liverpool ship 'neath his feet
Is the tallest of feelings, the top of the range,
Inheritance drawn from the Flags of Exchange.
Each Sea-Dog is human: some better, some worse;
Some heroes, some zeroes, some need a wet nurse:
But history shows that the record is sound:
Success is not gained when a ship runs aground.
The commonhold thread of each maritime note
Is, "Liverpool, Liverpool, keep it afloat."

Barrie Youde

Morning at sea

Merseyside Master Mariner's Club

Commodore Sir Bertram Hayes Hayes, K.C.M.G., D.S.O. in 1938 was the first President and the first Chairman was Captain E.A. Wood. The Club did not meet during the war and was re-established in 1946. The new President was Commander the Honourable F.H. Cripps, D.S.O., RN. The Club in its present form was founded in 1949.

President:		*Master:*
1949	Sir Burton Chadwick, Bart.	Commander The Hon. F.H. Cripps, DSO, DL
1950	Sir John R. Hobhouse, MC, JP	Capt. H.G. Dickins
1951	Capt. W.H. Coombs, CBE, RNR	Capt. H.G. Dickins
1952	Capt. W.H. Coombs, CBE. RNR	Capt. G.G. Astbury, DSC
1953	Sir Rex Hodges, JP	Capt. G.G. Astbury, DSC
1954	Sir Rex Hodges, JP	Capt. G.G. Astbury, DSC
1955	Sir Rex Hodges, JP	Capt. L.H. Des Landes
1956	Capt. G.G. Astbury, DSC	Capt. H.F. Pettit
1957	Capt. G.G. Astbury, DSC	Capt. G. Ayre, FRGS
1958	Capt. G.G. Astbury, DSC	Capt. V.E. Thomas
1959	Capt. L.H. Des Landes	W.R. Brotherton
1960	Capt. H.F. Pettit	Capt. D. Rankin, OBE
1961	Capt. G. Ayre, FRGS	D. Archibald, OBE
1962	D.Archibald, OBE	Capt. J.H. Wright, RD, RNR
1963	Capt J.H. Wright, RD, RNR	Capt. F.W. Skutil, CBE, RNN (R'td)
1964	Capt. F.W. Skutil, CBE, RNN (R'td)	Capt. J. Whitehouse, OBE
1965	Capt. J. Whitehouse, OBE	Capt. H.F. Pettit
1966	Capt. H.F. Pettit	Capt F.W. Skutil, OBE, RNN (R'td)
1967	Capt. F.W. Skutil, CBE, RNN (R'td)	
1968	Capt. F.W. Skutil, CBE, RNN (R'td)	J.D. Home, TD
1969	J.D. Home, TD	J. McKendrick
1970	J. McKendrick	N.P. Brooke
1971	N.P. Brooke	E.A. Jenkins, OBE
1972	N.P. Brooke	E.A. Jenkins, OBE
1973	E.A. Jenkins, OBE	E.P. Moss
1974	E.A. Jenkins, OBE	E.P. Moss
1975	E.P. Moss	J. Morton
1976	E.P. Moss	J. Morton

President:		*Master:*
1977	J. Morton	Capt. A.J. Braund
1978	J. Morton	Capt. A.J. Braund
1979	Capt. A.J. Braund	W.H. Bell
1980	Capt. A.J. Braund	W.H. Bell
1981	W.H. Bell	J. McKendrick
1982	J. McKendrick	W.H. Higgins
1983	W.H. Higgins	Capt. L.W. Roberts
1984	Capt. L.W. Roberts	Capt. R.H. Baldwin
1985	Capt. R.H. Baldwin	Capt. S.M. Threlkeld
1986	Capt. S.M. Threlkeld	Capt. J.P. Brand
1987	Capt. J.P. Brand	F. Whitehurst
1988	F. Whitehurst	Capt. M.H.D. Embleton
1989	Capt. M.H.D. Embleton	Capt. D.M. Belk
1990	Capt. D.M. Belk	Capt. W. Taylor
1991	Capt. W. Taylor	Capt. T.C. Mullings
1992	Capt. T.C. Mullings	Capt. G.F. Kay
1993	Capt. G.F. Kay	Capt. M.A. McClory
1994	J. Blaasse	Capt. M.A. McClory
1995	A.E. Proffit	Capt. A.G. Cruickshank
1996	T.H. Smith	Capt. G.M. Bryson
1997	E.G. John, MBE	Capt. D.A. Watt
1998	J. McKendrick	Capt. J.F. Scrivens
1999	P. Gannicliffe	Capt. M.D.R. Jones
2000	P.J.H. Tebay	Capt. P.H. Daniel
2001	G.R. Davies	Capt. B. Luke
2002	L. Ensor	Capt. G.M. Taylor
2003	E. Dickinson	Capt. G.M. Taylor
2004	W.F.B. Wood	Capt. D.N.B. Nutman
2005	D.L. Large	Capt. D.H. Allen
2006	Capt. D.l. Drummond	Capt. M.P. Bestwick
2007	C.E. Jones Esq.	Capt. R. Owens

12

Volume One Contents

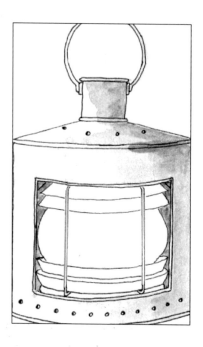

Captain Tony Braund
Master Mariner

Most seafarers are good talkers and good listeners, enjoying nothing better than the company of old friends … 'swinging the lamp'. Captain Tony Braund reminds us all that this exercise often blends sad thoughts with much pleasure. Tony is one of the senior Club members and his memories cover almost all of our history … I really have known him for ever! In fact, Tony is our oldest surviving Master and President and deserves to open the batting.

THE FALKLANDS

At school in Totnes many years ago a youngish B.A. taught us to note and remember quotations in order to widen the stunted growth of our Devonshire vocabulary. Then off I went to sea, where any remaining academic dreams were rapidly swamped by Thomas Grey and his ditty about Latitude, Longitude, Log, Lead and Lookout. But, seemingly there remained a message from some literary gentleman claiming that the great art of life was to have as many pleasant thoughts as possible.

My most pleasant memories of our Club seem to date back over the difficult gap years between Landfall and the Marina which we survived under the guidance of three wise men ... Eric Moss, Bill Skutil and Joe McKendrick. Thanks to the Padre Bob we were given hospitality, food and shelter at Kingston House where Harry Wilde headed a daily lunch group which gathered pace and popularity. But then came disappointment at the Atlantic Newsroom before the comfort and good humour enjoyed by a larger attendance at the Lyceum. Thinking back over those years, I recall one rather shy guest who attended a casual lunch at Kingston House, my friend Ian North, Master of ATLANTIC CONVEYOR.

After leaving Bullard King during 1951, Ian had joined Port Line where he was rapidly accepted as a promising member of the family. Some years later having told his father, a retired Headmaster, that his next voyage would be in command, he was advised to read 'The Art of Leadership' by Captain Roskill, R.N. This book opens with a Carlyle quotation, 'At all times a man who would do faithfully must believe firmly', and this Ian did. A member of the M.M.S.A. Council, a Liveryman of the Honourable Company and a Founder Member of the Nautical Institute, he was later portrayed by Michael Grey of 'Fairplay' as having a perception of worldwide shipping that was far out of the ordinary and that his practical good sense shone out like a beacon. Unfortunately a few weeks after his visit to the Club, ATLANTIC CONVEYOR was requisitioned for the Falklands Task Force and many of us unexpectedly came face to face with a new meaning for that word STUFT ... Ships Taken Up From Trade.

RANGATIRA was built on the Tyne for the New Zealand overnight passenger/vehicle ferry service between Wellington and Lyttelton which was unexpectedly discontinued. Following her return to the U.K., she was used as an accommodation ship at both Loch Kishorn and Sullom Voe before lay-up in the River Fal. She became the first of two ex-ferries accepted by the M.O.D. for the carriage of troops in the South Atlantic which

B.S.S.M. managed. The necessary rapid refit commenced at Devonport Naval Dockyard and it was during a return drive to Merseyside that I heard on my car radio the sad news of H.M.S. COVENTRY and ATLANTIC CONVEYOR.

COVENTRY was a Type 42 destroyer built at Camell Lairds and, from the turret windows behind my desk on the fifth floor of Albion House, I had seen her launch, various moves in the river and departure. My wife, Vera, and I were privileged to attend a commissioning party; it was a powerful vessel and the pride of a highly competent ship's company.

ATLANTIC CONVEYOR joined with the Carrier Battle Group on the 19th May, 1982, and six days later was struck by an Exocet missile, causing considerable damage and fire. Every effort was made to save the vessel, but finally the order was given to abandon. Five M.N. crew members, three members of the R.F.A. and three Service personnel lost their lives together with Captain North, the last to leave his ship, but sadly Ian failed to retain the grasp and desperate efforts made by a Royal Marine on a small life float. The Queen approved the posthumous award of the Distinguished Service Cross for Captain Ian North.

A wise man claimed that to understand the world and to like it are two things not easily reconciled ... and he was so right. Way back in 1938, I was the Senior Apprentice aboard a vessel homeward-bound from Auckland; a couple of days after rounding the Horn we boys were working together in and around the Starboard side lifeboats ... young Jimmy, a New Zealander, making his first voyage and my friend Colin, a South African, ex-Cadetship H.M.S. WORCESTER, who had sailed with me for the past eighteen months. Lots of fun and banter on that cold but dry day and then, just before lunch, Colin suddenly slipped or tripped and tumbled over the side. I could see his head and shoulders across the wake as we swung into a turning circle ... then he was gone.

Most mornings of the week my dog and I walk across Thurstaston Common, Royden Park or the Heswall Dales. It is surprising how easily the mind can fall into step and conversation with friends no longer with us. Yes, your oldest surviving past Master and President still enjoys the many pleasant thoughts of his life at sea, the ships and those who sailed in them ... but not those cold, cruel waters of the South Atlantic.

Captain Tony Braund recalls another memory of pre-war days at sea. He was a mere lad at the time ... just sixteen years and a bit.

A VERY BRIEF ENCOUNTER

As a youngster living in a West Country fishing port, I grew up with sounds from a not-too-distant yard building a variety of wooden craft. Industrial noises seemed less harsh in those days and the clink-clank-rattle of caulking irons was perfectly acceptable. Later, at sea, I soon learned to hate the brutal cacophony of chipping hammers attacking steel decks, but necessary noises, although tiresome, are in no way as frightening as the modern day sudden thunder as a low-flying jet screams overhead. Words such as 'unexpected' and 'violent' spring to mind.

Outward bound from London in the autumn of 1936, the second voyage of my Apprenticeship, we experienced reduced visibility down Channel and fog in the area the Met. Office now refers to as Plymouth. We lads were assisting the Bridge Watch and when I turned out at four the next morning the visibility had improved and was estimated as being not less than three miles. Our engines had been increased to near normal service speed.

I had been posted on the Starboard wing and just after

five o'clock the crow's nest look out struck three bells ... 'vessel right ahead' ... and almost immediately I heard the calm, competent voice of the Second Officer answering 'Fine to Starboard'. Within seconds our whistle was sounding the mandatory fog signal, the Master was back on the Bridge and our engines reduced to a safe speed.

I had become conscious of an increasing haze around our navigation lights and then suddenly just to starboard of our forecastle a vague loom of light transformed into a smudge of colour with navigation lights.

With a prolonged warning blast of her whistle there emerged a great clipper, bow flared up to a turtle backed fore-part, a Bridge and three majestic funnels. At a speed of possibly twenty knots and at a distance of maybe two or three cables, 1029 feet of NORMANDIE, displacing some 64,000 tons and carrying a compliment of passengers and crew totalling 3,000 persons, swept past in a fusion of power, light and sound, punctuated by thunderous explosions as high pressure steam from her main engine boilers exhausted into the atmosphere. Almost as rapidly this great shape, safely past, dissolved from sight in our wake.

Fortunately, the visibility rapidly improved with the early signs of dawn; the Master went below, our two four-cylinder Doxfords returned to normal service speed, and peace returned to the Bridge limits. Just the sounds of the Quartermaster's helm movements, the tick of the Sperry steering repeater and our Second Officer, also a West Countryman, chanting quietly to himself as was his habit, 'What a friend we have in Jesus'.

In my book, 'One Hundred and Fifty Years of the Mersey Mission to Seafarers', I told the story of the death of a young seafarer and with no apology here it is again.

A casual lunchtime conversation with Captain Tony Braund, at yet another Master Mariners' 'do' at the Liverpool Marina, a chance remark about ships' gangways, all this produced an unwanted floodtide of tragic memories. Captain Braund had been the Port Operations Superintendent at the time for Blue Star, Port Line Management.

Let Tony recall our memories.

In the early summer of 1970, Robert, a promising New Zealand lad from Pukerua Bay, was serving as an Apprentice aboard one of Port Line's modern reefer ships discharging at the Alexandra Dock. One evening he joined a small group of Cadets on a bulk sugar carrier berthed in the Canada Dock ... just a gathering of cheerful friends, who left to return to their own vessels at a very reasonable hour.

Unfortunately, Robert, leading the way, tripped on the lower step of the bulker's gangway and fell into the darkness of the water between the counter and the dock wall.

Immediately, two lads following dived in to find him and the shouting and commotion quickly attracted Dock staff and crew members returning to this and other vessels. After some little time, the Ship's Officers and Dock Police hauled six or more rescuers from the dock. The last two had been clinging to an exposed tip of the propeller blade, but sadly Robert had not been sighted.

After a distressing wait of more than a week, the body was retrieved, identified and following a post-mortem, Robert, who had died of a badly fractured skull, was finally allowed a peaceful funeral.

The only family relative able to attend this service, held at Thornton Crematorium, Sefton, was a cousin of Robert's father. Padre Bob Evans, who had been such a great help during this tragic period, officiated. On his suggestion I was asked to read the lesson, taken from the New English Bible, Romans 8, 31 to the end.

'Nothing in all creation can separate us from the love of God.'

This passage was mentioned in a letter from New Zealand a few weeks later in which the family spoke of the consolation they received from these encouraging words.

Thirty-five years later, Tony and I had remembered as we sat quietly together at lunch … our memories never really fade.

Thank you, Tony, for sharing your thoughts.

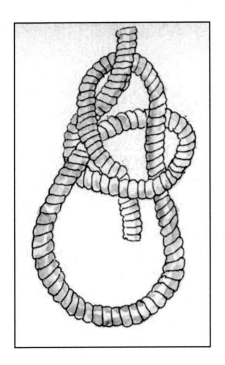

Captain John Philip Brand
Master Mariner

Captain John Philip Brand at the age of fourteen joined a holiday party of some thirty boys from Birkenhead Park High School in June 1934 ... the British India Steam Navigation Company ran cruises to the Norwegian Fjords, Copenhagen and Holland. At the vast cost of £12 young Philip Brand had acquired a taste for the sea.

THE BEGINNING

An interview with Ellerman Hall Line in Castle Buildings at the foot of Water Street on the Strand was successful. The Masters of the ships to which I was attached were to ensure that my education, in matters such as seamanship, was vigorously progressed. In return for this I was to be attentive at all times to the Master's commands, to serve energetically the welfare of the ship in which I sailed and that on no account was I to frequent taverns, ale houses or houses of ill repute unless this was on my Master's business. This intrigued me greatly to know just what would be my Master's business in such places as herein described. I am sorry to say I never really found out.

John was to join THE CITY OF BRISTOL in the port of Birkenhead on the 27th September, 1934. Captain Brand has written a lively and detailed account of those early years.

INDIA AT LAST

The Bombay waterfront, an engrossing sight I just cannot take my eyes off. The first building, that comes to my attention is, what I am advised by the Quartermaster on watch with me on the Bridge, the Gateway of India. It was erected for the Delhi Durbar in 1906 and as where all the dignitaries from abroad would land from their ships.

Dusk is setting in as it does so early in these eastern ports and the skyline of Bombay is silhouetted against the setting sun to the westward, presenting a very impressive spectacle. But sadly, I have to learn that distance lends enchantment. I am accompanied by an Irish Quartermaster by the name of Milliken who is sharing my anchor watch on the Bridge. As I am watching the spectacle of the sun setting behind and to the westward of Bombay, there is a sudden eruption of light from a much larger building immediately behind the wonderfully-illuminated Gateway of India. The Quartermaster sees my intense interest in the sight lying before me and comes over with the intention of giving me a bit of an education. "That, young feller, is the Taj Mahal". I pondered this information for a moment or two before saying, rather tentatively, that I always understood that the Taj Mahal was in a place called Agra somewhere near Delhi. "Young man, I am telling you that is the Taj Mahal and don't forget it". I was still not very happy with this piece of information and when the Chief Officer came on the Bridge, I cornered him and asked him to tell me what this building was. He said it was the most expensive pub in India and advised me to keep well away from it. He said it had nothing to do with the Taj Mahal I had in mind, which was indeed the shrine erected in Agra by one of the noble emperors, Shah Jehan in commemoration of his wife. I thought this sounded more in conformity with what I had always understood about the Taj Mahal, for even in those days I was very much engrossed in history, particularly of the Far East, and indeed have remained so ever since.

I talked to the Chief Officer for a while and was delighted to learn that the next morning we would have the day off to have a quick tour of Bombay with one of the Officers, which I thought was extremely good. I had some difficulty in getting to sleep that night as I could just not get my mind away from what I might expect to see the next day.

I was smartly out of bed the following morning to find, somewhat to my surprise, that the ship during the course of the night had berthed in the main Bombay dock without the assistance of we two Apprentices to ensure the ship's safe berthing. At the foot of the gangway, there lay what appeared to be quite a magnificent four-seater coach drawn by some poor dejected looking animal which I believed to be a horse. The poor creature did not appear to have eaten for many weeks and I did not feel our prospects were very good if they were to depend upon the poor animal assigned to the job of taking us on a tour of Bombay. So far as I can recall at this distance in time, motor cars were fairly rare in Bombay and the most popular means of transport was what we were now embarking in, known as a gharry. A less pretentious mode of travel was by rickshaw.

In due course we set off and toured the business area of Bombay ... the Taj Mahal Hotel, though we did not venture in, not with a mere 10 rupees in our pockets. Victoria railway station and Greens Hotel were all quite magnificent buildings though strangely interspersed with areas of the utmost degradation which had been converted into homes in the form of cardboard huts and heaven knows what and where all sorts of household duties were being performed on the pavement. A gentleman having a bath at a fire hydrant; a lady a bit further along cooking breakfast for someone at this time of day, again on the kerbside. Everywhere one went in Bombay one seemed to be eternally assailed by the rather beguiling smells of cooking, but sadly we were strictly reprimanded by the Second Officer to avoid this alfresco type of meal at all costs. Stalls sold fruit, beautiful melons ready-cut into slices, pineapples ready-peeled, awaiting consumption, but I did notice that there were a lot of flies about and I had to support the Second Officer's opinion that we would all die of cholera if we were to enter into the delights of that which was on offer.

Eventually, having covered the centre of the city, we set out on a journey to what was known as Malabar Hill. This lay a mile or two to the north of Bombay and we were informed that it was the sacred place of the Parsees. Here were the Parsee Towers of Silence where their dead were consigned. The poor old nag laboured up to the top of Malabar Hill and I noticed that this part was very heavily overgrown with large forest trees. Within these trees were three very large buildings, circular in shape, and in these were the Towers of Silence. The trees hereabout were absolutely full of the most repulsive looking birds known as Indian vultures, who were sitting in them patiently waiting for their next meal. As I remember these three Towers of Silence, one was confined to those who had died a natural death, one to those who had died of disease and the third for those who had died from physical violence. Although we were not allowed in the towers themselves as they were wholly sacred to the Parsee sect, we were given to understand that at the top of each tower there was a grating, or should I say three concentric gratings; the outer one being the largest was for the disposal of men, the next inner for the disposal of women and the innermost grating, the smallest, for the children.

We returned on board by about 3 o'clock in the afternoon when I observed that the ship was now engaged in coaling and I stood on the deck for some while watching the progress. Great baulks of timber had been laid from the shore up to the topmost deck of the ship. Hordes of small creatures seemed to be scampering up one baulk to the deck, where they dumped a basket of coal from their heads into a hatchway and into the bunkers and descending via another baulk, so there was a continuous stream of coal going into the ship. I stood looking at these creatures who were fairly heavily clothed, presumably to keep the coal dust off them as far as was possible. To my horror I realised that they were all women and they were watched over by a number of supervisors equipped with long willowy canes which they were not loathe to use on anyone who was holding up the job by reason of her slowness.

I next sauntered down into the bunker space to find out just where all this coal was going. It was of course going down into the main bunkers, but in the upper decks of the bunker spaces I was horrified to find a little area which had been screened off in the corner of the deck. When looking round the corners of the screens, I realised this was the creche. Here sat an old crone whose job was to keep a close eye on the children contained therein. Many of them were obviously very newly-born and were suspended in what looked like hammocks from the deckhead beams of the ship in lengths of material of filthy appearance. A most revolting smell pervaded the whole atmosphere. This left me quite shaken and taken aback, but I had much to learn about the squalor and poverty of India.

I suppose at the age of 17 going on 18, I was still a very impressionable sort of youth who did not take kindly to this sudden encounter with what is to be found all over India; the dreadful poverty which in all probability has little changed from those days as far as the vast majority of the working population is concerned. But it is surprising how rapidly one came to accept this poverty. It was many years later that I took my wife out to India when I had become the Master of a ship and with some trepidation I had to acclimatise her to what she must encounter in this respect, but even our womenfolk quickly learned to accept it as inevitable.

Walking round the hatches I realised that each hold contained a gang, men, who I later learned were known as 'Pathans,' a hill tribe from the Afghan hills. They were employed as stevedores paid by British Steamship Companies, which enabled them to return to their homes in and about the Khyber Pass and Kabul with their pockets full of Indian rupees with which to support their families. Any money left over could go to the purchase of a stolen British army rifle so they could continue their own private war with the British army.

They were most splendid looking fellows, not one of them under 6 ft, with great flapping pyjama trousers and beautifully embroidered waistcoats. Everyone had a most magnificent beard and did not really have Indian features, for these were men of the north of India. They were wonderful workers though a bit unpredictable in their ways and habits for they would suddenly leave and return to the hills at a moment's notice.

I felt very sad that I could cull so little from Captain Brand's early memoirs. At the end of his sea career, Phil became the Training Manager for his Company and in the final five years of his working life he reached the position of Examiner of Masters and Mates. Towards the end of his life he became 'registered blind' and encouraged by his friends he dictated his script and had hoped to complete his memoirs. He was a man whose friendship I treasured.

Captain Pete Redhead
Master Mariner

Captain Pete Redhead is, I believe, the oldest member of the Master Mariners and I always enjoy our conversations. However, there are two problems. I am not sure which title to use ... he is in fact a Commander in the R.N.R., Rtd., and has been awarded the Reserve Decoration and secondly he is a Captain in the Merchant Navy. Pete is very deaf and I, too, am fairly shot on the left side. When we chat we appear to be shouting at each other ... with smiles. We did have one ineffectual attempt to put notes together, but happily he pecked away on his machine to better effect!

I was a Cadet on board H.M.S. CONWAY from 1931 to 1933 leaving at the age of 16. At that time the CONWAY was anchored off Rock Ferry. I doubt if life aboard was much different than most boarding schools. I heard very few complaints and it certainly did us 'more good than harm'. We learned 'Discipline,

Respect for Rank and Responsibility'. In addition to the normal reading, writing and arithmetic, there was the theory of navigation and seamanship, including a knowledge of the Brown Gyro Compass to a high standard.

My only claim to fame is that part of my time on board I was the smallest Cadet. I played rugby for the bantam team. If my memory is correct, they were unbeaten and I can only remember one man scoring against us ... Dickie Guest who later was capped for England many times! He was good even as a school boy.

Fees were £40 per term plus required outfit, usually bought from the Sailors Home Clothing Store, whose rep was called 'Chicken', (the only name I ever new him by) and who visited the ship to deliver or take orders. Pocket money allowed was one shilling per week. Normally this equated to three two-penny bars of Cadbury's Dairy Milk (four if there was a lack of willpower) and either a poached egg on toast or beans on toast at the basement 'tuck shop' on the way back from the playing field on Saturday afternoon. I cannot remember which, but one was four pence and the other was sixpence. Wednesday afternoon, it was walk on by.

In the summer term we were allowed to go to Guinea Gap baths instead. One afternoon, my parents had met me outside the baths and we had reached the promenade to walk to Seacombe Ferry and were watching an empty B. T. tanker coming down the river. All of a sudden a man ran forward along the flying bridge and 'let go' the port anchor. The chain roared out, stopped, and parted. By this time the ship's head was swinging to port, curving round neatly alongside Egremont Ferry Pier, then listing to starboard the vessel leaned against the pier which partly collapsed. The span hopped up and down and fell off, leaving a few people stranded on the stage. The tanker's bow nearly made it to the sea wall. I seem to remember it was the BRITISH COMMANDER. Egremont pier has long since gone, only the buttress in the sea wall still remains.

I left to join Ellerman Hall line as an Indentured Apprentice. I believe that the cost was £50 and, provided that the Indentures were completed with good behaviour, this money was returned. Having done two years on CONWAY, which counted as one year's sea time for Second Mates Exam, I only required three more years. I had to wait some months for my twentieth birthday before putting in my papers for the Second Mates Examination. The B.O.T. examiners carried out an eye test. Their decision was final. If the candidate failed when subsequently applying to sit for Mate and Masters, not only was he barred from sitting but also his previous tickets were cancelled. I have several friends who fell at this hurdle.

Somehow I managed to get that prized BUFF SLIP and presented myself at the Marine Superintendent's Office with my brand-new Second Mate's Certificate. I was duly congratulated, my name was placed on the waiting list for a Third Officer's job and I was offered a job as a Quartermaster until there was a Third Mate's job available.

Fortunately, I was able to live at home and find my 'pocket money' doing various odd jobs on the sleuth gang at Ellermans' loading berths in Birkenhead Docks.

One Friday evening at 5 p.m., the police delivered a message from the Marine Superintendent requesting that I was to report to the office at 9 a.m. the following morning. It was normal to work Saturday mornings in those days. My father took the morning off to run me into the office where Captain Hanman said that the CITY OF SIMLA was sailing at 1400 and needed a Fourth Mate. We made a mad dash to the Sailors' Home Clothing Store and somehow they managed to kit me out. I was onboard, 'signed on' and sailed. At last I was on the Company Seniority List!

Pre-war pay started on 'signing on', normally the day before the ship sailed deep sea and finished when 'signing off', usually on arrival back in the first home port. There was no paid leave and we remained off pay until 'signing on' again, either Coasting Articles or Deep Sea Articles, for the next voyage.

A second voyage was as Fourth Mate of the CITY OF MARSEILLES and then came promotion to Third Mate of the KYOTO. Having joined the Royal Naval Reserve as a Temporary Probationary Sub-Lieutenant, I left the KYOTO to do a three months' drill with the Royal Navy during which time the Munich crisis occurred. On return to the Company, I was again appointed to the KYOTO as Third Mate (Officer if you were posh). I remained in her until arrival home after the outbreak of the war. I was then called up for service in the Royal Navy (approximately one month short of my sea time for Mates exam) until demobbed after V. E. Europe. The result was only 'canteen medals' from the U.K.

A FEW MEMORIES

KYOTO was in Port Said homeward for Liverpool at the outbreak of war. After a short delay, a convoy of approximately fifteen to twenty ships was formed ... KYOTO was astern of the Commodore in the B.I. DILWARRA. Some of the older Masters had First World War experience, the others and their Officers of the Watch 'learned on the job'. There were no escorts. About 10 p.m. off Algiers due to a foul up of an 'emergency turn to port', columns 3, 4 and 5 turned to port, 1 and 2 turned to starboard. Amazingly in the melee there was only one collision, 21 and 31. Fortunately the damage was above the waterline and both ships were able to continue. The convoy gradually got itself back into shape as the Commodore ploughed on.

To go back to the time I was an Apprentice, and it would seem for some time before, there were not enough Officers' berths to go around. Ellerman Hall Line carried Indian crews with the ships I sailed in carrying three white Quartermasters. As a very rough average, on the ships that I sailed in, two out of three were ex- Apprentices with Second Mates certificates, waiting for Third Mates berths or ex-Apprentices getting in the dreaded sea-time before having another go at the exam. Promotion was very, very slow. There were Chief Officers with anything up to twenty years in that rank and so on down the ranks ... one Third Mate had about nine years. There were many ahead of me. Where they had gone to when I returned to the Company after being demobbed ... "Don't ask!"

Most Deck Officers and Engineer Officers were watch keepers at sea which did not leave much time for socialising. There was no Officers' lounge in the older ships, only the saloon ... after meals had been cleared away. The Apprentices usually ate in the saloon at the second table along with the Third Mate and Purser. The Engineer Officers had their own mess room.

Very few people had radio sets. Once away from the coast you needed a very good short wave set. For those who got to New York, Courtland Street was full of radio shops and some potent sets were on sale. The shops disappeared when the Port Authority Buildings were built. Occasionally some-one had a gramophone, but along with records it was very heavy and bulky to carry.

One voyage crossing the Pacific, about as far away from anywhere that we could be, Sparks decided to do a bit of a leg-pull ... a bit cruel really, but most leg pulls are! There were only three radios on the ship ... Captain, Chief Engineer and Third Mate. The Chief's set was magnificent with a great array of valves, etc. and he was very proud of his equipment. Whenever he managed to find a station, he rushed round to Sparks and the others to see if they could get it.

My mate had a gramophone, so Sparks made a microphone

and hitched it up to his transmitter. When all was ready, the 'disc jockey' had been trained and the other owners had been primed. The rig was 'fired up' and Sparks went down to see the Chief receiving the 'broadcast' from the most distant station that we could find listed. Alas, Sparks was not impressed by the 'disc jockey' and a couple of days later he decided that he would give them a demonstration of how it should be done. The Chief happened to be listening to see if he could find any stations. Immediately he rushed round to tell Sparks, who unfortunately was just going into his next announcement. We were very unpopular for some time until the Chief came around to the send-up.

SOME HAPPIER MEMORIES

In New York in a suite of rooms at The Hotel Chelsea West 23rd Street, there was a British Apprentices' Club. Many Apprentices were very thankful to the two ladies, Mrs. Spalding and Mrs. George, who ran and maintained this club, I believe at their own expense. It really was an 'Oasis in the Desert' for any impecunious Apprentice who could only manage the ten cents fare each way on the subway.

Another very pleasant memory on my first visit to New York was when I and my fellow Apprentice were taken by one of these ladies to the Rockefeller Centre Cinema. In those days it was usual to have a stage show before the main film. If I remember correctly, there were twelve grand pianos around a raised part of the stage. Artur Rubenstein was the lead pianist, the others all being top names as well. The lights were dimmed, the pianist commenced playing the Ritual Fire Dance and the equally-famous Rockettes Chorus, in some sort of luminous costumes, danced on the raised part of the stage. My description falls far short ... all I can say is that I was impressed and can still 'picture it' in my memory.

My first ship was the CITY OF KOBE ... Persian Gulf, Calcutta and back home to U.K. One memory was that in the Calcutta Mission all rupees were 'bounced' to see if they rang true.

My second ship was the CITY OF LILLE ... Far East and home. This ship was unusual, being at that time the only diesel ship in the deep sea fleet. It was one of only three ships in the Company with Gyro compasses.

My last ship as Apprentice was the CITY OF BARCELONA, which then had a heavy derrick at No. 2 hatch which could lift 120 tons. There was also a 20 ton spreader beam for lifting locomotives. Nichols' 'Seamanship' has a photograph of this derrick lifting a large steam locomotive. Alas, the derrick was not used for a heavy lift during my time on board.

A FEW THOUGHTS

One incident I recall was when we towed a small ship with its engine room gutted by fire into Port Sudan. Picked up a bit of salvage money and a lot of paper work!

Another time, having a doctor on board, we answered a request for help. We took an injured man off a French tanker. The Doctor said it was urgent to get him to hospital, so the Chief was told to 'let her run' for Suez. Naturally, I expected a rocket for burning a lot of extra fuel. In due course, a letter arrived from Head Office. The French Company had offered to pay for any extra expense, etc. Ellermans had replied 'No charge - custom of the sea'. No rocket. Breathed again. Later, a letter arrived from the French Company thanking me and saying that getting the man to hospital as early as possible had been a great help and the man had recovered. We had done our best and were pleased to have helped someone.

Shortly before being demobbed, I was on leave and going to town on the bus in my best uniform. An elderly gentleman boarded at the first stop and sat next to me and in conversation he asked what were my future plans. When I explained that I had to put in a month's sea-time to pass for Mate, then get further sea-time in order to sit for Masters, etc., he assured me that there were special arrangements for taking Master and Mates exams after demob. He was a charming old gentleman. Shortly before getting off the bus he asked if I knew who he was. I replied, "No sir, but you seem to know a lot more about the sea than I do." He replied "I am Captain Keatings". I was in shock and nearly jumped off the bus in fright. This was the Chief Examiner of Master and Mates at Liverpool! Hairy ex-Apprentices used to shake and shiver at the mere mention of his name and the dreaded roar, "Get out" or "Put in another six months" or even "twelve months" extra sea time.

I did not want to stay at sea, but after being demobbed with nothing to lose and in deference to my father, I decided that I would 'have a go'. I was not very hopeful! I had hardly opened a book since sitting for Second Mate. No time was no excuse. So it was nose to the grindstone with a vengeance as a Master's ticket would be my only qualification.

I was even more in shock when I walked out of the exam rooms with another buff slip. The actual hard-back Certificates came some time after. Without looking or thinking that the slip was dated for the day of issue, down to the Office I went and was offered another 'quick' job as Second Mate of the old CITY OF DURBAN with my old seniority on the company roster. To cut a long story short, I felt that I 'owed' the Company so took the job.

I was 'hooked'. That shore job never turned up and in due time I was promoted to Command and exercised my warrant to fly the Blue Ensign until I reached retiring age.

Thank you, Pete Redhead, for your memories and especially for those pre-war recollections. Your full story could be a book. Keep on with the tablets like the rest of us!

Harry Hignet
Manchester Pilot

Harry Hignett is a source of many stories. His years in the Liverpool Nautical Research Society have produced gems. Here is a typical cameo that deserves telling. The article appeared in SEAWAYS in January 1987.

HOMEWARD BOUND

In the Spring of 1940, a director of a Liverpool cotton merchants left the U.K. for Egypt and the Sudan to secure the cotton necessary for textiles and even for making explosives (gun-cotton). With him was his Swiss-born wife. After a time in Alexandria and Cairo, they moved up the Nile to Khartoum to buy Sudanese cotton. Here, they heard news of the collapse of the Allies at the Western Front and Dunkirk. It was time, they thought, to return home and they made for Port Sudan.

In the uncertain conditions of the aftermath of the 'phoney' war they were unable to get passages either north through the Suez Canal or south via the Cape. Eventually the businessman and his wife returned to Khartoum where they were advised to make for Kenya and Mombasa; at the latter there was a better chance of catching a suitable ship.

The journey would have to be by riverboat, a couple of thousand kilometres of the White Nile and through a couple of lakes, and would take approximately a month. They passed through Lake Albert (perhaps 300 km long and 25 km wide) and around Lake Victoria (about 400 km across) ... a long tedious journey which in other circumstances could have been interesting. Finally, they caught a train to Nairobi, where they remained until there was news of a ship via the Cape that they might board at Mombasa.

At Mombasa, they boarded the Netherlands vessel, SPRINGFONTEIN, for a passage via Durban and Cape Town, spending a couple of weeks in each port before the ship left for Freetown, Sierra Leonne, where the convoys were formed for the hazardous run to the U.K.

The SPRINGFONTEIN anchored in Freetown harbour on Christmas Eve 1940, with orders to sail with the next convoy on the 1st January. After quite a jovial Christmas Day, the wife noticed on the 26th a slight haze coming from one of the ventilators at No. 3 hatch. She drew the attention of the Second Mate to it. He agreed it could be smoke, but said it was not unusual and that they could handle the situation.

Over the next few days, more vessels arrived in the anchorage, obviously for the next convoy north. As the number of ships increased, so the emission of smoke from No. 3 hold increased, but the Master and Officers remained fairly unconcerned until dinner on New Year Eve when the acrid smell of burning paint indicated something more serious. At about 2300 hours the deck became so hot that the wooden planking began to smoulder around the hatchway, and the crew were ordered to emergency stations.

At 2345 hours, emergency signals were made; distress flares sent up, a W/T SOS was sent and abandon ship signal blown on the ship's siren. The Third Mate called the naval signal station by Aldis, only to be told: 'Under war-time regulations the use of flares and the ship's whistle and all other frivolities were banned and in any case it was still only 15 minutes to midnight'.

A naval tug was sent across with an armed boarding party at about 0015, just in time to see flames shooting out of No. 3 hold. The SPRINGFONTEIN was not to sail with the convoy ... her bones were still to be seen on the beach near the anchorage, more than a decade later.

The cotton merchant and his wife sailed for the U.K. in another vessel ten days later. His wife, now over 80, told me this story a few months ago and brought to my attention the advantages and difficulties of travel on the Nile and in East Africa.

It reminded me of an Ugandan cadet, who quite some time ago, hoped to get a job on the vessels sailing on Lake Victoria ... until then I had no real appreciation of the size of that Lake or the others in East Africa.

Here is another Harry Hignett story.

THE KNOCKOUT

In May 1944, Colley and I sat on the deck of the FORT McLOUGHLIN enjoying the warm sun. Colley, who rejoiced in the name of Collingwood, an engine-room greaser, had been a professional boxer in his early days and was explaining his experiences in the ring. His voice, although quiet, was strong and matched his muscular body. "You always knew when you had knocked a man out ... the eyes look up to heaven and the jaws are wide open!" he told me.

We were waiting to sail on a fairly new ship, managed by a Newcastle firm for the Ministry of War Transport and about to join the Normandy invasion fleet on D-day. The grey paint of the hull and superstructure did not make the ship any better looking. We were moored in Bidston Dock, Birkenhead, towards the gate and a hundred yards from the nearest pub, the Pool Inn on the road opposite Poulton Church ... both local landmarks.

Colley nodded in the direction of the engine-room house, "Who's the young lad with the blond curly hair?"

"I think it's a new Cadet, and it looks as if he wants to speak to us."

The Cadet smiled at us "Do you live around here?" The voice came with a strong 'Geordie' accent; "I wondered if you could help me", addressing the query to me.

I responded, "No, I'm from over the water, Colley here is local".

Colley nodded "What's the matter?" he asked suspiciously.

The Cadet continued, "I want to take a girl to a dance tonight and need to sell some clothing coupons."

Clothing was rationed; coupons came in small books about the same size as the books of twelve stamps from the Post Office, but thirty coupons to the page ... in war-time merchant seamen got double rations. They needed to have clothing for the Arctic Circle and for the Tropics in any war-time voyage, but a few took a chance and used them to buy silk stockings for their wives and girl-friends, and more than a few sold coupons on the Black Market. Highly illegal!

Colley shook his head, and was reluctant to get involved, "Sorry son, I can't do it before tomorrow morning, I'm out of cash."

"That's OK", the Cadet said, brightening up, "The Second Mate will lend me the money until then."

"How many do you want to sell? How much do you expect to get?"

"A whole page, perhaps thirty shillings".

Colley shook his head "You'll be lucky to get thirty

shillings these days".

The Cadet looked crestfallen. "Well can you do your best for me, please?" he pleaded.

Colley nodded, "OK son, I'll try. See you tomorrow".

He turned to me, "I hear there's an old biddy who'll buy them. I'll see you in the Pool Inn later".

About six that evening in the Pool Inn, Colley pushed his way through the crowd to the bar.

"How d'you get on with the coupons, Colley?" I asked.

"Well I went along to the Eagle Arms and got thirty-three bob for them". He pulled out the book of coupons from his pocket to show us and studied the contents.

"Bloody hell, the old bitch!" he exploded. "She's cut two pages out instead of one and gave me the money for one page." "How the hell did she do that in front of you?"

"She took the book and held it under the table where she cut them out and then stuffed the money inside and handed the lot to me over the table".

"Hey Colley, do you want this drink?" He was halfway out of the door and didn't answer.

Colley didn't return that night. But, next morning just after breakfast, as I sat on the hatch, Colley came along and joined me. He clearly was not enjoying life.

"What's the matter", I asked. "Got a hangover?"

He shook his head. I persisted, "How did you get on last night, did she give you the coupons or the money?"

Colley shook his head, "She wasn't there when I went back to the Eagle Arms and naturally nobody had seen her before."

"What did you do?"

"I was in a right mood and after a few drinks along the road, I went across to the dance in the church hall opposite. When someone left the cloakroom for a moment, I went in and pinched a raincoat. This morning I pawned it and made up most of the money."

Just at that moment the Cadet appeared. Colley smiled. "I got the money lad," he said eagerly, "but to get the price I had to sell two pages instead of one. So here's your money, I got thirty-two bob a page for you. That makes three pounds four shillings; it was the best deal I could do."

A very crestfallen young man responded sadly "That's no good to me! Some bugger pinched my raincoat from the dance last night."

Colley's eyes looked up to the sky and his jaw was wide open.

Thank you, Harry Hignett. "It's the way you tell 'em!"

Captain Graeme Cubbin
Master Mariner

Captain Graeme Cubbin is an author in his own right. Apart from the article in this book concerning the history of the Liverpool Master Mariners' 'home ship', the LANDFALL, Graeme's real 'tour de force' is a superb history of one of Liverpool's major shipping companies, 'The Harrison Line of Liverpool. A Chronicle of Ships and Men, 1830 – 2002' … the saga of three hundred and thirty ships spread over a period of more than 160 years of incident-crammed history. It is a fantastic book. The story that you are about to read is recorded at length in that volume. Sadly, with apologies to Graeme, we have space for excerpts only.

Graeme is a much respected member of the Master Mariners, but his career almost ended in misfortune. He joined Harrison's SCIENTIST in 1940 … what happened next will follow … and over the years he was to obtain the obligatory Certificates of Competency, progressing steadily up the promotional ladder to reach the rank of Master in 1964. In 1973, he came ashore to assist the Marine Superintendent until his retirement in 1986.

But, let us go back to that rather shaky start in his career and let Graeme tell his tale. Remember that this was his first voyage as a Cadet, aged just sixteen and a half ... it could have been his last!

This account was published jointly by the World Ship Society, Gravesend and Ships in Focus Publications, Preston, 2003.

Kapitan zur See Bernhard Rogge, Commander of the German commerce–raider, S.H.K. ATLANTIS, gazed round his ship with feelings of satisfaction. Originally the converted Hansa Line cargo ship, GOLDENFELS, 7862 gt., she was now masquerading in a disguise as near perfect as makeshift ingenuity could contrive.

Overside were the national colours of neutral Japan; fresh paint glistening in the sunshine, emblazoned on the ship's black flanks. It was Friday, 3rd May 1940, and his ship had been at sea thirty-three days. His keen but untested crew, three hundred strong, stood to their battle stations, tense and excited, as they awaited the arrival of the first victim of their cruise, a British cargo vessel that was steadily overtaking on the starboard quarter.

There were few individuals in sight that sunny afternoon. A small group of sailors dressed in flapping white shirts leaned casually over the after rail; a lone Officer paced the bridge; and most innocent of all, a slim, slightly built cook's assistant wearing a gaily-coloured print dress, wide-brimmed hat, and a mutinous scowl strolled up and down the boat deck pushing a perambulator!

"5,000 metres and closing", intoned Leutnant Kasch, the Gunnery Officer, who, from his vantage point above the wheelhouse, was using to good effect a range-finder, cunningly camouflaged as a water-tank.

The moment-of-truth could not be delayed much longer. Eventually, Rogge spoke the eagerly-awaited orders.

"Clear guns! Hoist battle ensign! Make signals!"

In a flash, a flutter of bunting appeared on the triatic stay halyards, ordering the 'Englander' to stop, and not use her radio. The red, white and black Swastika ensign of the Third Reich swiftly replaced the Rising Sun of Japan. Flaps in the ship's side levered upwards, like so many suburban garage doors, to reveal the menace of the 5.9 inch guns. At Kasch's command, a smaller gun in the bow fired a shot across the freighter's bow.

Surprise was complete. There had been no enemy activity in the South Atlantic since the unlamented demise of the ADMIRAL GRAF SPEE in December. Captain George Windsor appeared on the bridge demanding to know who was meddling with that damned gun? He saw what appeared to be a neutral Japanese ship on the port bow, now swinging to cross ahead, and displaying a formidable armament. He at once came to grips with the situation.

"Hard-a starboard, Quartermaster," he roared.

"Double ring full ahead, Second Mate. Here lad" … to the Cadet … "tell Sparks he's got to get this message out".

The Old Man scribbled on a pad with a steady hand.

"QQQQ - G N G R – 1920S – 0415E - Challenged by unknown armed vessel".

There was no one within 300 miles to hear it. The message went out unheard and unheeded … except by an alert telegraphist on board the raider. He was on to the wavelength before three complete messages had been transmitted, and promptly jammed the signal with his own key.

"Enemy radio in action, sir!" he reported.

Rogge swore as he watched his prey turning away.

"Open fire!" he ordered.

Leutnant Kasch needed no urging, and salvo after salvo crashed out. Several shells burst in the after-holds of the target, igniting the cargo and sending flames leaping skywards. Another demolished the wireless cabin, leaving Radio Officer

Compton severely wounded in head and arms. Despite his injuries, and scarcely aware of his surroundings, Sparks nevertheless managed to retrieve his codebooks from the wreckage, transfer them to the specially weighted bag, and deliver them to the safekeeping of the deep. His duty done, he staggered dazedly to his boat station. The bombardment ceased.

SCIENTIST, after-deck ablaze, had stopped and Captain Windsor ordered the boats away. He and Chief Officer Alec Watson busied themselves collecting sensitive books and papers that might be useful to the enemy, and dumped them over the side. A group of walking-wounded stood quietly beside the medicine locker, patiently waiting for Chief Steward Harry Howarth to administer First Aid. Harry shook his head over one Lascar with a gaping wound in his stomach. He lifted him gently into one of the boats, but he died later aboard the raider. Meanwhile the boats were being lowered, and last minute thoughts took on a vital importance, though some were incongruous in the circumstance.

"Tell the Chief Steward ... he must bring the canteen accounts with him ... !"

"Fetch me some tobacco out of the top drawer ... Oh! And my tooth brush!"

"Please, Mr. Mate, have I got time to nip below for my bottom set?"

Quickly, the boats were manned and pushed away from the doomed ship's side. Their crews were eyeing the raider apprehensively as it bore down upon them with guns trained in their direction. Somewhat reassured by an amplified voice bidding them to pull alongside, they did so, staring up at the grinning faces of German sailors lining the rail, most of them bearing arms. One or two, however, slipped nimbly over the rail and into the boats, and began strapping the wounded into hammocks and stretchers before hoisting them on deck, where they were taken to a well-equipped hospital. The rest clambered wearily up the ladders and into captivity.

The SCIENTIST was at first peppered with gunfire, but the gunners failed to hit the waterline. As it was getting dark and a blazing ship would be a beacon to other vessels, the ship was dispatched by a torpedo and the raider slipped away into the night.

An hour or so later, the prisoners were herded below and were pleasantly surprised to be ushered into a cosy, well-prepared room. Alec Watson, the Chief Officer, was anxious to ascertain how our Asian crew members were accommodated. He was led away by the guard and returned some time later to report that they were in a similar, but more spacious, quarters further aft, and seemed in good spirits.

More unexpected surprises were revealed as time wore on. The Commander's ADC, Leutnant zur See Ulrich Mohr, was the designated Prisoners' Liaison Officer ... a tall, scholarly Officer with a genial manner, and a first class command of English. Leutnant Mohr went out of his way to win the trust of his country's enemies. The day after their capture, a loudspeaker was installed in the prisoners' quarters which broadcast music throughout the day, interspersed with news bulletins in English, not from Germany, but from the United States.

Prisoners were served the same food as the German crew ... except the Asians. With surprising sensitivity, the Germans

allowed them to employ their own cooks, to prepare the
traditional fare of rice, lamb and curries, avoiding the beef, ham
and pork relished by their captors. Drinking water, sometimes
laced with lime-juice, seemed plentiful, but water for washing
was strictly rationed.

A week after the SCIENTIST had been sunk, the raider
laid her cargo of some 100 mines off Cape Agulhas and then
steamed eastwards into the Indian Ocean. The weeks went by,
and nothing happened. The raider shed her Japanese disguise
and became instead the Dutch motor vessel ABBEKERK, with
a black hull, orange-brown upper works, surmounted by a black
funnel with an orange band.

Six weeks were to pass before ATLANTIS secured her
second victim, on the 10th June. This was the Norwegian
motor vessel, TIRRANNA, 7230 gt., and being of a good turn
of speed, she led the raider a merry dance before she was forced
to surrender. In fact, the raider was unable to close the distance,
and the one-sided battle became a stern chase fought at a range
of four to five miles. Although TIRRANNA loosed several
rounds from her gun, they were ineffective. However, the
Norwegian casualties were heavy, with five killed and several
more wounded. Ironically, it was announced later that day that
a peace treaty between Hitler and conquered Norway had just
been signed. The two nations were no longer at war!

After parting company with TIRRANNA, on the 4th
August, 1940, ATLANTIS moved north to cruise in the south
tropical latitudes of the Indian Ocean. During the next six
weeks or so, she sank four more ships … KING CITY (Smiths
of Cardiff), ATHELKING (United Molasses Co.), BENARTY
(William Thomson of Leith) and a French liner, that had
been requisitioned by the British in Fiji, the COMMISSAIRE
REMAL (Messageries Maritimes). The raider had been at sea
for six months and had cruised 31,638 nautical miles and had
deprived the enemy of nine ships together with their cargoes

… not counting certain unknown ships which had probably been mined off the South African Coast. There were now 365 prisoners on board the German raider.

A school for nautical studies had been set up since the earliest days of captivity. Requests for text books, almanacs, charts, and nautical tables did not go unheeded. Whenever a ship was boarded, Leutnant Mohr invariably came back with a selection of English books, charts and drawing instruments purloined from the victim's library and chartroom.

At the sound of the raucous klaxons, all the prisoners were confined to quarters; the steel door clanged shut and was promptly locked and bolted. An armed sentry remained on duty all throughout the action. The ventilation fans became silent, presumably as a precaution against the spread of fire; not a breath of air penetrated that crowded space. It became hot and stale and stuffy. The whine of ammunition hoists and the clatter of gun-ports being drawn up could be plainly heard and speculated on. The crash of the guns was like thunder in that confined space, invariably dousing some light bulbs and bringing flakes of paint down from the deck-head.

At first light on a new day, 22nd October, 1940, the DURMITOR of Dubrovnik, creamed along at all of seven knots, a pillar of smoke pouring from her rusty stack. Her buff funnel was surmounted by a black top, and the red and white and pale blue emblem of Yugoslavia was painted conspicuously on her rust-streaked flanks. A shot across the bow soon brought that ancient vessel to a halt. Would she 'do' as a prison ship? Rogge cruised around for four more days, hoping to find 'something better'. Nothing materialisd.

On the 26th October the prisoners were all ferried across to DURMITOR. She was full of rock salt which was levelled, then covered with tarpaulins and an ample supply of blankets. The ship had been built in 1913 by Russells of Glasgow and had originally been the PLUTARCH of Liverpool, a Lamport and

Holt steamer. The German Commander was Sub-Lt Dehnel, a stocky character with a blond imperial ... his first command! Conditions were grim and the prisoners had company ... rats! They ate mouldy black bread, Australian jam and cheese, and there was little of it. However, comradeship was strong. Card games were popular with fantastic stakes, but the main enemy was boredom. Soon they were short of coal; food and water was halved and speed reduced to five knots. Sails of tarpaulin were created and all timber was cut up for the furnaces.

Thus the days wore on until one afternoon, the twenty-eighth since parting company with ATLANTIS, the prisoners awoke from their 'siesta' to see a 'G' flag fluttering from the triatic stay: "I require a pilot". Sure enough, there was the land, a sandy waste pock-marked by a few stunted palms. No pilot appeared. So Dehnel, who could not have had a chart of the area, nevertheless headed boldly in for the cluster of huts that could be seen near the shore ... and ran his ship firmly on to the reef which barred the approaches!

The prisoners did not know whether to laugh or cry. The Germans looked angry and frustrated. After some discussion, a boat was lowered and a German delegation was rowed ashore by the Yugoslav crew. Eventually, the boat returned, minus the delegation, which the Yugoslavs reported had made contact with an Italian patrol. The order was given to abandon ship.

By that time, it was pitch black. As the boats approached the beach through the heavy surf, the prisoners suddenly became aware that armed native soldiers were deployed facing seaward and were looking extremely nervous. The men raised their arms, making it clear they had no weapons and then were marched off to the village, called Warshiek, under guard. There, the Italians arrested everyone, including Leutnant Dehnel and his German crew!

We had arrived at Italiana Somalia. A few days before, British cruisers had shelled Mogadiscio and the coast was on full alert, expecting an invasion. Unkempt, starved, wretched in appearance and bereft of any equipment, it was not too difficult to assure the Italian authorities that this was no invasion. An Italian Lieutenant was in charge of the local garrison and at length returned the weapons to the Germans. Soon the fires were lit and several kid-goats were slaughtered … throat cutting was not a pretty sight! There was a feast of goat meat, rice and vegetable stew, all washed down with generous measures of a rather harsh Chianti and fragrant coffee. All too much for their wasted stomachs. The next day, many were acutely ill, and remained quietly in their mud-hut prisons, pondering their recent gluttony and idly speculating upon an unpredictable future.

They awoke before dawn on the third day, 24th November, 1940 to the whine and clatter of motor lorries entering the village, assigned by the Army to transport the prisoners to the capital, 50 miles down the coast. That journey is described by Third Officer Ken Gorrie, formerly of the ATHELKING, in his diary.

I was in the second truck, along with twenty-four others and three guards. It was a nightmare journey. For the first two hours, we followed the coast, running over open desert covered with short, tough grass, almost brown with the sun. How those drivers managed the trucks, goodness knows; we were continuously climbing small, steep hillocks and dropping down the other side. At times we would heel over at an alarming angle, and frequently went bumping and crashing through ditches that would dismay anyone but an army tank driver. To add to our discomfort, the sun was getting higher and beating down on our unprotected heads."

After some four hours, we arrived in the leafy suburbs of Mogadiscio. The Italian populace in white suits and flowery-printed dresses turned to stare. Nobody cheered, nobody jeered and nobody threw anything. Arriving at a camp, we were housed in barracks holding twenty men each. So we settled into our new homes

Prison camp is the essence of boredom. Books, food, water were all in short supply. At least three men died of dysentery and other enteric ailments ... the only medicine was goat's milk and Epsom salts. There were no Red Cross parcels.

Early in the New Year we were moved to Merca, about 40 miles southwest along the coast. There was a beach nearby and we could supplement the rice and pasta diet with fresh fruit. News of the War filtered through and the days were tinged with hope. We learnt that on the 15th February, Kisimayo had fallen and that South African troops were across the Juba River. One day a flight of Hurricanes flew over the camp and Commandante Bracco allowed us to place white stones from the beach spelling ... "POWs – HELP" ... inside the camp compound.

Then came the 25th February, 1941.

A white flag flew over Bracco's office; the silence was uncanny ... not even the sound of gunfire. About four hours later a South African patrol car appeared at the compound gates and the camp went wild. The troopers looked bewildered, as well they might, for instead of finding the enemy they found themselves surrounded by a wildly cheering mob of happy 'rooineks'. The men were advised to stay in the camp until someone from H.Q. arrived.

The next two days were spent in camp, leisurely swimming off the beach or concocting imaginative dishes using the newly acquired stores. On the morning of the 28th February, we awoke to see that long, grey shape we had longed to see, standing off shore. A cruiser no less! H.M.S. CERES. The Navy had come to transport some 260 P.O.W.s down the coast to Mombasa.

On the 1st March, 1941, we disembarked, no longer P.O.W.s, but D.B.S. ...Distressed British Seamen. The many months of captivity were behind us. Shipmasters quickly descended upon the various Shipping Agencies, where, of course, they were well known and welcomed. Soon the wires were humming as Agents contacted their principals in the United Kingdom. The Companies promptly assumed responsibility for their own staff, informing next of kin, arranging cash and clothing allowances. They also authorised accommodation in several excellent local hotels. The crews, 'pool men' from the Merchant Navy Establishment, became the joint responsibility of the local Mercantile Marine Office and the Royal Navy. Most of them remained in the transit camp, but the sick and elderly were cared for by the Missions to Seamen whose priestly incumbents worked diligently for our welfare, organising local support, which was generously forthcoming.

It was mid-April that the ship came in. She was the troopship, NEA HELLAS, formerly the Anchor Line's TUSCANIA. Joyfully, the men packed up, bade hasty farewells to new-found friends and hastened down to Kilindini Docks to lay claim to a bunk in the six-berth cabins. Soon, Durban and Cape Town were behind us, and we sailed in the company of the aircraft carriers, H.M.S. FURIOUS and H.M.S. ARGUS, bound for Gibraltar.

Twenty-four hours after sailing from Gibraltar, we were forced to return by the news of BISMARCK's excursion into the North Atlantic. The carriers veered off to the north-west at full speed to join in the fray. Ten days or so later, Force H (RENOWN, ARK ROYAL, SHEFFIELD and several destroyers) entered harbour and Captain Bone of the NEA HELLAS was informed that it was safe to proceed ... at least, as far as BISMARCK was concerned.

We sailed into the Firth of Clyde on the 14th June, 1941 and worried about bottles and tobacco that we had all accumulated. We need not have worried. H.M. Customs Officers in Glasgow had just come out on strike!

The last word in this tale belongs entirely to Graeme.

The night train to Liverpool was crowded with servicemen and women, and we were lucky to find a corner of the passageway in which to squat uncomfortably and while away the hours in desultory conversation and fitful sleep. The journey seemed endless with numerous inscrutable, time-laden halts in wild countryside, but eventually the train coasted into Lime Street Station. It was six-o-clock on a Sunday morning and the streets were deserted. Opposite the Station, the old familiar buildings had been reduced to rubble during the May blitz and the tram trolley-wires looked like so much tangled knitting. The classic bulk of St. George's Hall still stood, although blackened by smoke and pock-marked by shrapnel. Its guardian lions, defiant as ever, were still gazing out over cratered Lime Street. My companions and I stared in awe at this ravaged scene for several minutes, then looked at each other and wondered what the hell we had to complain about? At last, we said "Good bye" and went our several ways.

My route led south and, as it was no use waiting for a tram, I trudged along the torn-up streets, sick at heart to see such wanton destruction. A passing motorist drew up and offered me a lift. I accepted gratefully and my benefactor proceeded to give me the benefit of his opinion on the latest air raids. At Princes Avenue, I asked him to drop me at the Church ... then realised that the Church was not there any more. With some trepidation, I walked up 'our street', past the broken houses, the sightless windows ... and there, still standing, was the home I had left one year and four months ago. The steps were gleaming white, the door was freshly painted, the brasswork shone, and draped proudly from a bedroom window was a Union Jack. I rang the door bell. I had come home.

In July 1940, the Admiralty had declared the SCIENTIST lost with all hands. The loose ends had been dealt with!

Allotments were stopped. The accounts of the missing seamen were made up and the monies passed to the next of kin. Women who had been 'widowed' nursed their grief and applied for the statutory pension. Some might have 'married' again. Parents received gently-worded messages of condolence from H.M. the Queen, but despite the odds, there were many who never gave up hope. It was tacitly agreed that those at home suffered the greater ordeal, not knowing what had happened or when to abandon hope.

When the euphoria had subsided a little, some unpalatable situations had to be faced. 'Widows' were obliged to refund to the State all the pension monies they had received. Premiums (i.e. the sums payable to an employer by the parents or guardians of Cadets and Apprentices ... £50 in those days), which had been refunded on 'decease' had to be paid again. Company accountants later re-calculated balances of wages, some inevitably in the red after the spending spree in Mombasa and 'adjustments' had to be made. But, in the eyes of kith and kin these were but a small price to pay for the miracle of deliverance.

There is just one more incident that Graeme recalls from the ATLANTIS story.

As the SCIENTIST'S crestfallen crew boarded the German raider, they were shepherded past a desk where a smartly dressed officer sat like a recording angel, noting down the names and ranks of his newly acquired prisoners. Eventually, the Master of the SCIENTIST stood before him, a pillar of righteous indignation.

"Name?" queried the Officer, whose English was faultless.

"Captain George Windsor", replied the Old Man, proudly. The puzzled officer looked at him askance and said sarcastically, "And my name is Adolf Hitler! Now, what's your real name?"

The Old Man stuck to his guns, of course, and even toyed with the idea of giving his address as Buckingham Palace, but thought better of it. Nevertheless, it was only with considerable difficulty that he persuaded the Officer that, despite the validity of his name, he was not a member of the British Royal Family!

Christmas 1942 found Graeme Cubbin serving as a Cadet aboard BARRISTER, sitting in Gibraltar Bay as a convoy assembled, bound for the United Kingdom. A continual source of menace was the occasional audacious sortie of enemy frogmen, operating from the Spanish port of Algeçiras, to place limpet mines on ships at anchorage. Gradually the convoy took shape as more ships entered the Bay and it eventually sailed on the 27th December. BARRISTER was homeward bound in ballast after unloading a cargo of supplies for the troops in Algiers. Graeme takes up the tale. (It appeared in the Harrison Line Newsletter, No. 38, March 1983).

By the 3rd of January, 1943, the convoy was in the Western Approaches and orders were given to split, the two outer columns to go North-about to the Clyde and the two inner columns to pass south of Ireland into the Irish Sea. BARRISTER, bound for the Clyde, was in the outer section. The bad weather still persisted, and visibility became worse, until it was very easy to lose track of the ship ahead. No ship had had sight of the sun or stars for several days. Dead-reckoning placed the BARRISTER some ten miles west of the Irish Coast, and, only too aware that D.R. positions are notoriously inaccurate, Captain and Officers were becoming very uneasy. However, they knew that some of the escort vessels were fitted with the new-fangled 'radar', a mysterious device whose qualities and limitations were virtually unknown to Merchant Navy Officers in those days. If landfall were due, then the inshore escorts would be sure to locate it and warn the convoy in good time.

During the Middle Watch on the 4th January, 1942, Second Officer Skelly found his next ahead, an American ship, to be an elusive station-keeper in the poor conditions. Surreptitiously, he eased the ship across to the next column to keep station on a large escort-carrier whose bulk was more readily discernable. At 4 a.m., he handed the watch to Chief Officer Wells.

The next few hours saw the convoy losing cohesion and by dawn, there was little sign of any other ship, apart from rather vague shapes on either side. The weather was heavily overcast and there was a persistent drizzle. Things began to happen with speed when a few minutes after 8 o'clock, the lookout on the starboard wing of the Bridge reported that he thought that he could see something ahead. Graeme takes up the story again.

Suddenly, out of the mist, and becoming more distinct with each leaden second, loomed the black silhouette of an enormous rocky crag ... its conical peak towering over the fore-yard! At its base, clouds of white spume rose high in the air as the Atlantic swells swept in. The Third Officer reacted swiftly.

"Hard-a-port! Two short blasts!" he yelled, casting an anguished glance aft to see whether our next astern was on our heels. There was nothing in sight.

"Get the Old Man up here!"

The ship's head was beginning to swing away from the dark menace of the cliff face, and it was only when we looked to seaward again that we realised that the ship was virtually surrounded by white water, the hallmark of rocky shoals. Captain Collins clambered up to the Bridge just as the ship struck.

The ship was vibrating madly under 'Full Astern' power

and the wash was sweeping forward, but the bow, held fast by the rocks, did not budge. The stern of the ship, on the other hand, was undulating ominously to the swell. There was a crack like a rifle shot from somewhere below the Bridge. Then another, quickly followed by a rattle like a burst of machine-gun fire. The rivets holding the ship's members together were bursting under the strain. Sadly, Captain Collins rang "Stop" on the telegraph and went to the engine-room voice pipe. He spoke to the Chief Engineer, who was down below.

"Shut down, Chief, and bring your men up from there!"

"Abandon ship!"

The first boat was launched just as the grey wisps of dawn were appearing in the sky to the south-east. Close to starboard was the lofty island rock that had been sighted at the beginning of their ordeal and which they discovered later was Inishshark. Another larger island called Inishbofin lay further eastwards and, beyond it the soft green hills and craggy mountains of Connemara. A corvette was standing off, available and ready to render assistance. Two more boats were launched and headed for the corvette that was later identified as the Canadian vessel, H.M.C.S. KITCHENER, (Commander Bill Evans, R.C.N.). Meanwhile, the end of BARRISTER was imminent. Amidships, the decks split asunder and the two winches at No.3 Hatch disappeared into the hold.

Most of the crew were picked up by H.M.C.S. KITCHENER and landed at Londonderry. For several days, three castaways remained on the island of Inishbofin to attend to formalities and the authorities. They survived in a large draughty house with a leaking roof. Eventually, they made their way via the Irish Customs and Excise to Dublin and home.

Many seafarers had a reasonably quiet war ... as wars go ... but, Graeme Cubbin had not quite finished his escapades.

In August 1943, he was at Baltimore in Maryland aboard DIRECTOR, loading a full cargo of military stores, munitions and transport vehicles, bound for the Eastern Mediterranean. They crossed the Atlantic in Convoy UGS 16 and from Gibraltar DIRECTOR headed for Alexandria in order to discharge her cargo. The next destination was Haifa, where they loaded a full cargo of high octane petrol in 'jerrycans', compact steel containers each holding about five gallons of fuel. They sailed from Haifa on the 11th November, calling at Alex to join a convoy of some twelve vessels and two corvettes. They arrived off Bari on the 21st and the Italian pilot informed them that a Royal Navy minesweeper, H.M.S. HEBE, had been blown up by a mine just outside the breakwater only a matter of hours before they had arrived. The ships waited for a berth, packed in like sardines, and a week passed before they could start unloading in the inner harbour. Graeme takes up the narrative.

Early on the Thursday, 2nd December 1943, another large convoy entered the harbour direct from the United States. That afternoon a lone plane circled high above the town, too high to be recognised, but was almost certainly German. No-one seemed to pay much attention, but anyone who had ever watched a high-flying Focke-Wulf Condor circling a convoy knew that it only meant trouble. Bari was like a well-stocked chicken-coop waiting for a predatory fox.

The raiders came over between seven and eight o'clock that evening. Early success was a direct hit on the U.S. Liberty ship, JOHN L. MOTLEY. She was laden with gasoline and explosives. She exploded with a roar and a flash that illuminated the entire harbour. The initial blast lifted all the DIRECTOR's hatchboards and tarpaulins from the hatches and blew them clean away. The open hatches gaped at the lurid sky from which, like a grotesque hail-storm, red-hot fragments of shattered ship rained down, some heavy enough to punch holes through the steel deck, others smashing the stacked jerrycans of petrol in the holds. Another near-miss tore a great hole in the masonry of the quay to which the ship was moored, blasting the men off their feet. The ship's side had been stove-in in way of the stoke-hold, the ash-hoist destroyed, several plates and a large number of rivets were sprung, some near the waterline. The surface of the harbour was ablaze.

The explosions, the leaping flames, the greasy, billowing smoke and the flying debris all combined with the blazing, oil-polluted water to form a magma poured from a crucible in Hell. But, unknown to the vast majority of victims and spectators of this infernal drama, until thirty or more years after the War had ended, another satanic ingredient had been added to the hellish brew. The deadly secret, known only to certain ship's Officers (who were all killed) was that the American freighter, JOHN HARVEY, had been carrying, amongst other cargo of a volatile nature, one hundred tons of mustard gas bombs. When the JOHN HARVEY blew up, the mustard gas was released into the harbour, some in gaseous form, but most of it mixing with the oil fuel scumming the surface of the water. Hundreds of seamen, forced to swim for safety were thus immersed in the deadly fluid, in many cases swallowing it or absorbing it into the lungs, eyes and skin.

As dawn broke on the stricken port, a dazed and subdued crew set about cleaning up the DIRECTOR. Of the twenty-six merchant ships which lay at Bari on the Thursday afternoon, seventeen had been destroyed and only a bare half-dozen sailed that Friday morning. DIRECTOR arrived at Port Augusta on the 5th December and lay there for a week, gas-freeing the holds and constructing an enormous cement box to contain the leaks in the stoke-hold. She returned to Bari on the 14th, just twelve days after the raid to unload the remainder of her essential cargo. Over a thousand men, mostly merchant seamen, died in the raid, and their sad remains were rising to the surface. Those of us who survived have never lost the memory of that horrid melancholy scene. DIRECTOR returned to England, having been diverted to Burriana in Spain to pick up an orange crop on behalf of the Ministry of Food ... a consignment of sunshine for Britain!

That was a horrendous picture! By 1948, Graeme Cubbin was the Second Officer of S.S. CRAFTSMAN and on Monday, 8th March, the ship was fog- bound in the Bay of Biscay.

Speed was reduced to 'Slow ahead' and the urgent beat of the engines subsided to a murmur. During the silent periods between the raucous blasts from their own steam-whistle, the Officers listened intently.

Minutes later, their attention was alerted. Faintly, from a point or so on the starboard bow, came the fog signal of a steamer under way. The engines were stopped and the ship quickly lost way. For some minutes the vessel drifted, several pairs of eyes trying to pierce the fog.

And then, they saw it! Captain O'Neil reacted at once.

"Hard-a-starboard. Full astern."

The Second Officer, momentarily mesmerised by the oncoming ship, like a rabbit in the headlamp's glare, jumped to obey, even remembering to sound the obligatory three short blasts on the whistle.

It was all to no avail! The SAMPENN ... the name was now visible on her port bow ... came on inexorably, her bluff stem ploughing into the CRAFTSMAN's starboard bow like a bulldozer! There was an almighty crash, the ship heeled crazily, and flame and sparks flickered ominously around the point of impact. Three-quarter inch plates from the forecastle-deck to below the water line were swept back like a drawing-room curtain, severed steel frames folded into the drapes. The forecastle-deck was uprooted, cargo in cases and drums

tumbled into the sea and the air was filled with the acrid fumes
of chemicals released from ruptured containers. It was a heart
stopping moment ... and 0918 by the chartroom clock ... to be
precise.

At 0920 hours, twelve minutes after the first distant fog
signal was heard, the ships drifted apart and the engines were
stopped. Clearly CRAFTSMAN was the more gravely wounded
and, true to the tradition of the sea, Captain John Styrin of the
SAMPENN stood by in case assistance was needed.

Aboard CRAFTSMAN, the initial shock had given way
to urgent, but orderly counter-measures. A team of sailors
under Chief Officer Les Williams and a phlegmatic Bosun
were running hoses along the foredeck, for the chances of a
fire or explosion among the volatile chemicals stowed in No.
1 'tween-deck were substantial. Another team of sailors was
preparing the boats for launching, for no-one at that stage had
any idea how long the ship might stay afloat. The Carpenter
was busily sounding tanks and bilges in the damaged sector,
while a few of the others with no specific task in hand went
back to finish their interrupted breakfast.

The Carpenter's report was encouraging. The fore-peak,
chain locker, and No. 1 Hold were flooded, but No. 2 was bone-
dry, indicating that the bulkhead was still secure. The Master
held a brief discussion with his Chief Engineer, who confirmed
that there were no problems in his department.

"Right, Chief, give her revs. for 7 knots and we'll head
for Falmouth. It's over 200 miles, but we should get there by
tomorrow evening. We don't want to overstress that bulkhead
by going any faster."

So CRAFTSMAN got under way and Head Office in
Liverpool advised that the salvage tug, ZEALANDIA, had
set forth from Falmouth to intercept and render assistance
if required. Shortly afterwards, at about 1.50 p.m., Captain
O'Neil released SAMPENN from escort duty and that vessel

headed up channel for Hull. The crippled ship, lying more than eight feet by the head, was creeping along at no more than 6 or 7 knots across the channel sea-lanes. The fog persisted. Cross traffic was heavy and the salvage tug never did meet the stricken vessel. At last, at about 7 p.m., they were relieved to see the light on St. Anthony's Head, which marked the entrance to Falmouth Harbour. At 8.30 p.m., the Pilot boarded and brought the ship safely to anchorage. The next day, the ship was moored to a buoy in Carrick Roads.

For five weeks, CRAFTSMAN lay at her moorings whilst an enormous patch of timber, metal rods and concrete crudely made the ship seaworthy for the voyage round to Liverpool where she docked on the 17th April.

Subsequently, a Ministry of Transport enquiry into the incident found SAMPENN 75% to blame, CRAFTSMAN 25%. It was a serious accident, but it might well have been far worse.

Captain Graeme Cubbin is certainly a born raconteur and his next tale is clear evidence of the fact. Graeme by this time was serving as Chief Officer.

NATURALIST AND MIDDLE MOUSE

The ship sailed from Avonmouth early on the 19th April, 1955, bound for Liverpool. In command was Captain John Ivor Jones, R.N.R. Ivor had been awarded the Distinguished Service Cross when in command of the corvette, H.M.S. HYACINTH, for sterling work during the battle for Crete in 1941. On November 26th, 1942, HYACINTH captured intact the Italian submarine, PERLA, single-handedly. This brought Captain Ivor Jones a Distinguished Service Order and a permanent place in the Royal Navy's hall of fame. The War over, he returned to the ranks and sailed as a Second Officer in Harrisons. Eventually, in November 1954 he became the Master of NATURALIST.

The weather on that voyage from Avonmouth was fine and clear. The ship passed the South Stack at about 10.15 p.m. on the 19th April and an hour later was rounding the Skerries. At about 11.25 p.m., with the Skerries light abeam bearing 148 degrees True, distance 3 miles, Captain Jones laid off the course for the Pilot Station off Point Lynas, Anglesey, about 12 miles to the east. He noted that the hidden dangers of Ethel Rock and Archdeacon Rock would be cleared by a good margin. Shifting the parallel-rules, he read off the course indicated ... 089 degrees ... almost due east. With his pencil he jotted down the figures on the chart, but by some freakish quirk of the mind, transposed them to 098 degrees!! Underneath, he wrote down the compass error, 10° W and applied it. Then he ordered Third Officer Dodds to steer 108 degrees (standard magnetic compass).

Undoubtedly, the Third Officer should have checked the course plotted, as is custom and practice, but the Old Man had given him a direct order and it was natural to carry it out right away. Then the compass error would have to be checked on the new heading with a bearing of a convenient star. All this took time, and by then it was getting near to one bell (11.45 p.m.), time to call the watch, write up the log, make the tea .... Consequently, that vital check was never made!

Unsuspected by anyone, the ship was forging ahead 9 degrees off course. Worse, the deflection in the course angle had the effect of placing the 4-knot, west-going tidal stream against the port bow, setting the ship down a further 5 degrees. It was a dark night, crystal clear, with every star showing in the celestial canopy overhead; the sea, darker than the sky, was calm and unruffled. However, Captain Jones must have been uneasy when the light on Point Lynas failed to appear when expected. He sent Second Officer Williams, who had just arrived on the Bridge to take over the watch, up to the monkey-island, where the standard compass was sited, to take a bearing of the Skerries light, still flashing with brilliant intensity on the starboard quarter.

Of course, the reason why Point Lynas light had not materialised was because the ship was still in the 'blind' sector, where the light was obscured by the lie of the land. Meanwhile, the Second Officer's bearing, projected to the course line, put the ship due north of Lynas ... which was ridiculous! Thoroughly alarmed, he went up the ladder to check the bearing again.

The impact, when it came at 12.24 a.m., was violent. The 10,000-ton ship, moving at over 11 knots, careered full tilt into a solid rock rising some 23 feet above the surface of the sea.

I was sound asleep at the time, and the force of the impact threw the ship on her side so violently that I was flung out of my bunk. Still half asleep but unhurt, I reached for my jacket and lurched out on deck. Outside it was bedlam. The ship was still, immobile, but mingling with the roar of steam escaping from the relief valves was the screeching of a million demented birds. Overhead they swooped, weaving and diving amid the rigging, their wings, ghostly pale, reflecting the light shining from the masthead lamps, their beaks agape, screaming their raucous protest at this sea-monster that had driven them from their quiet roosting places on the rock.

I ran up the ladders to the Bridge, feeling the vibration as the engines began working astern. The roar of the steam ceased abruptly, leaving only the angry shrieking of the sea-birds to disturb the silence. Captain Jones was standing on the bridge wing.

'Where are we? What's happened?' I asked.

'That', replied Captain Jones dazedly, pointing towards the rock looming over the bow, 'That, Mr. Mate, I believe is the Middle Mouse!'

I went to the Chartroom, glanced at the chart ... at the course running almost due east ... at the pencilled figures ...

and realised at once just what had happened.

Three rocky islets stand off the northern shore of Anglesey, the East, West and Middle Mouse, all of them 'blind', for none of them is lit ... and NATURALIST had hit the middle one. She was transfixed by her forefoot, held fast, and making no response to the engine's stern power. The ship's position was precarious, for the tide was still ebbing. Chief Officer, Carpenter, and Second Engineer Mike Merrifield checked the ship for damage and found all compartments tight, except the fore-peak and No. 1 tank, which were flooded. Their thoughts reverted to the Old Man's lonely plight and they felt a great sadness.

A vessel showing the white-over-red signal for a pilot boat was approaching cautiously. It was the Lynas cutter coming to find out what on earth a ship was doing in that position. An Aldis lamp flashed across the dark waters.

"Do you require a pilot?"

The question occasioned some rather hysterical mirth. "Affirmative" was the reply. When at last the large frame of Dick Lund, the Company's appropriated pilot, climbed over the rail, his bluff reassuring manner was like a tonic.

"The tide will start making in half-an-hour or so", he said confidently. "Then she'll float off."

And so she did, and we resumed our voyage to Liverpool ... down by the head, but under her own steam.

Graeme has written at length the stories of his colourful life. Sadly, we only have room for one more ... he was Master of the GOVERNOR at the time, the year 1969 and the title is intriguing.

THE DAY THE MANCHESTER SHIP CANAL RAN DRY

From our berth alongside Trafford Wharf, we watched MANCHESTER COURAGE back out of No. 9 Dock with detached interest. It was 6.50 p.m. on the 16th March and our pilot, Bill Walker, was keeping a professional eye on things from the wheelhouse. The breeze was fresh from the east and the two Canal Company tugs, SABRE and SCEPTRE, seemed to be having difficulty holding the big ship up to windward as she headed towards the lock. In fact, she was clearly in danger of hitting the 'bullnose', that end of the lock wall which jutted out into the basin. One would have expected to see the screw churning astern at this crisis … but the dark, polluted water under her stern was still. There appeared to be engine trouble.

At last, the tugs had her moving astern, but the ship still continued to fall down to leeward. Professional curiosity turned to alarm as it became apparent that MANCHESTER COURAGE was in grave danger of falling against the GOVERNOR! I made a hurried exit from my cabin to rouse the Officers and men to have the fenders on hand, ready to cushion the anticipated blow. But they were already on their way and I darted up to the wheelhouse to confer with Pilot Walker, who was also showing signs of perturbation. Gradually, however, the tugs began to win their battle and the ship began to draw away. As her Bridge drew level with ours, the two Pilots had a lively and colourful conversation. The cause had been engine rouble. There was nothing for it but to wait patiently for an hour or so until the ship's engineers had completed their task, while berthed alongside Salford Quay.

When the time came, there were no hitches and the Manchester Liner passed easily through the lock and into the Barton stretch. GOVERNOR followed shortly after, entering Mode Wheel Lock at 9.15 p.m. However, when the ship was secured in the lock, Pilot Walker advised against immediate departure.

"We'll wait until we know whether the sonofabitch has cleared the next lock" he growled. So, we stayed, until the Lockmaster's office declared that Barton was all clear.

Our lock was lowered and we pressed on through the next section, securing in Barton Lock about forty minutes later. Pilot Walker's wariness was not yet mollified, however, and the fact that the Liner had not yet cleared the much shorter Barton/ Irlam section was a sign that all was not well. We played the waiting game, determined to stay in high level until Irlam was reported clear.

It was well that he did. The unthinkable had happened. A disaster of such proportions that it was likely to figure only in a nervous Pilot's worst nightmare had overtaken the MANCHESTER COURAGE!

Briefly, she had charged through the lower lock gates, emptied the lock, and was now perched across the sill, wedged by fallen masonry and other debris. The upper gates had not been closed ... there had not been time ... and they had been swept away in the rush of water. The level of the two-mile Barton/ Irlam section of the Canal fell sixteen feet and rapidly drained off into the Latchford section. Two Manchester Corporation sludge vessels, the MANCUNIUM and the PERCY DAWSON, both lying at the Corporation's berth, were stranded in the mud, the former sustaining some damage.

There is no escaping the awesome conclusion that, if GOVERNOR had moved into the next stretch of water on cue, she too would have been lying high and dry, listing drunkenly in a noisome bed of the Ship Canal mud and slime.

It was not until the 21st March, 1969, that tugs were able to tow the MANCHESTER COURAGE clear of the shattered lock and proceed to Gladstone Dock in Liverpool to discharge her export cargo. Work on the main lock went ahead, new gates were installed and on the 18th April, 1969, the Manchester Ship Canal was fully operational once more.

Thank you, Captain Graeme Cubbin ... there should have been so much more!.

Captain Arthur Sugden
Master Mariner

Captain Arthur Sugden went to sea at sixteen years of age at a time when the War was at its height of danger for the seafarer. The learning curve was steep!

THE AMERICAN SURVIVORS

I joined the S.S. CITY OF WELLINGTON on the 11th May, 1941, in Birkenhead. We sailed a few days later to Oban for orders. We were told to proceed to the 'Tail of the Bank' and wait for the convoy to assemble. As soon as we gathered, we sailed for Halifax, Nova Scotia ... incidentally, we were bound for Calcutta via the Cape for 'bunkers'.

It was an uneventful convoy, but I think we were very fortunate because during the crossing, BISMARK slipped through the Denmark Straits. H.M.S. HOOD blew up with almost total loss of lives and H.M.S. PRINCE OF WALES was damaged in the subsequent engagement. However, we almost made it to Halifax, because the day before we were due to arrive, the Commodore instructed us to open our sailing orders and proceed independently at our full speed, 11 knots, as against the convoy's 8 knots.

Off we set following the Admiralty course and zig-zagging on southerly courses, never in sight of land, skirting the West Indies and with constant look-outs, we eventually crossed the Equator ... no celebrations, naturally ... and proceeded on southerly courses in the South Atlantic.

It must have been over ten days and we had never sighted anything, not even a smudge of smoke on the horizon, when suddenly the Third Mate at about 1100 hours thought he saw a lifeboat. He blew one blast on his whistle, which meant that I had to report to the Bridge. The Captain was there. He was elderly and obviously, his eyesight was not as good as someone younger. He told me to go down and to call the Chief Officer and ask him if he would please come to the Bridge. So, down I went, knocked on the Chief Officer's door and gave him the Captain's message.

He was dressed in his white longs and a singlet, being quite warm, and he was having a game of crib with the Second Officer. He immediately jumped up, put on his patrol jacket, uniform cap and proceeded to the Bridge. The Captain said, "The Third Officer thinks that he can see a lifeboat." The Chief Officer's immediate reply was "Can it be a decoy, Sir?" That was quite logical because some submarines had used this method to induce a merchantman to slow or stop, thus presenting an easier target for the sub. We did not reduce speed and were closing by now on what was quite clearly a lifeboat.

The Captain was getting impatient. We had now reduced speed so he asked the Chief Officer, "Surely, by now, you can make something out!" The Chief Officer was using the telescope. He turned to the Captain and said, "Looks like a bunch of dagoes to me, Sir!"

We stopped and slowly drifted closer until the Captain said, "Use the megaphone and ask them what ship?" The reply came back. "We are an American ship, S.S. ROBIN MOOR, out of New York bound for Cape Town. We have been fourteen days in an open boat!"

The Chief Officer turned to the Captain and said. "Something fishy here, Sir! S.S. EXMOOR is written on the side of the lifeboat. We'll ask again. You said ROBIN MOOR, why is S.S. EXMOOR on your lifeboat?" The reply came back that she was EXMOOR, but had been sold to the Robin Line just before sailing from New York. "We changed the name on the bow and stern, but we have not got round to the lifeboats." That made sense, so we picked them up ... the Captain's boat first, with the Captain's wife, a young couple with a two-year old boy called Robin, a Mr. and Mrs. Cohen (more about them later), other Officers and crew.

A pilot ladder had been thrown over the starboard side of the foredeck, just forward of the Bridge. The Officers and crew climbed up quickly, but as soon as their feet touched the deck, they collapsed ... legs giving way after sitting so long. We laid them out on top of the hatch. Then came the women and little Robin. Our Second Officer, the late Captain Reg Bushell, went down the ladder and a heaving line was lowered. He secured it round Robin and himself, we took in the slack and he brought Robin on board. Later he was sent a Gold Medal inscribed by President Roosevelt. He showed me it when I sailed with him some time afterwards on the CITY OF SYDNEY.

Then we proceeded on our course and eventually picked up survivors from two more lifeboats, 35 souls in all. A fourth lifeboat, under the command of their Third Mate, made Permanbuco in South America.

Thirty five extra mouths to feed presented quite a problem aboard with a crew of sixty already, although most of the crew were Indians and they carried their own sheep on the poop, along with a few hens. For the Europeans we had run out of potatoes ... no fridge on board and the ice had long melted in the ice-box. There was no running water and the pump was kept locked. There was one bucket in the morning and one bucket at night ... that was for everything, drinking, washing, dhobie, etc. We were down to hard tack and bully beef before we reached Cape Town. The ship's biscuits were so hard that the Chief Engineer always used a hammer to break his.

Eventually, we arrived in Cape Town and the American survivors disembarked. We found out that one of the passengers, Mr. Cohen, was on his way to Durban to become manager of the Metro Cinema. As he left he gave me a pat on the shoulder and said "Now don't forget, son, if you are ever in Durban, come and look me up. I'll see that you get the best seats in the house."

It so happened that some eighteen months later I was one of the Apprentices on the CITY OF SYDNEY and two of us decided to have a walk round Durban ... needless to say we had no money. There was the Metro. In we went and asked the lady to telephone Mr. Cohen and just say 'CITY OF WELLINGTON'. He was down in a flash and we happily ended up in the best seats in the house.

You must remember that America was neutral at the time of the ROBIN MOOR sinking. The Captain of the submarine had ordered the vessel to stop in order to check the manifest. He considered that the cargo could be of use to the Allies and decided to sink her. But firstly, he told them to provision the lifeboats and make sure that they had plenty of water.

The CITY OF WELLINGTON was sunk in August 1942 south-west of Freetown. Sixty crew members and five gunners were rescued by H.M. Destroyer, VELOX a day later and landed in Freetown. Seven of the crew were lost.

As you read this anthology, it will be obvious that the seafarer has a special code of life, the origins of which are mostly lost in time. Traditions by the nature of the word are passed down from age to age. Captain Arthur Sugden reminds us of one or two.

NEW YEARS EVE

I was on board the S.S. CITY OF WELLINGTON in 1941, outward bound for South and East Africa via Ascension Island and St. Helena with supplies.

We were on our own, having left the Atlantic convoy, but I forget which one it was. I was instructed to report to the Bridge at 'one bell' (quarter to midnight) on New Year's Eve.

I was then given precise instructions on my duty, which was as follows. About five minutes before midnight go for'd and stand on the Fo'c'sle Head near to the bell which was generally very big. On a whistle from the Bridge ... there were no phones in those days ... I was to strike eight bells i.e. to let the Old Year out and then another eight bells to welcome the New Year which would sweep over the bow before engulfing the whole ship.

These sixteen bells had to be struck by me, because I was the youngest member of the crew (17 years). I can assure you that it was quite eerie standing on your own on a dark night in the middle of the Atlantic with the ship heaving under you.

I was glad to strike the bells, report back to the Bridge and then get into my bunk.

BURIAL AT SEA

On the same ship, we were homeward bound from Calcutta. We had a 4.7 inch gun on the poop. I was in the gun crew. Just before sailing we had been told that we would carry five gunners and their ack-ack gun (anti-aircraft), which I think was a Bofors. The ack-ack was lashed aft and the gunners kept watch round the clock. We rounded the Cape and eventually joined a convoy at Freetown. Our escort was one armed trawler and a Sunderland flying boat.

Everything seemed normal in the convoy until about 0200

hours one morning when a shot from the poop was heard on the Bridge. Upon sending someone along to investigate, it was found that one of the army gunners had blown his brains out. Obviously, burial at sea was necessary.

If you were on day work, you had to report to the Chief Officer before 0700 hours and he gave you the job or jobs for the day. On this occasion, he said "Come to the Bridge and see me at 0900 hours." When I reported, he said "Oh! I want you to go with the Quartermaster and the two of you can sew up the body! The engine room will send up a couple of fire-bars, which you can lash to the legs and I'll be along to measure up the canvas."

Whilst we were waiting, the Q.M., who was an old hand and had obviously done all this before, said "The Mate won't be very pleased with this chap." I asked "Why?" He answered, "Look at the size of him. Think of all the canvas he will take."

We lashed on the fire-bars and then the Mate arrived with a bolt of No. 2 canvas. He measured up very carefully and we set to work. The Q.M. kept chatting away and said to me, "Of course, you know that the last stitch has to go through the nose." I replied, "Surely not!" "Oh yes", he replied. "The Mate will be along to see you do it. Never mind, we'll get a tot when all this is done."

So, we sewed away. The Q.M., being a crafty old hand, made sure that I had the job of finishing off. It was not a pretty sight when you saw the poor chap's head with quite a large hole and his brains half-oozed out!

Sure enough, the Mate arrived to make sure that I put the last stitch through the nose. Thus, the tradition of Nelson's time, and maybe before, was still being carried on in the 20th Century.

The Captain signalled the Commodore asking permission to drop out of line for the Burial. Back came the reply to remain on station and commit the body to the deep in the usual manner. This we did by sliding him off a couple of hatch boards from the port side of the aft well-deck.

I heard that, after we safely docked, the Second Mate had to make a court appearance since he was the Officer on Watch at the time of the suicide and nobody even knew that the gunner had a revolver.

WRONG SHIP TORPEDOED

Ellerman Hall Line, CITY OF JOHANNESBURG, ex-MELFORD HALL, built 1920. Position sunk … 33°20'S, 29°30'E.

We were homeward bound from Calcutta and Colombo via Cape Town with 7,750 tons general cargo including pig iron, cotton, jute, rubber and tea. Deeply laden, we were routed south in the Indian Ocean well to the east of Madagascar until south of Durban and then headed west towards Cape Town.

A torpedo struck on the port side midships about 2300 hours. I jumped out of my bunk, we were already listing to port and, of course, there was a strong smell of cordite. I grabbed my life-jacket, put it on, tied securely; my station was starboard lifeboat on the poop and my duty was to enter the lifeboat, fit in the plug and clear the lines ready for lowering. The main problem was reaching the poop, since we had an after well-deck, already awash, with a narrow flying bridge and since all our Indian crew lived aft there was a mad stampede of Indians charging forward to reach the four other boats, namely two jolly boats abaft the Bridge and the lifeboats at the after end of the boat-deck, so head down I just had to charge through.

Our lifeboat was lowered successfully and the crew climbed down the rope ladder until the last two, the Third 'Sparks' and the Third Mate. We had drifted a few feet away from the ship's side and 'Sparks' wouldn't jump, so the Third

Mate pushed him off the ladder into the water before boarding the boat himself. Then we had the job of fishing 'Sparks' out of the water. I never realised how difficult that can be with a heavy body in waterlogged clothing. It took about three of us to finally get him over the gunwale and into the lifeboat. We then shipped our oars and started pulling away from the ship. Then there was a large explosion as our ship was struck by a second torpedo, after which she sank almost immediately.

Our lifeboat had been on the lee side so now we felt the full force of the wind, and the sea was quite rough, when the moon suddenly shone through a break in the clouds and being low its rays lit up the water. Then I got the fright of my life because the U-boat surfaced right in the middle of the moonlit water and not too far away. However, he was closer to another of our lifeboats with a neighbour of mine who was the Q.M. in charge, and the German Captain hailed him and asked him what was the name of our ship. The Q.M. told me afterwards there didn't seem any point in giving a false name, so he told the German, who replied, "Are you sure? Because I'm waiting for the CITY OF WINDSOR from Australia". We found out later of course that there was a spy in the railway yards in Cape Town with a transmitter advising the U-boat of impending arrivals and departures and U504 commanded by Fitz Poske was part of the 'Eisbar' (polar bear) patrol group of five U-boats in the Indian Ocean, S.E. of East London.

We finally set our sails, but the wind freshened considerably and I think our canvas had partly rotted with too much monsoon weather and it blew out. We then tried the sea anchor, but there again the line carried away so we were left with just a jib and a couple of oars to keep her steady.

Thankfully, late the next day, we were spotted by the FORT GEORGE and were rescued, only to find when we boarded that she already had picked up the Q.M.'s boat crew. So she had 54 extra souls on board. The Captain called us together and explained that the FORT GEORGE was on her maiden voyage, having been built in Vancouver and she was bound for Trinidad and would take us there, but she didn't have enough food on board. She was managed by Ropers. This caused a few smiles, however he said he would try and land us at our naval base, Simonstown. Of course, he couldn't break radio silence so the next day, as we steamed into Simonstown, a 4" shell was fired across our bows. After some quick Morse on the aldis lamp the Navy allowed FORT GEORGE to enter and even warped us alongside where we disembarked and were put on the train for Cape Town. As a memento of the FORT GEORGE, I kept the breakfast menu card for 24th October 1942, which I have in front of me now and copy as follows:

MENU
24th October, 1942

BREAKFAST
Grapefruit, Curried Beef & Rice
Grilled Sausage & Mashed Potatoes
Tea, Preserves

DINNER
Vegetable Soup
Steak & Kidney Pudding
Baked Potatoes & Cabbage
Rice Pudding
Cheese & Biscuits
Coffee

TEA
Scrambled Egg on Toast
Fried Steak & Onions
Cold Roast Beef & Salad
Tea, Preserves

In conclusion, I must say how kind the people in the Cape were to all survivors, because when we reached Cape Town there were already 500 from the troopship ORCADES, plus survivors from many other merchant ships. We had to wait a month in Cape Town before a ship was available to take all the D.B.S. home. A Dutch passenger ship called the M.V. SIBAJAK, which used to be on the Java run, brought us safely to Liverpool where we tied up alongside the stage in the pouring rain with all my worldly possessions in a paper carrier bag. We had been given £10 for clothing when in Cape Town, which was enough for a pair of shoes, socks, a set of underwear, shirt, slacks and sports coat. You knew that everyone in Cape Town with brown shoes, slacks and sports coat was a survivor.

NEAR MISS IN CONVOY

I was one of four apprentices aboard S.S. CITY OF SYDNEY, outward bound in an 8-knot convoy from UK to Freetown, Sierra Leone.

This would be in 1943 and by that time, British Merchant shipping was much better protected. For example, most ships had an anti-aircraft gun in addition to the 4" or 4.7" guns, also Oerliken guns were generally mounted on the Bridge wings. In fact, I had attended the training dome in Durban and was allowed to fire an Oerliken. Hence, when on lookout, my station was alongside an Oerliken. The other big improvement was that ships were fitted with very high intensity parachute flares in case of night attack.

On this particular night, I was on the middle watch (midnight – 0400 hours) with the Second Officer, when about 0200 hours we were attacked by submarines. The first we knew was when a Scandinavian ship way on the port side of the convoy was hit; we knew she was carrying ore because she was so deep in the water and she broke in two and sank as we were watching.

Our alarm bells were immediately sounded and the Second Mate told me to collect the charges for our snowflakes out of the chronometer locker (kept there for safety), fit them in our two rockets and cock the firing pins, which I did. I had just cocked the pin of the last rocket when there was a blinding flash and there must have been a tremendous explosion. All that I remember was picking myself up from the after end of the Monkey Island and dropping down the short vertical wooden ladder on to the wooden deck on the after end of the chartroom. I turned and then stopped for a moment because all around our ship were huge geisers of water, just as if we were being bombed. I must have been in shock because it took me a second to realise that the ship directly ahead of us in convoy must have been full of explosives, had blown up and pieces of the vessel were raining down on us. The next moment, a large piece of phosphor bronze crashed past my head and landed at my feet.

I thought it was about time I moved, so I ran to the after starboard corner of the chartroom intending to report to the Second Officer, when, just as I rounded the corner, a huge stringer plate from the ship ahead landed on top of the Oerliken gun on the starboard Bridge wing where I had been for the previous two hours. The Captain appeared out of the starboard wheel house door, saw the damage and spotted me. "Take the wheel, Sonny". He always called me 'Sonny'. So I went in the wheelhouse and took over the wheel; strange, but once I was steering and in the wheelhouse, I suddenly felt safe. Of course by this time it was brighter than daylight with all the numerous parachute flares and I remember the wonderful sight of one of our escorts, the sloop H.M.S. WELLINGTON, steaming in the opposite direction to the convoy between our column and the next column on the starboard side. She must have been doing over 20 knots, creaming it up at her bows … a wonderful sight! Incidentally, the same vessel is now moored in the Thames and used by the Honourable Company of Master Mariners. The Chief Officer was the next to appear on the starboard side of the Bridge; on the previous voyage he had been torpedoed on the CITY OF ATHENS and his room was on the deck below, near enough to where the plate landed to nearly blow him out of his bunk. Naturally he thought we had been torpedoed and said to the Captain, "Shall we take to the boats?" All the Captain said was "Full ahead" since the Mate was standing by the engine room telegraphs. The Mate must have been in shock because he repeated his enquiry about taking to the boats. The Captain, who was a man of immense strength, just picked the Mate up and moved him out of the way and gave the telegraphs a double ring which of course meant extra full speed.

I knew what would happen next, and sure enough, the engine-room, voice pipe whistle blew. Chief Engineer: "We have burst oil pipes down below". The Captain's reply was swift and brief "If you don't give me full speed Chief, you will end up in Davy Jones locker like the poor Dutchman ahead". I immediately felt the throb of our quadruple expansion engine increasing the revs ... she could do over 14 knots. The next thing the Captain ordered "Hard-a-starboard" followed by "Midships", then "Hard a port" and then, I realised what he was doing. He had me line the ship up between the columns and steering in the white wake which H.M.S. WELLINGTON had left. By this time we were really moving. So we steamed straight out of the convoy and made our own way to Cape Town, where we spent a week undergoing repairs. We were also carrying cased aircraft on deck and you can imagine the mess they were in. The Dutchman which blew up was a big ship with goalpost masts easy to steer by in the dark. All I saw was some floating timber and a few flames as we steered over where she had been. The plate which landed on our gun was ¾ inch thick and just looked as if some giant hand had twisted it ... it stunk of cordite of course. Incidentally, next to the

Oerliken gun which was smashed by the ship's plate was a tube, which all ships had at that time, in which you placed a distress rocket if required. The tube served as a convenient spot to hang my tin hat on a warm night, but the next mornmg I found my tin hat on the after end of the boat deck about 150-200 feet away.

Captain Arthur Sugden enjoyed his time at sea. Starting at sixteen in Ellerman and Hall Line, he sailed as a Third Mate during the latter part of the War and was lucky to survive. He joined S & J Thompson's Silver Line with their 16 knot twin screw cargo vessels. On V.J. Day, he had docked in Birkenhead, needing a few more months to take his Mate's 'ticket'. Next came Athel Line, molasses from Cuba to UK and runs to the Gulf and Shanghai, Australia and Singapore, etc. By this time, he was married and joined Moss Hutchinson late in 1949. He was in command for 21 years, the last eight under the P & O flag. Arthur finally retired in 1984 after some four decades at sea. He is a good companion.

18ᵗʰ Century Swedish Poop Lantern
(Candles)

Captain Cyril Roberts
Master Mariner

Captain Cyril Roberts had a lifetime at sea ... he obtained his Extra Master Certificate, became a Ship Master, a Board of Trade Marine Surveyor and Examiner before he retired. I record some of his memories.

THE LOSS OF M.V. DEFOE

(In position 52 11 deg. North, 19 32 deg West, SW of Rockall.)

I joined Lamport and Holt Co. Ltd. in January, 1941. In the February, I sailed on DEFOE as the junior of two Cadets, headed for South America with general cargo.

In the September of 1942, I was on my third voyage as Senior Cadet in DEFOE and we left Manchester for Famagusta. The cargo was war materials, aircraft dope, cylinders of liquid chlorine gas, bombs, ammunition, rockets and Very lights, etc. A motor torpedo boat and a motor patrol craft were secured on the foredeck.

DEFOE joined a convoy of about sixty ships off the Scottish Coast and proceeded north of Ireland to set course for the Straits of Gibraltar.

On the 24th September, I was keeping the 0400 – 0800 watch, taking the first shift, 0400 – 0600, at the wheel. At about 0630, as the stand-by, I heard and felt a large explosion and the General Alarm bell went off. On reporting to the Bridge, I saw that No. 1 Hatch had exploded and was blazing furiously.

After collecting my papers from my cabin, I relieved the helmsman at the wheel so he could do the same.

At this time, the DEFOE was steering a course to try to limit the spread of the fire but this was a collision course with the rest of the convoy. The other vessels kept clear of us.

The steering position's window had a steel plate, with a slit in it so that the helmsman could see ahead, that could be lifted for protection. This I did, fortunately as it turned out.

At about 0700, the fire party decided to inject steam into Hatch No. 2 by means of deck valves. Five crew members, including the other Cadet, were working on No. 2 hatch cover, dumping any inflammable material. Before steam could be injected, No. 2 Hatch exploded killing all five and injuring some others.

The Master then gave the order to abandon ship and we proceeded to the lifeboats. The DEFOE had lost most of her forward hull and, with engines stopped, she lay almost end on to the wind.

My boat was lowered on the starboard side, but drifted away half-empty, as the ship was making a lot of leeway.

The port lifeboat could not immediately clear the ship. The chlorine cylinders had been shattered and this gas pervaded the ship, particularly on the portside. Two men had jumped into the sea to escape the gas, one being the carpenter. Eventually, the port lifeboat was rowed away from the ship.

At about 0730 with ten crew members I retreated to the crew accommodation aft to escape the gas.

When the chlorine gas had nearly cleared, those remaining on board decided to leave the vessel in the dinghy. The Master,

Captain Scott, stayed and started to search the ship for any remaining crew ... none were found.

The Chief Officer and I lowered the dinghy with eight crew in it and when it reached the water it promptly drifted away from the ship. I went down a life-line into the sea and swam to the dinghy and was pulled into it. The Chief Officer followed down another life-line and we rowed the dinghy back to the ship and picked him up. The water was very cold and the Chief Officer and myself were freezing, but the convoy rescue vessel, a passenger vessel called INCOMATI, came alongside our dinghy and we scrambled up nets on the ship's side.

The INCOMATI's crew looked after us well and those badly burned by the explosion received very good medical care. I received a cut on the forehead, from glass which had come through the slit in the wheelhouse protective plate. When the medical team washed my face, one said to me, "You are not as ugly as I thought", but it was only a slight wound.

Captain Scott finally left the DEFOE on a raft which I had previously released, but failed to launch. He was finally picked up by a Naval escort vessel.

The INCOMATI landed us in Freetown, West Africa, fourteen days later. After a week in an hotel we boarded the ACQUITANIA for Liverpool where we arrived two weeks later.

It was very sad to loose my shipmates, particularly the Junior Cadet whose total sea-time was only five days. The injured crew members all recovered ... some badly scarred.

On the 11th June 1943, I was notified that I had been granted a Commendation by Winston Churchill.

After leave, I joined the M.V. DEBRETT ... a sister ship to DEFOE. I served in her until my first Certificate.

After serving in other ships, I re-joined DEBRETT as Third Officer and took part in the invasion of Sicily at Syracuse. Other trips around the globe included the Far East and Australia. The DEBRETT was in the middle of the Pacific when the atom bombs were dropped.

The DEBRETT escaped bombs and torpedoes to finish the War intact.

Captain Cyril Roberts continues his thoughts

MAN OVERBOARD

Our ship, a medium size fruit carrier, with a cargo of bananas from the West Indies to Liverpool, was proceeding just north of the Canary Islands, on an early September morning in 1955.

It being a Saturday morning, the crew was engaged in cleaning the accommodation and deck areas as was routine.

The inspection party, comprising the Master, Chief Engineer, Chief Steward and myself (Chief Officer), having inspected the midship accommodation, was proceeding on the after deck to inspect the crew quarters in the poop.

Suddenly, we heard the shout of "Captain, Captain" from the sea on the starboard side and we were surprised to see a long-handled broomstick sticking right up with a head of hair floating at the surface. It turned out to be a seaman who had been engaged in hosing down the boat-deck. He had been holding on to the lifeboat grab-line which had parted and sent him on the way overboard.

All hell broke loose. The Bosun, with the voice of a foghorn, immediately informed us of the emergency, together with the Third Mate on the Bridge sounding the whistle, ringing the alarm bells, releasing the lifebuoy on the Bridge wing and stopping the engines.

The Captain headed for the Bridge, the Chief Engineer to the engine room and I to the motor lifeboat on the starboard side. The Captain manoeuvred the ship and gave orders to launch the lifeboat.

I picked five seamen and two engineers to man the lifeboat. Unfortunately, the ship's head was not quite right for the launch and the ship was rolling heavily, causing the lifeboat to bang heavily against the ship's side.

Our two engineers valiantly tried to start the engine, but to no avail. So, we had to out oars and row towards the lifeboat. The boat's planking had been sprung and we were filling with seawater, but our engineers were game to the last, still trying with the starting handle under water!

We sighted our colleague and pulled him on board. We stretched him out on the thwarts' benches and were relieved when he was promptly sick.

The lifeboat was now floating on the buoyancy tanks with a free-board of about five inches, making it impossible to row any distance. The Captain was waving for us to return and I was waving to him to come to us, which he eventually did.

Lifting the heavy boat was an uncomfortable operation … very slow as the falls were hand-operated.

On reporting to the Bridge, the Captain wanted to know why it had taken so long. I asked the Third Officer to check the logged times and it actually had taken just fifteen minutes. The Captain gave us a "Huh" and left the Bridge.

Needless to say, we cancelled our routine boat drill on the Saturday afternoon.

Thank you, Cyril. You seafarers have some very off-beat experiences, not just in wartime.

18th Century Poop Lantern
(Oil Lamp & Wick)

Captain Mike Curtis
Master Mariner

Captain Mike Curtis is well loved and respected by us all and in this story we are taken back to the start of his sea-going career. We little thought at that time of the hard years that lay ahead for this country and for the rest of the world ... the European War became a World War and young Mike Curtis became part of history.

SINGAPORE INCIDENT 1942

On 29th September, 1941, I joined the cargo liner TALTHYBIUS in Liverpool as the senior of four Midshipmen. By no stretch of the imagination could she be called a beautiful ship. Built in 1912 in Greenock as one of a pair of ships designed for world-wide trade, she was, at over 10,000 tons gross, one of the largest carriers afloat at the time of her launch and for some years after. Due to the fact that she had twin masts forward and aft, set abreast of each other and joined by a catwalk near the top of each pair they were known amongst seafarers as 'goalposts' and by the dockers of Merseyside as 'football boats'. She was propelled by twin reciprocating steam engines and coal-fired boilers.

89

TALTHYBIUS had a wartime complement of 77 men made up of … Master, 4 Navigating Officers, 4 Midshipmen, Chief Engineer Officer, 7 Engineer Officers, 3 Radio Officers, Doctor, Chief Steward, Second Steward, Bosun, Second Bosun, Lamptrimmer, 4 Quartermasters, 10 Sailors, a Sailor's Cook, 5 Stewards, Chief and Second Cook, Baker and Galleyboy, 2 Fitters, a Leading Fireman, 12 Stokers and Trimmers and the Firemen's Cook. From the Bosun down, all these were Chinese. For defence purposes, there were 8 Gunners from the Maritine Anti-aircraft Regiment Royal Artillery, a Leading Seaman Gunner, R.N., and 2 Merchant Seamen Gunners.

The ship left Liverpool the same day in a coastal convoy bound for Cardiff and Swansea. At Cardiff, she bunkered to capacity under the coal tips and also loaded coal into the four main holds to a height, when levelled, of about ten feet, which took out all the awkward shapes at the bottom of these holds including the twin propeller shaft tunnels, and made a solid surface on which to load vehicles. At Swansea, a variety of wheeled service trucks, Bren gun carriers, ambulances and artillery of different kinds were loaded on top of the coal, while into the other holds went the thousand and one items required to keep an army in the field.

From Swansea, we sailed to Milford Haven to join the convoy that set off up the Irish Sea to be met by a section from the Mersey and, in the St. Georges' Channel, by the Clyde contingent. We headed west into the Atlantic in company with about 50 other ships, bound ultimately for the Middle East. We remained in convoy as far as Freetown in Sierra Leone and from there sailed independently south around the Cape and up the South African coast to Durban.

It was while on this leg of the voyage that we heard of the Japanese attack on Pearl Harbour, followed by America's entry into the war. It came as no surprise therefore, when our destination was changed to Bombay.

Having bunkered at Durban, we sailed via the Mozambique Channel to Bombay where, hastily topping up our fuel supplies, once again we joined the convoy bound for Singapore. Our route led down the west coast of India, round the south tip of Ceylon and then in a south-easterly direction to the Sunda Strait between Sumatra and Java. At this point, the convoy formed two lines and, passing Krakatoa, weaved its way northward across the Java Sea, through the Banka and Rhio Straits, finally coming into the Singapore Strait arriving in the Western Roads of Singapore shortly before noon on the 25th January, 1942.

That afternoon, we moved to the western wharf in Keppel Harbour and commenced discharging the military cargo. Outwardly the scene on the Singapore waterfront was the usual bustle associated with this port; the traders came on board and set up their stalls, the ice-cream man was still selling his 'Eskimo pies', but occasionally the air-raid siren added its strident note to all the other noises of the port. Air raids at this time were spasmodic, probably reconnaissance more than anything else. By dint of working round the clock with all the labour we could employ, the cargo, except for the coal, was discharged in 72 hours!

On the 29th of January, orders were received to commence unloading the coal from the bottom of the four main holds. However, due to the increasing incidence of air raids, the dock labour was becoming less than enthusiastic about working in an area that was obviously a prime target for the Japanese bombers. Only about 50 tons had been unloaded before the labour supply, which that morning had been reduced to a trickle, finally dried up altogether. The coal had to remain in the ship. That evening, we moved to the main wharf and awaited further orders.

These came on the afternoon of the 30th of January. We were instructed to commence loading, the following day, a cargo of airstrip construction equipment, consisting of bulldozers,

91

graders, dump trucks and all that that goes with them. It was part of a unit operated by the Royal New Zealand Air Force and we would be taking the personnel with us. Destination was to be Telok Betong on the extreme south point of Sumatra. That evening the machinery started arriving on the wharf and the next morning all that was required was labour to load it. No one turned up, so the four Midshipmen instructed the Kiwis in the art of handling ship's derricks and driving steam winches. Work was able to commence.

Japanese air activity was increasing daily, which hampered loading operations considerably, but by the morning of the 3rd of February all the equipment, with the exception of one large grader, was aboard and stowed. As this final piece of machinery was swung into position, the air-raid warning sounded once again. The by-now familiar sight of a formation of 27 bombers was observed approaching from a northerly direction maintaining course to pass directly over the ship. As always, they made their way quite undisputed by allied aircraft and at a height, as far as we could judge, above the bursts of anti-aircraft fire which always seemed to explode well astern of their line of progress.

We took cover and almost immediately bombs began falling unpleasantly close. Within a few minutes all was silent again, except for distant ack-ack fire, and we emerged from the doubtful shelter in the half-deck to watch the planes. Having passed over the neighbouring island of Blakang Mati and part of the way across the Singapore Strait, they wheeled on to a reciprocal course and commenced their return run. We returned to the cover of the half-deck. This time there was no mistaking their target, the ship shuddered and lurched as bombs fell on and around her with ear-splitting explosions. Then silence for a few seconds. This was followed by the sound of running feet along the steel deck as we all emerged from the deck-house to ascertain the extent of the damage. The most serious area appeared to be on the fore-deck where smoke was billowing from No. 2 hatchway, the place where the last of the machinery was being loaded. Of the squad of RNZAF men who had been working in the hold and had elected to remain below for shelter, their Warrant Officer had been killed outright while five others, plus one of the ship's gunners, were very severely burned by flames ignited by the bombs falling on to the vehicles, with full fuel tanks, standing on a floor of coal.

Having hauled the wounded from the hold, we fought the fire throughout the afternoon and just as we appeared to be gaining the upper hand, the water pressure on the hoses was reduced to a useless trickle. Our emergency petrol-driven pumps were brought into use and the local Fire Brigade, which had been dealing with more fires on the wharf, turned their attention to us. The cause of the failure of the ship's fire main then became all too apparent. While the direct hits had started the fire, a string of near-misses all along the starboard side had caused far more serious damage by peppering the hull side plating with shrapnel as they exploded just below the waterline. The volume of water pouring into the stokehold and engine room was more than the ship's pumps could cope with and, although they kept going as long as they could, in the end it was a losing battle and inevitably the time came when fires had to be drawn to avoid an explosion. The steam pressure fell and both engine and boiler rooms had to be evacuated. Attempts to staunch the ingress of water by rigging tarpaulins over the ship's side were made, but this operation was not successful and a further heavy raid during the late afternoon caused more damage to the hull and started another, smaller, fire in one of the after holds. By this time, the Chinese crew had decided that discretion was the better of valour and headed shorewards. The Officers and gunners carried on fighting the fire until the evening, when it was finally extinguished. However, the ship had developed a considerable list to starboard and was obviously settling on the uneven bottom of Keppel Harbour.

That night, as nothing further could be done, the Junior Officers and Midshipmen were sent up to the Mission to Seamen Club for a meal and a night's rest, returning early the following morning to the ship. It had been decided that every effort must be made to get the ship afloat and into dry-dock without delay. To achieve this, two items were essential ... a diver and salvage pumps. The ship was completely dead, no power or light was available. Fortunately, the galley was coal fired so it was possible for the Chief and the Second Stewards to provide meals, although all water had to be carried to the ship from Singapore Cold Storage premises some 500 yards distant, a job performed twice daily by the four Midshipmen.

Attempts to obtain assistance in pumping the ship out from the harbour tugs failed as their crews had deserted, but the Company's Engineer Superintendent, resident in Singapore, was able to spirit up a salvage pump. As it weighed in the region of four tons, it posed something of a problem to lift it from the wharf. We rigged a heavy rope tackle from one of the derricks and, by the time this was in position, we had obtained the services of a company of the Singapore Defence Force Volunteers. With all their men hauling on the rope tackle and the rest of us on guy-ropes, the Chief Officer acting as shanty man, the pump was hoisted aboard and positioned by brute strength.

No time was lost in starting the pump up and soon an estimated 400 tons of water an hour was being pumped out of the ship. After several hours of pumping the list eased considerably to ten degrees, and the water in the ship fell about a foot, but after that remained constant.

It had been hoped to pump enough water out of the ship to tow her into the Empire Dock to effect repairs. In retrospect, it seems remarkable that even at that date, the 4th of February, the myth of Fortress Singapore was still intact as far as we were concerned. We were advised that the tugs, now manned by Europeans, were back in operation and it was decided to attempt to move TALTHYBIUS the following morning, February 5th. Shortly before zero hour the Canadian Pacific liner, EMPRESS OF ASIA, was steaming through the Strait with troop reinforcements when she was attacked by Japanese bombers and set on fire. All harbour tugs were immediately ordered to her assistance and our plans cancelled. She became a total loss.

The evening of the 5th of February saw the arrival of a second salvage pump and once again, with the assistance of the Volunteer Force, we were able to manhandle it slowly aboard and, by the early hours of the 6th of February, it too came on stream. Both pumps worked steadily throughout the day resulting in a reduction in the water level to the pitch where plans were made to move the ship direct to dry-dock. Ever more frequent air raids, however, forced the cancellation of the project.

It was about this time that we noticed a massive pall of smoke rising steadily higher and higher into the northern sky. The only place in that direction capable of supplying enough combustible material for such a huge conflagration was the Naval Base at Seletar. Either it had been hit, or it was being systematically destroyed to deny its use to the enemy. Whichever it was, it was a sign, if any were needed, that we were working against time.

We also noticed that the ships were getting scarce in Keppel Harbour and that when they sailed they carried with them large numbers of non-essential Europeans. More and more abandoned cars on the wharf were the outward indication that the situation ashore was becoming daily more serious.

On the morning of the 7th of February, a check showed that the steady pumping had succeeded in lifting the ship clear of the bottom and with the list reduced to 5 degrees, plans were again put in hand to move the ship from the Main Wharf to the Empire Dock. Some of the Chinese crew had returned, so with them to handle the ropes ashore and helped by the arrival of two tugs, we at last started to move the ship slowly along the wharf and into the more sheltered water of the Empire Dock. All went well and the ship was finally tied up in her new berth. We were now able to turn our attention to getting the pumps in the optimum position to keep the water under control, but before we could achieve this, one of the pumps developed a fault and had to be stopped. The other was unable to cope on its own and was shut down, and the ship settled back on the bottom again.

On February 8th, the long awaited diver arrived; some of our Chinese Stewards also turned up. The four of us Midshipmen were able to hand over the water-carrying duties to the Stewards and concentrate on working with the diver, our main task being to cut and shape pieces of timber into various lengths for him to plug the holes in the hull. Progress was slow and at one point, an air raid caused us to seek shelter once again. No bombs fell close and as the planes moved away, somebody said … "The diver!" We tore on deck and looked over the side at the diving boat; the air-pump was still and a very thin line of bubbles was coming up to the surface in stark contrast to the usual surge of air rising. We swarmed down the rope ladder and started to wind the pump handles. Out of the boat's cabin came the Indian pumpmen and attendants. At that point, the diver broke surface alongside and the attendants unscrewed his helmet glass and removed his helmet. The diver, an Australian, then proceeded to tell the fortunes of each of his crew in terms that left us speechless with admiration and in no doubt about what he thought of them and all their antecedents.

Both pumps were restarted and the water level in the stokehold and engine room reduced again, but at around the 14-foot mark they seemed unable to make further headway.

That afternoon the Stewards were carrying water across from the Cold Storage Depot when they were caught in the open by a sudden unannounced air raid. Before they had time to take cover, a stick of bombs fell across their track and one of them was killed outright by a bomb splinter. There but for the grace of God!!! After that, we saw no members of the Chinese crew again.

The diver was ordered to another job that evening and, as there was no further improvement in the water level, the pumps were stopped until we could be sure of getting the diver back.

During the night, we were aware of a steadily increasing rumbling noise in the distance, which at first we took to be thunder, but as it continued unabated hour after hour, we realised that it must be an artillery barrage of large proportions. Up to that point, I don't think we realised just how critical the situation had become. We knew that the Japanese were moving down the Malay Peninsula, but it came as a shock to realise just how close to Singapore Island they now were.

On the morning of the 9th of February, rumour was rife that the enemy had forced the Johore Strait and had landed on the Island. We tended to ignore these stories and continued to rig staging and prepare timber bungs against the divers return. To our delight, he and his squad turned up that afternoon and, once more, the pumps were started up and plugging of holes continued.

While we were concentrating on this operation, we heard a loud whistling noise followed by an explosion on Blakang Mati, the island opposite the wharf about half a mile away. This was repeated steadily at irregular intervals and it dawned on us that we were now under artillery fire. Air raids had also been stepped up and were concentrated on the port area. Transit sheds on the wharf alongside the ship were hit and set alight. We therefore turned our attention to fire fighting with our portable fire pumps until we had the fire under control and it was no longer a threat to the ship. That night the continuous artillery barrage to the north of us was resumed.

Early the following morning, the 10th of February, work on plugging holes in the hull was resumed with the diver tackling the plating by way of the engine room, but after breakfast the port was subjected to a very heavy series of air raids and it was judged too dangerous to carry out further diving work. There was also an artillery duel going on between the guns on Blakang Mati. However, the pumps were thumping away and it did begin to seem that the work done by the diver was starting to pay dividends. Measurements of the rate the level was falling indicated that we were going to need a lot of time, and that was something we didn't have!

Our thoughts and conversation now turned more and more on how we were going to extricate ourselves from the position we found ourselves in. There was a small tug, not much bigger than a large launch, lying just ahead of the ship, completely deserted by her crew. It was proposed to fuel and provision it for use as a getaway vessel should it become necessary. These plans were put to the Master who vetoed the scheme on the spot. Nobody, he said, would leave the ship without his permission and that would not be given until Naval Control issued instructions. There was little that we could do for the rest of the day. The noise of gunfire seemed to get steadily closer, and more Europeans were boarding the few ships left in Keppel Harbour, all of which sailed that evening. We heard on the grapevine that a general evacuation had been ordered.

Early the next morning, the 11th of February, the largest ship we had seen in the port for some days, EMPIRE STAR, steamed slowly through the harbour and berthed at the Main Wharf. She immediately commenced to embark evacuees. We could now hear the rattle of small arms fire not too far away and there was no doubt in anybody's mind that things were critical. A group of soldiers, utterly weary and demoralised, appeared on the wharf and advised us to sail immediately. We showed them the flooded engine room and they went on their way.

By mid-morning, it was apparent that if anybody was going to get away, a move would have to be made promptly. The Master, still awaiting orders from Naval Control, realised this and calling us all together said that it was now a case of every man for himself. Asked what he intended to do, he replied that he would remain with his ship. The Third Officer and the Second Steward both said that they would remain with him. The rest of us, looking along the wharf to where we could see the EMPIRE STAR some half mile distant and still alongside, decided that he who fights and runs away lives to fight another day!

On numerous occasions, I have looked back on this episode with a twinge of conscience. My loyalty should have been to the Master, but common sense told me that there was no hope of the enemy being repulsed at this point. I had already, less than a year previously, been 'in the Bag' in Vichy-controlled territory in West Africa and had decided that life behind barbed wire was not to be recommended. True, the French had politely offered the alternative of joining the Foreign Legion, which I and the rest of my shipmates politely, but firmly, declined. But now, at this particular point in my career, I was starting to wish I had accepted!

However, the decision was taken, and each of us with a small bag containing treasured possessions and a change of clothing went down the gangway. There were a number of abandoned cars on the wharf and, selecting several of these, we drove off towards the EMPIRE STAR, hoping that she would still be alongside when we got there. It must have been shortly before noon when we reached her and all was bustle and hurry in preparation for imminent departure. As we got out of the cars, we noticed a few hundred feet along the wharf, another ship, tiny by comparison, the only other ship alongside. She was flying the White Ensign and appeared to be some sort of patrol craft. It was almost uncanny the way we hastily changed direction; perhaps it was some sort of sixth sense brought on by a period of bombing and shelling, but the same thought hit all of us, ... 'big ship, big target, small ship better chance'. We drove along to the small ship and our Senior Officer explained our position to the First Lieutenant. He in turn reported to his C.O. They were both Royal Naval Reserve Officers (men in the Merchant Navy in peacetime), and the C.O. immediately wanted to know where the Master was. "He is remaining with his ship," we replied. Commendable, but foolish in the circumstances was his summing up. He called one of his Sub-Lieutenants, a man built like a prop forward, and instructed him to take one of the cars to TALTHYBIUS. He was to tell the Master that he had come from Naval Control with orders for him to 'abandon'. He was then to bring him back without fail, together with the two Officers who had remained with him.

Meantime, we had a brief chance to examine the ship that we hoped would get us out of our predicament. Rejoicing in the name of H.M.S. PING WO, she was typical of the small cargo passenger vessels that plied the Yang-Tse River ports from Shanghai between the wars. About 200 feet long, she had a remarkably shallow draft of about six feet. The Bridge stood on top of a block of passenger accommodation right forward, overlooking the fo'c'sle head and bows of the ship. The accommodation stopped short about fifty feet further aft, where a long cargo hatchway was built at main deck level, served by a mast and two derricks. This took up about another 50 feet and the after half of the ship was the engine and boiler room, over which was built another high block of accommodation through which the funnel passed. She was a coal-burning ship and was designed to work in relatively smooth waters.

On being taken over by the Navy for patrol work, a 12-pounder gun had been fitted forward over the foc'sle head and just below Bridge level. A light machine gun graced the top of the after accommodation. She was hardly likely to strike terror into the hearts of the enemies. On being sent to Singapore, her crew had been made up of local Chinese and Malay ratings. With our arrival on the scene, these local men left the ship with the exception of the Chinese carpenter and ten engine room ratings. We wholeheartedly agreed to work our passage in their place to get the ship away.

Top priority was fuel and food. We split into three working parties ... one on the wharf shovelling coal into tubs, one on the ship working the steam winches hoisting the coal aboard and tipping it into the bunkers, while the third party, of which the four Midshipmen were part, took hand trucks to the transit sheds, forced open the doors and filled our trucks with anything edible, taking them back to the ship. The first shed we tackled appeared to be full of Guinness and condensed milk, but we found a more general variety of food in the next one. We only took the Guinness on the final run!

The Sub-Lieutenant returned with our Master and the two Officers whereupon work stopped briefly to check that everyone was present. During our stay in Singapore, we had sustained two other casualties besides the Chinese steward. One was the Seaman Gunner severely burned when we were first hit, and the other was the First Radio Officer who had been injured in an air raid while he was ashore some days previously. He was not fit enough to travel and had to be left behind in hospital. The muster showed that we were still two Officers short; they had last been seen earlier that day bent on a scorched earth policy to prevent the contents of the ship's bar from falling into enemy hands.

Once again, one of the abandoned cars was pressed into use. The Fourth Officer and Junior Midshipman being detailed to locate the two missing men and bring them back to PING WO, the sailing deadline being in half an hour. Meantime the working parties completed storing and coaling the ship and made ready to sail. In the interval between all being ready for sea and the return of the remaining Officers, the rest of us pushed all remaining cars, lorries and cargo handling equipment in the vicinity into the murky waters of Keppel Harbour.

The missing duo were duly located and bundled into the car. Deciding they had a bit of time in hand, the rescuers went aboard TALTHYBIUS one last time, the Fourth Officer to get his binoculars and the Midshipman, getting his priorities right, collecting his cabin trunk full of clothes.

By the time they returned to PING WO, the moorings were singled up and all was ready to sail. We got the missing men aboard and pushed the faithful car into the harbour. As we were jumping aboard, the C.O.'s voice shouted to the Fourth Officer and myself to remain ashore in order to cast off the mooring wires. The ship was lying with her stern to the current. "Let go the stern rope and back spring" came the order. We complied, and ran along the wharf towards the bow of the ship as the stern started to swing away from the quay. Seeing the manoeuvre, we anticipated the next order, "Let go the head rope", and it came off its bollard in an instant. Almost simultaneously, the bow moved off the quay as the order came to cast off the forward back spring, the last rope holding the ship to the wharf. Momentarily, we looked at the ever widening gap and both knew that to comply meant, quite literally, missing the boat. We hurled ourselves at the receding hull and thankfully both grabbed the side rails and tumbled on board. There was a yell of warning to stand clear as the engines went full astern and a judder as the wire tightened then parted, the two ends snaking dangerously back in opposite directions, thankfully not doing any damage. The two of us made ourselves scarce. It was by then mid-afternoon on the 11th of February.

The ship moved out the short distance from Keppel Harbour and into the Eastern Roads; here, off the breakwater, she anchored and began to collect evacuees from all manner of small boats and launches which came out to us from Clifford Pier. In the three hours before dusk, we had picked up nearly 200 people, mainly Europeans and Eurasians, some in uniform but most were civilians, business men and a few women. The largest contingent was from the British Malayan Broadcasting Company.

That evening, after dark, we weighed anchor and steamed out of Singapore. It was an unforgettable sight … fires blazing in the port area and in the city, but all of them dwarfed by the massive conflagration on the nearby island of Pulo Bukum which contained the fuel storage tanks. The flames roared up in the still night air to a fantastic height illuminating the underside of a huge black billowing cloud. Almost like a chain of beacons spreading the message of defeat, the Dutch oil installation on the south side of the Strait and to the east of us was set ablaze as we watched. The two fires of about the same intensity gave a weird glow as we headed west towards the Durian Strait and away from any possible enemy naval thrust. Off the northern end of the Durian Strait, and with the fires still blazing in the distance, we anchored as ordered until dawn on the 12th of February. Then, as dense black smoke was still rising, we turned south-eastwards down the Durian Strait bound for Batavia, some 550 miles away.

By this time, we had got into a seagoing routine. The Senior Officers kept their normal watches with their Naval opposite numbers, the Senior Engineer Officers did the same in the engine room, where the Junior Engineers acted as greasers and the Chinese greasers became stokers. The Fourth Officer and the two Senior Midshipmen acted as Quartermasters and steered the ship from inside an armour-plated pillbox in the wheelhouse. The Radio Officers helped in the wireless room, while the Chief and Second Stewards organised meals with the assistance of volunteer cooks from among the passengers. The

Gunners kept a lookout in the two gun positions.

All the evacuees settled themselves down in cabins and the public rooms and in any spare corners of the accommodation.

Rifles and ten rounds of ammunition were handed out to those crew members who knew how to use them, so apart from the boost it gave to individual morale, at least they had a token weapon to hit back with. They were very little use against aircraft flying at the height the Japanese bombers maintained.

During the morning of the 12th of February, there was considerable enemy air activity as we moved through the Durian Strait and the decision was taken to lie low among the multitude of islands and reefs that abound in the vicinity. We dropped anchor close to a heavily wooded island just about on the equator and remained there until dusk. A steady stream of aircraft flew overhead, but none of them spotted us. As darkness fell, we weighed anchor and headed across a relatively open stretch of water towards the Banka Strait. By dawn on the 13th of February, we were close to the eastern exit of the Banka Strait and again the Captain of PING WO sensibly decided to seek shelter close to the coast for the day, rather than present a target for marauding aircraft. At dusk that evening, we hove up the anchor for the last time, and skirting the coast of Sumatra we headed south for Batavia, arriving there on the afternoon of 14th of February, 1942.

The coastline in the approaches to Tanjong Priok, the port for Batavia, is very low-lying and apart from a backdrop of distant hills, the first signs that we saw as we neared the land was a large number of merchant ships at anchor off the port. In spite of their uniform battleship-grey colour, we could easily pick out at least four of our own company's ships by their distinctive silhouettes and tall funnels. Speculation was rife as to which of the ships we would be allocated for the voyage home.

Having been given clearance, we entered Tanjong Priok

harbour and secured at our berth; arrangements were made for all the evacuees to disembark and await re-allocation to ocean-going ships. We, however, were instructed to remain aboard PING WO and were joined by a small Naval draft of about 15 Boy Ratings who we understood to be survivors from the Battleship PRINCE OF WALES and the battle cruiser REPULSE. We also embarked a squad of Australian dockyard policemen, who had arrived at Batavia some days previously from the Royal Naval Dockyard at Seletar. Late that afternoon, it was confirmed that we were to remain on temporary loan to the Navy and continue to man PING WO on the next leg of her voyage, to Australia!

During the evening, we moved to the coal tips and commenced bunkering for the long trip ahead of us. The bunker spaces were to be filled and additional coal was to be loaded into the only cargo hold to ensure that we had enough to see us as far as Fremantle. The Junior Engineer Officers worked watches up in the gantry crane to check the weight of each grab full of coal to ascertain the precise amount that was put aboard, every lump counted. In the early hours of the following day, several truck-loads of food arrived and we had to turn out and store ship. It seemed to consist of tinned stew and biscuits and precious little else.

On the morning of 15th of February, we cast off from the coal wharf and moved out of the harbour. Just outside the break-water we were met by a harbour tug, towing a disabled Australian destroyer, H.M.A.S. VENDETTA. A veteran of the First World War, she had been undergoing a refit at Singapore when the Japanese attacked the Malayan Peninsula and had been towed to Batavia for safety. Our job was to tow her from Batavia to Freemantle!

Shanghai river boats were designed to operate in shallow and comparatively smooth water, hence their very light draft, while the one thing a tug needs is a fairly deep draft so that the propeller can bite the water at all times. It was not going to be a comfortable voyage.

By the time the tow line had been rigged and the ship was ready for sea, the day was wearing on. We got under weigh and, with VENDETTA weaving along astern of us, we headed west towards the Sunda Strait. A full day had passed before we were abeam of the volcanic island of Krakatoa and setting a south-easterly course towards Australia, the best part of 2000 miles away. Once clear of the Sunda Strait and with nothing between us and the African continent, the ship started to roll and continued rolling for the next sixteen days. My main memory of that passage is of bracing myself against the large brass steering wheel during my two-hour spells of steering and wedging myself in a corner of the accommodation to try to get a few hours undisturbed sleep. She was not an easy ship to steer in the best of weather, but with another ship tied on behind it was almost impossible to steer a decent course.

At one stage, the strain on the steering gear began to tell and it was necessary to rig relieving tackles to help ease the strain. During the early part of the trip, we were escorted by the sloop H.M.A.S. YARRA, but, as we moved at a snail's pace towards our distant goal, she left us and returned to join units of the Allied fleet in the Java Sea. We understood later she was lost on her way there.

On the 4th of March, we finally anchored in Gage Roads under the lee of Rottnest Island, off Freemantle. By this time, the Japanese had overrun Sumatra and Java and three days later, all Allied resistance in South-East Asia had ceased.

Food, fresh water and fuel had just been adequate and indeed, in spite of the incessant rolling all hands were remarkably fit, probably due to the fact that all those not directly concerned with running the ship worked steadily throughout daylight hours shovelling coal from the cargo hold to the bunkers. The ship had maintained an average speed of just over 5 knots during the seventeen day journey and at no time was there any serious problems with the tow rope. Doubtless, if we thought the trip had been pretty tedious, it must have been sheer hell for the crew of the VENDETTA, a completely dead ship wallowing in our wake.

Our arrival at Fremantle coincided with the return of a convoy bringing Australian troops home from the Middle East for defence of their own country and we had to wait all day at anchor due to port congestion. Harbour tugs took over VENDETTA and we ultimately berthed late in the afternoon. Meanwhile the Padre at the Missions to Seamen had been very busy arranging billets and accommodation for all members of TALTHYBIUS crew in private houses in and around Fremantle. The response to his appeal had been overwhelming. The four Midshipmen stayed with two related families outside the town. With the passage of time, one can't help wondering whether the kindness and hospitality of all these people was ever officially recognised.

After about a week, the Master was on his way home and the rest of the Officers followed at intervals, more or less in order of seniority, as berths became available on ships passing through Freemantle en route for Britain. The Midshipmen, being as it were on the bottom of the pile, got by far the best of the bargain, six weeks holiday practically living on the beach at Cottesloe; swimming, surfing, tennis and riding, all in ideal weather. Thanks to the foresight of the Junior Midshipman in collecting his trunk at the last minute, we even had one uniform between the four of us which we took in turns to use to impress the girls at the local dances. Our hosts, the Broomhalls and the Palmers and later the Lovegroves and the Laws, were kindness itself and, I can't help thinking, pretty long-suffering in their dealings with four teenage seafarers with healthy appetites. But, one by one our turn came and by July 1942 we had all arrived back in the U.K.

The Master was awarded the O.B.E. for his leadership during the episode, the Third Officer who had so gallantly stood by him was lost two years later when his ship was torpedoed by a Japanese submarine off the East African coast, and the First Radio Officer survived the Japanese prison camp after recovering from his injuries.

TALTHYBIUS, as expected, was raised by the Japanese and pressed into service by them after being renamed TARUYASU MARU. When they surrendered in 1945, she was located in the Japanese port of Maizuru instantly recognisable by her distinctive goal-post masts.

She was repossessed by the Ministry of War Transport and given the name EMPIRE EVENLODE. The company sent out a crew to bring her back to the U.K. via Singapore where a full cargo of scrap iron was loaded. The combined effect of old age and lack of maintenance by her captors resulted in serious problems with her machinery and boilers on the homeward voyage to such an extent that it was considered too risky to send her through the Suez Canal. She took the longer route via Durban and the Cape of Good Hope, retracing her outward voyage. After a protracted stay in Cape Town to replace 1200 boiler tubes, she finally arrived back in Swansea in May 1946, five months after leaving Japan and nearly five years after her previous call at the port.

After a survey, it was decided that she was no longer fit for further service and was sent to the ship-breakers yard where she followed her cargo to the scrap heap.

Thank you Captain Mike Curtis. That really was a memorable tale and a piece of our maritime history.

Eric Proffit
Company Director

Eric Proffit was a Director of the Blue Funnel Line and eventually President of the Master Mariners Club 1995 – 1996. Happily he has looked into the past and given 'the lamp' a mighty swing. Eric is a well-known character. His 'nostalgia' relates to life aboard a Trooper ... Eric was a 'brown job' in the Army on board the troopship, BRITANNIC. My experiences were similar. I was a Royal Air Force 'Brylcream boy' in the MONARCH OF BERMUDA (outward bound) and REINA DEL PACIFICO (homeward). Let Eric tell his story.

My story starts in March 1943 when, after a year in the ranks (East Lancashire Regiment) I was sent out with a draft of Officer Cadets to be commissioned in India. We were taken by troop train to Liverpool and embarked aboard the troopship BRITANNIC at Gladstone Dock. We were shown our 'quarters' ... hammocks down on 'E' Deck, packed in like sardines. We sailed on 11th March, 1943 round to Greenock, where next morning we joined a large convoy assembling there.

The ships and their escorts sorted themselves out and off we went. History would eventually relate that we were to pass through the most intense U-boat attacks of the War. Allied losses would be the highest ever ... March 1943 was the most successful time for the German submarines.

BRITANNIC was flanked on her port side by a destroyer. Over the next few weeks, I was to develop a deep affection for that destroyer. She was steady as a rock, despite the seas often covering her. Years later, I was told that the convoy was WS28 and 'my' destroyer was H.M.S. REDOUBT. Other escorts included H.M.S. QUADRANT, RACEHORSE and RELENTLESS and the merchant ships carrying thousands of us to the Middle East and Far Eastern Theatres (in addition to 'my own' BRITANNIC) were DUCHESS OF BEDFORD, MONARCH OF BERMUDA, ORANTES, OTRANTO, REINA DEL PACIFICO, STARTHNAVER, WINCHESTER CASTLE, SOBIESKI (Polish) and TEGELBERG (Dutch).

Progress was relatively uneventful, apart from the occasional alarms and flurries of activity by the escorts on the fringes of the convoy as they signalled and dashed about dropping depth charges, presumably when the presence of U-boats was suspected.

Gradually, a sort of routine euphoria set in amongst the troops ... after all there was nothing we could do about it ... we were but helpless pawns in this sector of the war at sea. What was obvious to us was that, as a large troopship, we would be the main target of any enemy attack that might develop from U-boats, either individual loners or, a major German tactic at the time, from several of them hunting in packs. The convoy's route appeared to be an extended circle out into the Atlantic, keeping out of range of German aircraft operating from airfields in France. We then turned back towards the coast of West Africa. It was at this stage in our voyage that several ships and an escort left us to enter the Mediterranean destined for North Africa.

The rest of us sailed on down the West Coast of Africa and when we reached a point a few days steaming from the

Cape, we were told that we were to leave the convoy and go it alone, at full speed, for Cape Town. The rest of the convoy was destined for Durban. We were all reminded to wear our life-jackets at all times and armed (why I wondered) lookouts were posted on all decks to spot for any threat from sea or air. I was given a party to operate on the forward part of the main deck where we were to remain in shifts, until we docked in Cape Town.

Off we sailed, and gathered speed ... this was very impressive to us after the previous weeks of trundling along at the convoy's requirement to maintain the speed of the slowest ship. Very soon the rest of the convoy disappeared over the horizon taking with them the escort that we had come to regard with great affection ... particularly for me, my own personal destroyer!

Then suddenly, without warning, at about 2 a.m. it happened! We had an engine breakdown and we were left wallowing like a stranded whale with no escort of any sort. To make things even more dangerous, the night was clear and the moon was full. It was an eerie experience with just the lapping of water to be heard and everybody on all decks at action stations watching out for the dreaded bubbling trail of a torpedo. The tension could be felt throughout the ship and, as dawn was breaking, the sound of aircraft engines could be heard. Two South African Catalinas arrived and commenced circling us, spotting for danger. Then, to our even greater relief, about mid-afternoon, three South African destroyers arrived from Naval Base at Simonstown. All this time we remained completely helpless. Eventually, to a rousing cheer of relief from all hands, our Captain announced that repairs were completed and we were about to proceed at full speed. Accompanied by three destroyers we sped through the night and, early next morning, the welcome sight of Table Mountain loomed dead ahead. To farewell hoots from the destroyers and welcoming sirens from the shore, we berthed at Cape Town. It was only then that we were informed that we were to leave BRITANNIC and move into a Transit Camp in Cape Town prior to being carried to our ultimate destination by another ship.

Our draft of officer cadets was assembled on the quayside and we were marched off to a Transit Camp at a place called Retreat. Compared with the way we had been living since Liverpool, the camp's Nissen huts with two-tier bunks and hot showers were absolute luxury and bliss! Also, after the rationing at home and the Spartan life aboard the troopship, we found ourselves in the land of plenty ... huge tins of jam, fruit of all kinds, chocolate, gallons of milk ... indeed everything we had almost forgotten about since the outbreak of War!

We had no duties whilst awaiting our next ship and were allowed out every afternoon and evening and, if invited, we could join a local family for a weekend. We were to witness at first hand the quite wonderful hospitality extended throughout the War by the South African people to troops who were transiting their country en route to the War.

After six wonderful weeks of luxury and pampering, the orders came through to pack our kits and be ready to embark at 6 a.m. the next day. Very fond farewells all round and we marched back to the docks to board the troopship ATHLONE CASTLE which was to take us to Bombay.

After an uneventful, unescorted, full-speed voyage, with the danger of attack limited to the outside chance encounter with a Japanese submarine, we berthed at Bombay, India, on the 11th June, 1943 ... exactly three months after sailing from Liverpool. The journey was complete and, although I didn't know it at the time, more than three years in India and Burma lay ahead.

Precisely three years and eighty days later on 5th September, 1946, I was a Major in the Fourth Battalion, the Frontier Force Regiment (Indian Army) at a place called Tavoy in Southern

Burma. A signal from Divisional H.Q. came in to say that my release group was now operative and I was to proceed to Rangoon to join a troopship there for repatriation. Ten frantic days later, after an horrific journey through the monsoon (that's another story) I boarded the S.S. ORMONDE and we sailed via Bombay to Tilbury, arriving U.K. on the 12th October, 1946.

Thank you Eric Proffit. Trooping to me meant playing bridge with the same partner everyday, washing for eight weeks in salt water, rejoicing in the sight of the White Lady of Durban and then flying aircraft in Rhodesia. I, too, spent time at Retreat and made many friends. Memories!

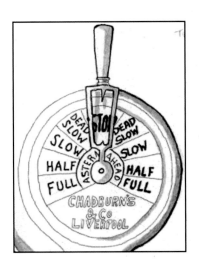

Captain Brian Hodges
Master Mariner

Captain Brian Hodges starts his story at the beginning ... where better?

BOY TO MAN IN FIFTEEN MONTHS

My story really is about my first voyage at sea, which was indeed fifteen months long, in wartime and all the things that happened during the voyage which I hope will make interesting reading.

I suppose one could ask the question what makes one want to go to sea. Well, my father always wanted to go to sea, so who else to send but his eldest son, but there was maritime blood in the family. Grandfather on my mother's side of the family was a Master with the Bristol City Line and my great-uncle, my grandfather's brother, was the Senior Surveyor and Examiner of Masters and Mates with the, then, Board of Trade in Bristol and based in Queens Square. Enough I suppose to send me on my way.

I was educated at St David's Collegiate School in Bristol and stayed there until I was 16, having passed the Junior Oxford Exams in Mathematics. I then worked for the Bristol Evening

Post while all the paperwork, interviews, and Indentures were sorted out and until I was given an appointment to join my first ship.

So really my story begins on the 8th October, 1941 (a date that I'll never forget) the day that my father and mother travelled with me to Newport from our home just outside Bristol to join my first ship the M.V. CORNISH CITY of the Reardon Smith Line (known as Smiths of Cardiff). After a tearful farewell on my mother's side, not knowing whether she would see her son again, my father took me down to the docks, where I was deposited into the hands of the Chief Officer, Idris Williams (who was in later years promoted to Master), who assured my father that I would be in capable hands. So my parents left me and I was left to my own devices. I was shown the Apprentices' living quarters, which were in the midships section, and to me it looked like a small box with four bunks, two over two, a small locker each and a drawer each under the bunks, a small table and a wooden bench. The messroom was off the cabin and had a table with a bench either side and a locker to stow foodstuffs and crockery, such as it was. After dinner ... I cannot remember what it was ... I was advised to put on working gear while one of the other Apprentices showed me around on a sort of orientation trip. The CORNISH CITY had had her day of fame as she was the Commodore ship of the JARVIS BAY convoy and she had a few battle scars to show for it in the way of shrapnel dents from gunfire on the poop house.

The ship was just completing loading a much-needed cargo of military supplies for the Middle East, and we sailed from Newport two days later. I was allowed two days to get myself used to shipboard life. Perhaps I should mention that the CORNISH CITY was under the command of Captain D. C. Lennie, who was also from Bristol ... not that that gave me any special favours. We sailed to Belfast Lough and then met up with the rest of the convoy to the north of Northern Ireland.

Life was not too bad to start with. Fortunately I was not seasick, but I soon learnt that the Junior Apprentice was the lowest form of life onboard ship. There were four of us Apprentices ... the Senior one, named Buckholtz, who was in his last year, was from South Africa.. Next to him was Mike Sharpe from Bideford, then a chap called Kennedy from Newquay, Cornwall ... I believe his father owned a couple of fishing boats ... and, of course, yours truly to make up the four.

Being on day-work to start off, I was working under the Bosun from whom, with his wealth of knowledge of ropes and knots etc. you learnt fast, but I had to collect all the food from the galley, dished up in kits, some of which looked pretty repulsive. Also, as Junior Apprentice I had to clean out the Officers' toilets and wash-places, as well as our own that were shared and used by the Junior Engineers.

I soon learnt the nautical lingo ... ceilings became deckheads, walls were bulkheads, floors were decks, left was port, right was starboard, the fo'c'sle was where the crew lived and so on. We has a crew of about 45 including gunnery personnel. The Engineers had their own accommodation block above the engine-room and the gunnery personnel lived in the poop house, which housed the stearing gear as well. The ship was armed with a 4-inch gun, a 12-pounder anti-aircraft gun and two Oerlikens on the Bridge wings. As well one can imagine, we went to bed with our clothes on and slept with a life-jacket close to hand and a few personnal possessions wrapped up in plastic to keep them watertight in case of emergency.

About a week after leaving Belfast, there was an almighty crash in the engine-room and the ship was stopped, leaving us to our own devices as the convoy sailed on. We were in a very vulnerable position. Apparently one of the main engine pistons had cracked the cylinder cover, and after the engineers had

117

made temporary repairs we limped into Ponta Delgada, Horta, the main port in the Azores, to make more permanent repairs, allowing us to proceed on 3 cylinders instead of 4. The engine was a 4-cylinder Doxford diesel which would give a speed of about seven and a half knots instead of eleven. Stopping off there was a bit of an education, it being my first foreign port and going ashore I tasted beer for the first time, which I did not like at all thank God. Something else which stood out in my mind was that I saw pineapples growing, as I thought, wild along the side of the road, but in fact they were actually cultivated.

Leaving Ponta Delgada, the honeymoon was over for me, as the ship was sailing independently. I was rapidly taught to be able to steer the ship, box the compass, so that I could be put into the watch system and release an A.B. for day work, which for me meant a ten hour day plus two hours look-out duty ... quite a long day.

Feeding conditions got worse as we were on our way to Pernambuco, I don't know why. The ship had a small ammonia refrigerator that kept on breaking down. The potatoes in the spud locker smelt, the soup we had at lunch time, you had to scrape the weevils off the top, and the same with the bread. The Chief Steward had put us on our Pound and Pint (Board of Trade's feeding scale) which was pretty meagre. We ended up with rice cakes instead of potatoes and only one egg a week, and that was on a Sunday. So in the end we were glad to get to Pernambuco for much-needed fresh supplies. We had to have our lime juice every evening to keep scurvy at bay. Of course, I was sent on all the stupid errands that are part of shipboard life, like asking the Chief Engineer for air on the organ for the Sunday service that never materialised, go down to the engine room for a left hand monkey wrench, or a long stand, but after a couple of these pranks you got wise and became wary of anything that did not seem quite right. In the tropical evenings while it was still light, I learnt to play cribbage, something

I learnt to enjoy. The tropical evenings did not last long as blackout at sea was very strict, even to smoking on deck after sunset.

From Pernambuco, it was on to Cape Town and then Durban, where the ship stayed for six weeks waiting for a spare piston to arrive from the UK. which took us over Christmas and New Year 1941/42. This was a very welcome break and one enjoyed by all the crew. In Durban, the Senior Apprentice had a visit from his mother who lived in Port Elizabeth and I must say she ensured that the four of us had an ample supply of fresh tropical fruit to supplement our diet. I was introduced to avocado pears which I still enjoy to this day.

Being in port over Christmas, we had two days off, so on Christmas Day I took myself off to church, having been made to go as a lad at home. It must have been my lucky day as I and a guy in the R.A.F and one in the Army were asked to spend the holiday at the home of a Mr. and Mrs. Payne, who I found owned a department store in Durban. So we were whisked off to their country home at a place called Kloof about 25 miles outside Durban, where we were wined and dined and then entertained by a group of Zulus doing various war dances with beating drums for their accompaniment. We all returned to Durban the following day by being put on the local train. What a memorable first Christmas this was away from home.

We had an uneventful journey north to Suez. Perhaps I should mention another rude awakening I had was having to do your own washing, and as the ship only carried 30 tons of fresh water and this was for domestic use only, the only thing you could do was to plead with the engineers to give you a bucket of water from the donkey boiler and heat it up with a steam jet on deck. Thank goodness most of our washing was working gear as I am sure better clothes would not have stood up to the sort of treatment we gave them. Then it was through the Suez Canal. Another experience ... it is still called a 'Big Ditch' in the sand ... and so on to Alexandria, where it took ten days to discharge our cargo. Whilst in Alex we went to the pictures one evening and could not get any transport back to the ship, so Mike Sharpe thought we should take a gary. The driver was asleep on the side of the road, so we piled on to this rickety form of transport and Mike drove it down to the dock gates. He then turned it around, gave the mule a flick of whip, and it was last seen running back up the road empty. Another night Mike enticed a mule up the gangway and left it on deck by No. 3 Hatch. One can imagine the Chief Officer's dismay to see this animal outside the accommodation block and having to get a proper sling to lift it back ashore. Of course, we all pleaded ignorance as to how this animal got onboard.

Leaving Alex it was back through the Canal to Suez to be fitted out as a temporary troop carrier, and the between decks in No. 4 and 5 hatches were converted to accommodate 200 Australian troops with all their equipment bound for Colombo and with a Warrant Officer in charge. Our food was still pretty drastic so another of Mike Sharpe's escapades was to raid the Aussie stores in the holds, which meant such things as Bully Beef and tinned fruit to supplement our supplies. We had come to understand what the black 'S' on the funnel meant ... starvation. The Warrant Officer did not realise that his stores had been tampered with until we had been in Colombo a few days and then he was going to take us all to court. Fortunately we had an air raid on Colombo, their first on Easter Sunday, 1942. The Japs dropped a pattern around our ship but none of them exploded, and because of this raid we were dispatched to sail immediately, so we heard no more from the Aussies. The crew was given the job of dismantling all of the temporary troop-carrying gear, with the bits and pieces to be discharged in Durban.

Arriving at Durban, we had to anchor off, awaiting a berth. I was on the 8 to 12 evening watch, when quite suddenly the ship started to pitch violently. I was on anchor watch on the fo'c'lse with great swells rolling in as can happen round there. I say I was never so frightened in all my life, because when the ship fell into the trough of the swell you were literally airborne. The Third Mate, realising what it must be like, called me back to the Bridge where at least I felt safe.

From Durban we sailed to Trinidad, still uneventfully, and by this time I had learnt word perfect the 31 Articles (Rules of the Road). The Third Mate had taught me where to look for the stars and I also learnt some elementary navigation. It was early in June when we arrived in Trinidad. After spending two days there, a convoy was to be formed to sail into the Gulf of Mexico. We were to be the Commodore ship, our Captain being the most experienced of all.

Sailing from Port of Spain in the afternoon, the six ships of our convoy had just formed up outside the Bocas when a submarine got to work and by 6 p.m. had sunk five of the ships, with the loss of all hands in each of them. We managed to escape under cover of darkness. What an afternoon!

We arrived in Galveston to load a full cargo of rock sulphur for Melbourne. During the loading, we had to wear goggles and face masks … it was so dangerous.

So it was back through the Gulf of Mexico, the Caribbean, the South Atlantic, round the Cape of Good Hope into the Roaring Forties. It was really terrible climbing into the crows nest to keep a lookout. It was so cold, but it was wonderful to see the Albatross swooping so gracefully over the sea, such magnificent birds. Eventually, we sailed up the Yarra River to Melbourne to discharge in full. I asked the Captain if I could have a couple of days off to see an aunt and uncle who lived in Geelong. He refused, but I took off for a couple of days anyway, only to face his wrath on my return. The Chief Engineer spoke kindly for me and I was let off with a caution to not do it again, and my punishment was to be night-watchman for the rest of the voyage. I did not mind as it was overtime for me.

Cleaning the holds was a nightmare after the cargo of sulphur and could not be completed by the crew alone, so shore cleaners were brought in. Sailing from Melbourne we were bound for Port Pirie in the Spencer Gulf to load a part cargo of phosphates for the U.K, good news all round as at long last we could see the end of the voyage. It was while we were loading that I had my first introduction to the putting up of shifting boards and feeders as after leaving Port Pirie, we went to Port Lincoln to load grain, which by its very nature is liable to shift in heavy rolling. The grain in the feeders allows for any settling. The loading of the phosphates and grain did not take long, as it was done by conveyor belt. We loaded down to our marks and then set off for Wellington, with routing orders for the Panama Canal.

After arriving at the Balboa anchorage, we eventually got clearance to proceed through the Canal. In those days, canal transits were only done from 0600 to 2200 hours. Before we left Balboa we were boarded by 12 military personnel as well as the pilot. They were heavily armed, as the Americans were very security-conscious. They made sure all the orders given by the pilot were carried out properly. These people were stationed on the Bridge, the fo'c'sle, poop and the engine room. To the Chief Steward's dismay, he had to feed them and not with the rubbish he had been dishing up to us.

Safely through the Canal, it was on to Key West, Florida, but two days before we got to Key West I went down with a mysterious illness. My face became swollen so much so that I could hardly see. After the ship had been boarded by the Port Health Officer, he had me sent ashore to the local hospital where they kept me for two days. I think they pumped me full of penicillin. I had dreams of being sent home D.B.S. along the Florida Keys and by train to New York, but no such luck. I was sent back to the ship. I never did find out what was wrong, but the doctor did say I was suffering from anaemia, so for a week I had the same food as the Captain.

We were routed independently to Halifax where we joined a convoy for the U.K. and, strangely enough, we experienced no enemy action at all during this part of the voyage. We arrived in Belfast just before Christmas, 1942 to discharge the grain, and then on to Swansea for the discharge of the remainder of the cargo. I don't remember anything of that Christmas and I eventually left the CORNISH CITY on the 27th December, 1942. During the 15 months away I had grown three inches. None of my clothes would fit me, and I must have looked a right mess as I boarded the train to take me back to Temple Meads, Bristol, with my pay-off of some £20 in my pocket. I only got 16/8d a month, plus overtime at 6d an hour and War Bonus of £6 a month. I did not really want to go home as I had grown away, and was going to find it hard to settle down to a new life. I had learnt to swear like a trooper in the true nautical fashion. The Captain gave me a glowing report for my first voyage, but alas, he did not survive the war.

During this voyage I had done practically every job one could possibly do onboard ship. Helping to paint the funnel from a Bosun's chair, painting the mast down, also from a Bosun's chair, swaying around some 70 feet above the deck, chipping and painting over the side in port from stages, cleaning out the bilges, setting rat traps in the holds, etc., etc. I wonder what the Health & Safety people would have to say today. So I went home, spent five weeks there before joining my next ship on the Tyne.

Reardon Smith taught me seamanship, how to give and take orders, and enabled me to sail as Second Mate at the age of twenty and take my first command at the age of thirty-two.

Thank you, Captain Brian Hodges. That first voyage might well have been your last. Brian left the Reardon Smith Line in about 1946 and joined the Elder & Fyffes Shipping Line, and served with that Company until his retirement with 26 years in command. He also obtained an Honorary Panama Canal Pilot's licence, transitting the Canal in excess of 120 times. He thinks he is the only person in the U.K. to hold this Licence. Read on.

In the June 2002 issue No. 23 of 'Shipmates' (the twice yearly magazine of the Reardon Smith Line) was Captain Louttit's report of the sinking of the S.S. VERNON CITY, hit by one torpedo from U-boat 172 in the South Atlantic on 28th June, 1943. Here is part of Captain Malcolm Louttit's report about the survivors in a lifeboat.

THE SINKING OF THE VERNON CITY

I impressed upon my crew that if a submarine came along they were to say that the Captain had gone down with the ship. Within a few minutes the submarine surfaced on the starboard side of the ship and closed my lifeboat. We were addressed by what appeared to be the Second-in-Command, who spoke to us in perfect English, and asked for the Captain. My crew, in a very convincing manner, shouted that he had gone down with his ship. At this, the German officer asked for one of the sailors to go on board. Cadet Hodges, a young apprentice, who was sitting in the bow of the boat, immediately volunteered and was pulled on board. There were two ratings standing on deck, one with a tommy gun. The following conversation took place:-

German Officer   Are you English or American?

Cadet Hodges   English

German Officer	What was the name of your Ship?
Cadet Hodges	SANTA CLARA VALLEY

(a ship that was sunk a little while back belonging to the same Company)

German Officer	What was your cargo?
Cadet Hodges	Coal and coke
German Officer	Where did you come from?
Cadet Hodges	The North East coast of England
German Officer	Newcastle? Where were you bound?
Cadet Hodges	Round the Cape Horn to the West Coast of South America
German Officer	What course were you steering?
Cadet Hodges	S.E.
German Officer	I saw you altering course, are you sure there are no officers there? (meaning the lifeboat)
Cadet Hodges	Positive. You can go and look if you like.

Cadet Hodges was then taken to the conning tower and on the way was told that he might be taken prisoner-of-war. The Commander was informed of what the cadet had said, and made him write down the name of the ship on a piece of paper. The cadet was also asked some personal questions, such as, "What is your rank?", "Where do you live, where were you educated, name, age, etc." On being asked his opinion of the War, Hodges said, quite frankly, that he thought that Germany had the best of it at first, the Allies now had the upper hand. The German officer asked if the boat had sufficient food and water, and told the cadet to steer west. Cadet Hodges was then put back into the lifeboat, after the German officer had shaken hands with him and wished him the best of luck. He expressed his regrets at the Captain going down with the ship, and said he was sorry that he had to leave them so far from land, but hoped that he would make land safely. All this took about half an hour.

Captain Louttit continued his article about the episode.

All my crew behaved well, but I think that Cadet Hodges was particularly outstanding. Although aged only 17 or 18, he showed great courage in promptly volunteering to board the submarine, fully knowing there was a possibility of being kept as a prisoner-of-war. Despite the shock of being torpedoed, he displayed great initiative and quick wit in misleading the submarine Commander by giving false answers to his questions.

Cadet Brian Hodges received a Mention in Despatches from Winston Churchill for the episode with the German submarine.

As I expected, along came another tale from Brian.

CARRIBEAN INTERLUDE

This story begins in San Salvador (Watling Island) in the Bahama group of Islands ... this is the reputed landfall of

Christopher Columbus in 1492. The island is on the eastern extremity of the Bahamas, some 200 miles south-east of Nassau. It is 13 miles long and 5 miles wide. The main town, Cockburn Town, is situated on the western side of the island, this being the leeward side. The main industries are fishing and farming. There is an airstrip for light aircraft. On the west coast is an obelisk painted white about six to seven feet high to mark the spot where Columbus landed.

A banana ship, the M.V. MORANT, of some 6,500 tons gross tonnage, was on passage from the United States to Central America with a cargo of rolls of liner board, which is used for making banana boxes. She also carried six passengers.

On the morning of Sunday 9th October 1979, with perfect weather conditions, as the ship was passing San Salvador, the Captain decided to call the passengers to the Bridge. He took the ship close to land to give the passengers a better view of Columbus's landfall. He misjudged his position by getting too close and struck a coral reef, tearing the bottom out of the ship in the vicinity of No. 2 and 3 holds with disastrous consequences.

The ship was stopped and slowly manoeuvred to the anchorage at Cockburn Town, a port and anchorage used mostly for pleasure craft and fishing vessels.

At this stage, the author of this story comes into the picture.

I was at home on leave in Ireland. As I was the Senior Master in the Company, I received a frantic telephone call to report to the Head Office a.s.a.p. in order to receive a briefing on the situation. A ticket had already been booked on a flight from Dublin to Heathrow and I arrived in Southampton on the 11th October. There I was duly briefed on the circumstances and demise of the MORANT. I flew out to San Salvador by regular airline to Miami and Nassau, and by charter flight to

San Salvador with a full brief to take charge of the proceedings until the ship had dry-docked in Savannah for 'full and complete repairs'.

Going on board on the 12th October, everything looked like a complete disaster area. Already there was an oil barge and tug in attendance. The first thing to do was to relieve the Captain of his command, arranging for him to fly home as soon as possible where he was to have an internal disciplinary hearing and his release from further Company service. Then, I had to repatriate the passengers to the United States. This completed, I was able to get down to the 'nitty gritty' of the task in hand.

One of the most surprising things of this catastrophe was the lack of oil leaking into the sea. It was as though all the oil that was in the D.B. (double bottom) was being kept there by sea water pushing the oil upwards to the tank top, which fortunately was not punctured. However, with the arrival of the oil barge and tug came a so-called Salvage Master. He suggested that we get to the oil through the air pipes of the ruptured tanks, which had been located by a local deep-sea diver. This made sense, and so began the tedious task of pumping some 200 tons of oil into the barge. I maintained that he had placed the suction pipes too far down the air pipes. Being a typical American he told me that I did not know what I was talking about. On the 15th October, the barge left us to be towed to Savannah. On the following day, I managed to get a clearance from the Local Customs Officer for the ship to proceed to Savannah for repairs, with the understanding that a Company representative would take a copy of the clearance to the Chief of Customs in Nassau.

So, on the 16th October, we weighed anchor and proceeded to sea under tow at an agreed speed not exceeding 6 knots. We were unable to use the main engines due to vibration that would have knocked the engines out of line, but we were able to use one generator for domestic and navigational purposes.

The following morning, I received a radio telephone call from a very irate Chief of Customs wanting to know who had given me permission to proceed to sea. At the time, we were still in Bahamian waters. I tried to explain to him that the Company representative had left Cockburn Town yesterday afternoon and that he should have received a copy of the clearance that morning. Unbeknown to me at the time, the Charter aircraft, which should have taken the Company representative to Nassau with one of the officer's wives, had developed engine trouble and had ditched in the sea off the Island of Eluthera! After the aircraft had ditched, the pilot had been able to inflate his rubber dinghy and, with the aid of a shirt as a sail, they made it to the island of Eluthera. There, they were taken in by local inhabitants. It was three days before they could finally get a boat to take them to Nassau.

All seemed to be going well and we were blessed with fine weather throughout, with just normal trade winds and slight to moderate seas.

On the 20th October, the electrician fell ill. Apparently, he was suffering from a duodenal ulcer and should never have been passed fit for duty when he visited the doctor some two weeks previously just before he had joined the ship in the United States. He was treated on board and we made him as comfortable as possible. Unfortunately, the ulcer burst during the night and he died on the 21st October.

I managed to get in touch with a local medical team that is available in most places throughout the world. They sent a paramedic out to the ship which was then in the Florida Straits. She pronounced him dead and asked what I wanted to do with the remains. As the ship was under tow and not knowing if the U.S. Coast Guard would detain us before entering port, I decided to evacuate the remains to the hospital mortuary at Melbourne, Florida, until arrangements could be made to fly the body back to U.K.

Arriving off Tybee Island, the entrance to the Savannah

River, at midday on the 22nd October after six days under tow and a distance of some 642 miles, the ship was met by a Pilot and the U.S. Coastguard. The ship was examined thoroughly to make sure there was little or no chance of pollution as fines for this are extremely high. After two hours, they gave us permission to proceed to the discharging berth, where an oil boom was placed around the ship to contain any possible oil leakage. Discharge of the paper cargo took place on the 23rd and 24th October.

The Agents advised me that I would have to go and identify the remains of the crew member that had died. So, I chartered a plane to fly me to Melbourne. I was met there by an undertaker who took me to the mortuary for the formal identification. Then, I selected a casket and in true American style a suit of clothes for him to be buried in. Next, I arranged for the casket to be air-freighted back to Liverpool, his home town, for a family service. Ironically, the casket was too big for the British crematorium so he had to be re-casketed! In hindsight, I wished that I had performed a burial at sea, which of course I am allowed to do.

To bring this saga to a close, the vessel was finally dry-docked in Savannah ... one of the few ports in U.S.A. that has a dry-dock ... at 0800 on the 26th October, 1979. When the dry-dock was pumped out, all the oil that the barge should have taken fell into the bottom of the dock. What a mess! Then the true extent of the damage was revealed. It took about four months of steam cleaning, cutting away the defective parts of the hull, welding all the new plating back and for the engine to be realigned. Next came the shipyard trials before she was finally seaworthy.

I left the ship after she arrived in dry-dock and was present long enough to see most of the mess cleared,

What an experience!

Thank you, Captain Brian Hodges ... that was fascinating.

Captain Edward Burling Clarke
Master Mariner

During my research for information when writing 'A Dog Collar in the Docks', I told the story of Captain Edward Burling Clark. Further digging has produced more details and I tell the story with pride. It truly is a memory of an old friend.

One of the greatest opportunities that is afforded a parson is the privilege of being asked to conduct a funeral for a loved one. In this way, I have met some remarkable families. It is sad that so many of the stories have not been recorded and that the legacy of the past is so quickly forgotten. But this is a story that I can tell.

Over many years, I had involved myself with the Sea Cadet Units on Merseyside and was Chaplain to the Central Unit in Liverpool. As a result of all this, I was asked to attend a conference at the Royal Naval College at Greenwich.

Only those who have worshipped in the College Chapel can understand the real beauty and majesty of the building, especially in the early morning hours when ecclesiastical buildings are at their best. However, the high spot of that week for me was the 'Dining-in-Night' in the Painted Hall. After an excellent meal, the port circling, the loyal toast behind us, the Mess President invited the Band Master to take wine with him at the high table where happily I, too, was seated. We raised our glasses to the musicians and thumped our tables, until the Band Master stood on the cleared table top and at a merry tempo played the Post Horn Gallop. Tradition is impressive when you are in the middle of it.

During that week we had been invited to spend an afternoon in the National Maritime Museum, which is vast and wonderful. For the allocated two and a half hours, I selected the horological department as my guided tour. The time passed quickly!

With hindsight, I should have chosen the Medal Room. In that room, I might have seen a Croix de Guerre with Bronze Palm, which had been awarded to a small Naval vessel in 1944. That would have been the link between Greenwich, France, Liverpool and this story.

Captain Clark was truly a remarkable man. In 1951, he was promoted to the rank of Captain, R.N.R., and had the distinction of being the first shipmaster in the 'home trade' to be promoted to that rank. His sea-going career had started in 1919 as an Apprentice in the Elder Dempster vessel, RHODA. After eight years in that Company and two years with the White Star Line, followed by a year's course in the Royal Navy, he joined the Belfast Steamship Company in 1932 as Second Mate (he held an Extra Master's ticket!) of the old ULSTER PRINCE. He obtained his first command ... the ULSTER HERO ... in 1936 and went on to be Commodore and to command all the company's vessels.

He was promoted to the rank of Lieutenant-Commander, R.N.R., in 1939 and served as Navigating Officer in the DUNLUCE

CASTLE, which was converted into an accommodation vessel and taken to Scapa Flow. In the middle of 1940, he took command of the French destroyer, ARRAS. Six months later, he served in H.M.S CORINTHIAN, an Ellerman Wilson ship that had been converted into an armed boarding vessel. Then followed a period of command of a small French trawler called the TARANA ... more of her later. That small craft was employed on the hazardous duty in the Mediterranean of landing our agents in enemy-occupied territory and bringing out people pursued by the Gestapo, as well as R.A.F. pilots and aircrew who had been shot down, and assisted by the Resistance in making their escape from France and Italy.

Captain Clark afterwards was involved in the preparation for the North African, Sicilian and Italian landings. He subsequently moved up to Molfetta, on the east coast of Italy, and was engaged in the North Adriatic in liaison with Yugoslav forces until the end of the war. He was promoted Commander, R.N.R., and in 1944, went out to India after V.E. Day to take command of the AUSONIA, then a Fleet Repair ship. On demobilisation, Captain Clark resumed his appointment with the Belfast Steamship Company.

But, let us return to the Croix de Guerre with Bronze Palm awarded by the French Government, the Gold Cross of Merit with Swords from the Polish Government, and TARANA. When his daughter, Rosemary Fitzpatrick, asked me to conduct his funeral some forty years later, I was able to uncover his remarkable story.

During the year 1942 H.M.S. TARANA would sail from Gibraltar, black hull, grey upper works and funnel, White Ensign flying ... just another armed trawler going about her business. However, once the Rock had dipped over the horizon, all hands were mustered. She was repainted to look like a fishing trawler, gear was strewn about the deck and all the men dressed like fishermen. Over the stern hung a tattered Portuguese flag. This was TARANA's war rig!

The Pat O'Leary Organisation, together with a Polish group, ran a very successful escape line and TARANA was part of the system. Many hundreds of men and women were transported safely out of France. On the return journey to Gibraltar, the disguise was reversed and TARANA would again become a Naval ship.

Anthony Deane-Drummond, later a Major General, was one of the men who escaped from France aboard TARANA and he wrote about his experiences in his book 'Return Ticket', published in 1953 by Collins.

"All that we had to do was wait for the rowing-boat which might be twenty minutes coming in. Half an hour went by and no sign of the boat. We gave some more flashes on our lamp, but these were not answered by the ship. What could have happened? Had we dreamt those blue flashes? However, we decided to give it another twenty minutes before we did anything more.

"The twenty minutes went by and another twenty minutes as well. It was now ten-past two and still no sign of any rowing boats. We just went on flashing, while hoping for the best and giving our lamp as wide an arc as possible in case the ship had drifted down wind.

"At half-past two there was still no sign and our guides began to look very worried. We were a very big party and would have been no easy problem for them. They would have to get us away by 3 a.m., if they were to have a reasonable chance of hiding us somewhere by daylight. My heart was sinking and I was trying to be cheerful and not depressed ... I remember telling Whitney Straight that it was bound to be all right as 13 was my lucky number and today was July 13th. 'Well, I hope you are right,' he said, 'I am not too happy myself.'

"The words were hardly out of his lips when a blue flash came from the sea and not more than a few hundred yards out. Soon we heard the padded noise made by muffled rowlocks, and at 2.45 a.m. the rowing boat beached. A midshipman in naval uniform was in the stern and a couple of husky A.B.s were at the oars. Apparently, the off-shore wind and current had been very strong and, after making one abortive effort to row ashore, they had returned to the ship for another hand.

"We piled aboard and pulled off after saying good-bye with many 'au revoirs' to our brave guides. Two of us lent a hand at the oars, and in ten minutes we sighted the small ship against the night sky, and had soon climbed up a scaling net helped by many willing hands on deck. We were then taken to the fo'c'sle and had enormous mugs of Navy cocoa, bread and jam and cheese thrust into our hands. It was wonderful to hear the cheery naval slang going on all around and English being spoken again. Even while we sipped the boiling cocoa, the ship's engines started to murmer and we were heading out to sea and away from our bay.

"The Captain of the ship came to speak to us and see who we were. He told us it was so nice to pick up Englishmen, as usually he had nothing but Poles. We asked him how on earth he managed to sail so close to an enemy shore with so small a ship, and he told us we would see how in the morning when we took a look around. A twinkle came into his eye, as he said,

'You see, we look just like a peaceable fishing trawler.' 'And by the way,' he said as an afterthought, 'if any planes come out and have a look at us in the morning, I want you all below decks. All my crew have the right clothes to keep the make-believe going, and I don't want any plane to become suspicious at the numbers we are carrying aboard.' He bade us a cheery good night and we turned in to some spare bunks. We were soon sleeping the sleep of the just and thankful.

"Morning came with a bright blue sky, and I was on deck to see what sort of ship she was. Outwardly, she looked a dirty, brown trawler, with bits of rope strewn everywhere and nothing at all shipshape. Some of the crew were working in old reefers, and the Captain was on the bridge in a garb not much better. It was on a closer inspection that the little trawler became interesting. The big steam winch was a 3.7 inch gun. Another gun was fixed aft under the guise of an engine-room hatch and machine-guns galore all over the ship could be swung into place in a jiffy. It must have been something like World War One's Q ships and looked quite effective.

"We were going to be taken to Gibraltar, but first we had a mid-ocean rendezvous with a tiny coastal ship from which we would take about eighty Poles. This was quite a regular occurrence and many hundreds of Poles came out of Europe by this method. Our trawler never went in close to shore, but this was done by a little coastal ship about a quarter of our size and captained by a very gallant Polish Captain. His disguise was so good that he sailed right into small ports on the southern French coast to take on board a new load to ferry out to our trawler. It was almost like a bus service, and was never suspected because of the tiny size of his craft.

"We were at sea two days in a really bad storm, which made our little trawler stand on its head and tail alternately, with great seas sweeping over us from stem to stern. At times the Bridge was the only part of us above the waves, and for the first time in my life I was seasick. So, too, were most of the crew, for it was one of the worst summer storms that they had experienced in the Mediterranean.

"We made our rendezvous with the Pole, but he was even worse off than we were and in addition had eighty wretched Polish refugees aboard, packed like sardines in the open boat under a tarpaulin that served to keep out most of the weight, if not the wetness, of the sea. After about twenty-four hours cruising slowly around, the storm died down as quickly as it had blown up, and the eighty weary Poles climbed aboard us. The poor devils had not eaten or slept since they had embarked four days before, and their few possessions were soaking wet.

"We dried them off and, with a good meal inside, their spirits perked up and they began to look like human beings and less like half-starved animals. The little boat pushed off with its Polish Captain, and we set course for Gibraltar at last. All the time that we had been waiting for the weather to quieten, we had been cruising between the Spanish-French frontier and Sardinia. We were never much more than fifty miles from shore and it was an anxious time lest a plane or ship should come out to see what we were doing. We were getting so close to home that it would be terrible if we were discovered now.

"Everyone felt a bit easier when we had our load of Poles aboard, and even the crew could be seen going about their tasks a little more cheerfully than before. It must have been a thankless and dangerous job that they were carrying out, and they received no recognition for it in the newspapers. All they could tell their friends and relations was that they were serving in H.M Trawler, and that was all. They had the dangers and nerve strain of the submarine service without any of its glamour.

"With thirty-six hours sailing yet to do before we arrived at Gibraltar, our Captain announced that tonight would be 'painting night'. It was the thirteenth complete coat of paint that he had given his little ship in four months and by morning we had to be a nice grey H.M. Trawler in all its glory with White Ensign flying, guns oiled, decks scrubbed and ropes neatly coiled everywhere. Everybody was dished out a pot of grey paint and a brush, and all night we painted, until by 4 a.m. the transformation had been completed and our little ship had had its face lifted again.

"I don't think even we who had lived on the ship for close on six days had realised that there were so many guns aboard her. They seemed to sprout from every corner, and we would have given an attacker something to think about if he had poked his nose too close.

"All the following day we sailed on westwards in the lovely Mediterranean sunshine, and now we began to feel we were really getting somewhere. We were due in Gibraltar that night, but would have to wait until dawn next morning before we were allowed in through the boom.

"The authorities in Gibraltar were most surprised to find a party of escapers mixed up with the Poles, because nobody had warned them that we were coming. Everybody was very helpful however, and somehow we were squeezed into a troopship that was sailing for Britain the next morning."

This was just another episode in the wartime adventures of Captain Clark. I thought that I had known Captain Clark well, but had no idea of his story. His activities received no award from his own country!

On returning to England, he resumed his work with the Belfast Steamship Company and became the Master of the ULSTER PRINCE and the ULSTER MONARCH, proudly flying his Blue Ensign. By that time, he was the Commodore of the Line. He finally retired in 1967.

At the time of his death in 1981, I had known Nobby Clark for twenty years. He never talked of his adventures, but I am pleased to be able to tell a little of his story.

There were so many others like Captain Clarke. We forget at our peril.

Captain Cliff Mullings
Master Mariner

I seem to have known Cliff for many, many decades and casually I asked how it all began ... a series of documents arrived by post and here they are.

IT STARTED WITH A BANG

My life began at Horley, Surrey, and then there was a move to Hove and that obviously was where I caught the seagoing bug. There were day trips on Campbell's paddle steamers to Boulogne from the Palace Pier in Brighton. Then it was Newhaven to Dieppe on British Rail Steamers. One of them was the S.S. PARIS and a friend of the family knew the Master. I was allowed to steer the ship and seeing the Old Man with his brass hat pushing the telegraph handles, I thought that it looked good and would suit me! I recall the Spithead Review when on the return trip a heavy swell was thumping under the paddles and spraying everywhere.

141

A move to Oxford came, where I finished my schooling. I had thought it was a waste of time taking the School Certificate, so with the help of my father I enrolled in a three month pre-sea training course at Sir John Cass, Aldgate in order to join the Donaldson Line, the Daily Mirror paper boats. However, due to heavy war losses they were unable to accommodate me and I signed indentures with Houlder Bros. This was in 1943. They assigned me to the M.V. EL ARGENTINO at Plantation Quay, Glasgow together with eight other apprentices. At this point I started off on the wrong foot! Being rather keen on dancing in those days and finding Joe Loss was on in the Playhouse, I was off ... but was soon dragged back by two other apprentices, sent by the Chief Officer, as I was due on board.

Our accommodation was three converted passenger cabins, two for sleeping and one as a day study cabin. Messing was in the saloon on one large table outside the pantry where we queued with our plates for our meals. The Chief Steward was delighted to have nine young apprentices under his wing, but we soon realised that he had to be watched.

The ship had been under repair, having been run at maximum speed with a U-boat behind her! We all went on a gunnery course and finally sailed in mid-July, 1943. Watches were set and my spot was a gun platform by the funnel. The vessel was a 16-knot 'reefer' in a large 7½-knot convoy and we were positioned at No. 1 on the starboard corner. I believe that we were the largest ship, destination Buenos Aires, with part of the convoy for the Mediterranean and the remainder for Freetown.

At 1715 on the 26th July, about 200 miles west of Lisbon, just at meal time, action stations were taken up as enemy aircraft were in the vicinity. At 1800 hours a Focke Wulf at about 10,000 feet dropped a stick of bombs which exploded about fifty feet abreast the Bridge, engulfing the ship in smoke and spray.

At 1835, another aircraft flew over the ship at the same height, dropping five bombs that pierced No. 5 and 6 hatches. Derricks were blown off and a Samson post collapsed.

At 1840, 'Abandon ship' was issued and Nos. 1, 2 and 4 boats were lowered ... No. 3 was holed. Nos. 2 and 4 cleared the ship, but No. 1 was overturned by wreckage.

The vessel foundered at 1845 ... she sank by the stern and stood upright before disappearing below the sea.

Seventy-seven of us were picked up by a corvette, H.M.S. MALLON. We in No. 2 picked up those in the water. Unfortunately, the Second Engineer was lost. He was seen climbing the escape ladder to the Engine Room skylight. Those that saw him said that he was very badly burned, lost his grip and fell back into the Engine Room. H.M.S. MALLON remained with the convoy overnight and, due to shortage of water and stores, headed for Casablanca. The remaining crew were picked up by a rescue tug and taken to Gibraltar.

En route to Casablanca, two of the Firemen, who were badly burned, died and were buried at sea. One night I tried to sleep on a hatch, marked 'Explosives' ... there was no choice. Most of us were in the clothes that we stood up in, but on arrival we were kitted out in Army battledress and R.A.F. equipment. The injured were quickly taken to hospital and we were taken to an American Army camp ... most of them had departed to the North African Coast. We were allocated mosquito nets and camp beds and were under canvas. The toilet was a large hole in the sand with a plank across. I am afraid that the mosquitoes were a very angry and hungry bunch! The crew of what I believe was a Clan Line ship ... it had been sunk the morning after us ... were also in the camp, having been landed from a frigate.

The problem was transport home. After about three weeks we were sent to a French ship, called the SIDI BRAHIM for passage to Gibraltar. The Lascar crew from the Clan Line ship were in No. 2 hatch. I was allocated the Third Mates' cabin and never saw so many cockroaches before or since. On arrival at Gibraltar, we transferred to the troopship CAMERONIA, Anchor Donaldson Line, although there was some trouble with the Master, not wanting a load of survivors on board! Being a troopship, no booze was allowed, but some of the Engineers took care of us en route to Glasgow!

When I arrived home, I noticed that the Chief Steward must have found time to collect the ship's account books before she sank as my tobacco account was deducted!

A spell of leave and I was again on an overnight train to Glasgow to join the QUEEN ELIZABETH (1938) as a passenger with the rest of the crew to join a 'Samboat' called SAMEARN at Portland, Maine. However, on route, we were accommodated in the Hotel Bryant on Broadway and 52nd Street in New York ... so Christmas 1943 was at sea and New Year at the Hotel and Times Square!

We eventually joined the ship in Portland, Maine ... there were engine trials whilst moored to the wharf ... and then sailed back to New York and loaded war materials for the Mediterranean.

Whilst anchored in Naples Bay, Vesuvius was in full eruption ... quite a sight at 4 a.m.! We had trouble with some air raids, but there was no damage. Next came another Atlantic run, loaded with more war materials, this time for various ports in India. At Calcutta we loaded aluminium ingots and tea from other ports, ending up in Columbo and finally we sailed to our discharge port, Liverpool.

After a spell of leave, I then joined the S.S. MARQUESA (1917) in South Shields for passage to Halifax and Liverpool with frozen produce. After this came some time in another 'Samboat', the S.S. SAMPEP. She was the convoy Commodore ship, trading between Tilbury, Antwerp and Hamburg.

Hostilities over, I joined the M.V. RIPPINGHAM

GRANGE (1943) in London Docks, sailing to Buenos Aires to load a full cargo of frozen meat for the Mediterranean ports. This was to be my last voyage as a Senior Apprentice before going for my Second Mate certificate. The first port of call in the Mediterranean was Haifa where the Bridge and main 'tween decks were discharged from No. 2 hatch. The next port was Port Said.

Whilst I was off watch and still asleep, around 0600 hours, at the Pilot station, I was rudely awakened by a heavy impact and another Apprentice shouting. A ship that turned out to be the CITY OF HONGKONG had hit us in No. 2 and we were starting to sink. I thought 'Oh! Not again!' I grabbed my lifejacket and went to see what had happened.

The two upper decks had been discharged at Haifa, but the three lower decks had 700 tons of frozen carcases. The hold was flooding due to the rivets popping out and the plates springing open. Luckily, the bulkheads between Nos. 2 and 1 and Nos. 2 and 3 held up and eventually all the cargos from 1,3, 4,and 5 and 6 were discharged into local storage. No. 7 was left for discharge at Malta. After about a week, the warm water had made the rotting meat smell everywhere. The discharge was done using a grab and we dumped the mess into small Army landing barges. Port Health stipulated that it was emptied some 20 miles out. We used AFS pumps to wash it all off. Arab stevedores were in the hatch pulling the carcases out from the wings to the centre of the hatch. After about two weeks of this, everything came to an abrupt halt.

Discharge had been at night and we dumped all day. At around 0100, I and everyone else were called when the Third Officer on cargo watch raised the alarm. When the stevedores removed the hatches and plugs to go down for the next deck, they had just passed out. By the time that I got there, six of the stevedores were on deck and I started artificial respiration on one of them. I told the Chief Officer that I was not getting anywhere ... this bloke's dead! All six died, and the Third Officer and Master were arrested on manslaughter charges.

The foredeck was out of bounds without a respirator or face mask. All the white paint turned black on the deck. Apparently, the mix of salt water, galvanised insulation and rotting meat created a deadly gas. The ship was turned around so the prevailing wind took the awful smell away from the accommodation. The crew demanded shore accommodation ... of course, the officers and apprentices remained.

About ten days elapsed whilst Siebe Gormans, U.K., gathered the necessary protosorb gasmasks and other equipment together and had it shipped out to Port Said with a representative. The Egyptian Fire Service Staff volunteered to work with this equipment down the hatch with one of our officers in charge. Hatch boards were strapped together, plus rails around to take three men and an officer and they were hooked on to a cargo runner as a cradle to lower them into the hatch. Canvas pools were rigged on deck and it was our mucky job to wash off the stinking fat as they were lifted up on to the deck. They only spent short spells in loading the slings. When the barges were full, they went out to sea. Later they were allowed to go up the coast, discharge the meat on the sand and burn it. One 'Z' craft in the charge of the Third Officer was washed beam-on to the beach, as the kedge anchor was not let go in the right spot. One propeller was damaged, so we had only one craft. This caused further delay.

Meanwhile, a diver worked on the plates below the water-line and I believe that about a thousand wedges were hammered up in between the plates to reduce the ingress of water. A water barge was employed to pump the water out from the hatch and a tug employed to tow it 20 miles out to sea. Discharge continued in this way until the hatch was cleared. A large cement box was constructed over the holed plates and we proceeded to the Tyne via Malta for repair about three months after we had arrived at Port Said.

I was past my sea-time required for Second Mate's, so I enrolled at King Edward School as soon as possible. On passing, I joined the DUNSTER GRANGE, a sister ship of the EL ARGENTINO. After eighteen months I was transferred to an Empire-type ship, nine knots in a following wind! I also found out that the Company was updating its wartime tonnage, so I thought there were better ships around. On arriving in Liverpool from Buenos Aires with a bagged cargo of linseed oil, I spotted an Elders and Fyffes ship that was the seventy-five passenger, CAVINA, fitting out after war service in order to carry war-brides to the U.S.A. That, I thought, was more in my line.

The linseed oil expelars were over-heating with smoke coming out of No. 3 hatch ventilator. Being Sunday, no work was going on, but a scratch team of stevedores was mustered and the hatch was opened up with the fire service standing by. A number of bags in the hatch were smouldering. After discharge, we proceeded to Glasgow for dry-docking and refurbishing.

Entering through the docks, a number of ships were passed under repair, one of which was the GOLFITO. She had developed a turbine problem on sea trials ... this delayed her maiden voyage. Little did I know that I would eventually spend a year in her as Second Mate and almost a year as her Master!

I left Houlder Bros. in August 1949 and joined Elders and Fyffes. I sailed on numerous ships, promoted to Second Mate in 1951, and passed for Master in 1953. It was then Company policy to have a Second Mate with a Master's Certificate on the GOLFITO and I was appointed to her in 1955. The next year I became Chief Officer of a number of ships and in 1960 was given my first Command.

Captain Cliff Mullings takes us back some thirty-four years in Fyffes Line.

MEDICAL PROBLEM

In the barmy days of the sixties and seventies, my Company signed on a Ship's Doctor, newly qualified, who wished to enjoy a working holiday on our passenger/cargo ship for a twenty-six day round voyage to the West Indies.

As tended to happen on the first night out, I was sitting at the dining-room table making small talk with the newly acquainted passengers. I became aware of a strange dragging noise on my left. Trying to ignore this the best way I could, I was suddenly aware that it was the Chief Steward and Headwaiter half-dragging, half-walking, the Ship's Doctor out of the saloon!

I later found out that his head with the aid of alcohol had been slowly falling into the soup and at this point it was deemed advisable to remove him from the table.

After a few words with him the next morning, the voyage progressed. The passengers, paying ten shillings and six pence for the privilege, all reported very highly of his attention and ability as a doctor.

Ships with less than twelve passengers were not required to carry a doctor and were, I presume, at the medical mercy of the Chief Steward or other such 'quack', armed with the medical book. The Master, of course, was still ultimately responsible for all and every activity on his ship! However, Cliff recalls other problems which can befall the intrepid traveller!

KILL OR CURE

After an illness, Mrs. X decided that a twenty-six day voyage to the West Indies on a 100-passenger/cargo vessel would do her good. All luggage was loaded as normal and items marked 'not wanted on voyage' were stored in a special baggage locker for handy access for passengers, if required. Fool-proof!

An hour from the berth, still in pilotage waters, the Purser came to me on the bridge and said "Mrs. X cannot find her baggage". My reply was simple "Oh! My Gawd!"

The Purser and Chief Steward then searched all the cabins and all the items in the 'not wanted on voyage' locker. The conclusion was that it was not on board. An R.T. call to the Office advised them of the position of Mrs. X who had sent her baggage in advance. Next morning a cable was received from the Office advising us that in fact the baggage had arrived a day late and would be forwarded by air.

Meanwhile Mrs. X had only the clothes she was wearing with her. The other lady passengers and the Stewardesses had a whip-round and kitted her out. Everything was fine from Trinidad where all her baggage was waiting and she was enjoying the trip ... until the next incident!

The return voyage from Jamaica was via Bermuda and had become a bit of a problem because of drug smuggling. Suspicious last minute reservation for a passenger and with plastic bags being thrown over the side to be picked up by powerful speedboats had become common practice. Because of this activity, if a daylight arrival was not possible, the vessel was stopped and drifted about fifteen miles outside the pilotage area.

Mrs. X was in a cabin on the Promenade Deck, immediately abaft the Stewards' slop locker. About 0300, the Night Steward reported water flooding about the mid-ship staircase to the lower deck. He located the problem as being a burst salt water pipe in the slop locker.

There was a low swell causing a gentle roll, and the door sill being about an inch high, this water also ended up sloshing around in Mrs. X's cabin! She awoke in fright and said later that she had thought that the ship was sinking and that she had been forgotten!

Her fright was such that the ship's Doctor needed to see

her. On top of all that she had a fur coat stowed in a suitcase on the deck under her bed.

Mrs. X left the ship a week later feeling far worse than when she had joined, and went ashore with an insurance claim form in her bag!

That was a splendid series of happenings to be smiled upon after the event. Thank you, Cliff. Your next memory is probably common to many a seafarer ... the strange thing about your tale is that you almost missed it.

FLYING IS QUICKER ... MAYBE

My leave ended and the Company advised me that I was to re-join the Cristobal in Panama. At the time I was on medication for a skin rash, probably caused by a urea cargo (banana fertiliser) recently carried to Central America. This was causing me to feel sleepy.

I always cleared my baggage U.K. to destination, but at the transfer point I would verify at the check-in desk that my suitcases were accounted for ... in the late 60s this I found could be quite easily done. In this instance it was just as well that I did as one was missing. Arrangements were made to take me to the baggage loading area, where I was fortunate enough to see my suitcase in a container destined for India, not Panama.

The flight to Lisbon was uneventful; an evening meal, a 'noggin' and my pill. I was off to sleep in my window seat. Departure was around 0130, shortly after which the fun began. In my sleepy condition, I was just aware of an announcement from the Captain that due to a problem we were to return to Lisbon, but first we would be circling Lisbon Bay and dumping fuel. In my hazy condition, I thought O.K. he is the boss and dozed off again.

The next thing that I was aware of was approaching the runway. I thought that my luck had changed as the nun sitting next to me grabbed my arm, crying and saying 'Will we be all right?' I replied 'Yes, we would be O.K.!' Looking out of the window I could see the full reception committee tearing along beside the plane ... fire engines, ambulances, police, the lot! So I quickly got my head down in the crash position.

The landing and disembarkation was normal and the Captain had obviously done a very good job landing a fully-loaded D C 10 on only two engines without incident. I was later told that passengers at the back of the plane had heard a bang. When I disembarked I could see that the cowling around the engine on the tail was hanging off.

The next problem was what to do with 400 passengers at around 3.30 a.m. A fleet of buses was mustered and we were dispatched to various hotels. Only hand baggage was available ... the electrics to operate the hold baggage doors were powered by the damaged engine. In those days I always kept tooth-brush, paste and shaving gear in my hand baggage, so was able to tidy up a bit later in the hotel.

Later in the day we were all bussed back to the airport, where the KLM representative was trying to sort things out. What annoyed me was the hard time the KLM representative was having from some of the passengers, one woman was screaming at him 'Get me out of here! I'm going to a ship in Caracas.' He just told her and everyone else that he was doing all that he could. He then disappeared round the back somewhere, probably to get out of the way!

I later asked him what the chances were for an early departure as I was to join a ship in the Canal Zone as Master. He then told me that he had been in the Portuguese Navy and had given up the sea for a job in KLM. I commiserated with him over the hard time some of the passengers were giving him. He said that it was not uncommon.

He said that boarding time would be about 2200 hours. I finally saw him at the check-in barrier where he was issuing the boarding cards and he said 'I've up-graded you to First Class!' I nearly got on my knees in thanking him, as my Company could never afford to up-grade Master or Chief Engineers.

So it was 'champers' on take off from Lisbon and again at Caracas. The overall delay was around twenty-one hours as the relief plane came in from Belgium.

I never saw my potential new girl friend, the nun, again and joined the ship in Panama Bay with no further delay.

Thank you, again, Captain Cliff Mullings. It seems appropriate to let Olga Mullings have the last word.

I have many happy memories of days on board when I travelled with my husband. Since my childhood I have wanted to go to Holland. Then the opportunity came, never having been abroad, to find myself sailing towards the Hook of Holland.

I flew to Bremerhaven with a member of the catering staff and was very amused and somewhat confused to find on arrival at the airport to see that there was a placard waiting for Mr. Cook. We got the message! He was, in fact, the ship's Cook.

A voyage to the West Indies was interesting and memorable. The weather in the Bay of Biscay could not be described as good and, sadly, it took me a few days to make an appearance in the dining room!

The passengers were interesting and there was a fine social life on the ship. On the previous voyage, my husband had welcomed Princess Alice, a grand-daughter of Queen Victoria, who apparently made frequent visits to the West Indies.

I found it strange not to see land each day, but it was an unexpected pleasure to pass near the Azores at night and see the bright lights on the horizon. The schedule had been Barbados and Trinidad, but this time Trinidad was cancelled as there were problems at the quayside and we only called at Barbados. It was truly beautiful with light-coloured sand and a turquoise sea. I enjoyed seeing yellow birds in the trees overlooking the beach ... memorable! Then we travelled through the sugar plantations.

Next in line was Jamaica. I watched the bananas being loaded as the bearers sang in unison. Then we went to the colourful straw market. We had received a number of invitations. How can one forget that trip in a boat with a glass bottom that enabled us to wonder at the coral beneath us.

Our final destination was Bermuda ... quite unlike the Caribbean ... but totally enchanting.

Thank you, Olga ... the years tumble by but memories are undimmed. Actually, I intended to give Olga the last word, but Cliff had more to add.

OH DEAR!

In the late 60s I was moored at the banana berth in San Pedro, L. A., and I had just come out of the shower. I watched the cargo hatches being opened up when I became aware of a tanker turning around in the basin without tugs. There was a tug strike in progress. It was rapidly becoming apparent that no stern power would stop her headway. The only thing that could stop it was our ship. I pulled my clothes on rather rapidly, dashed up to the Bridge and sounded the emergency alarm to get everyone up.

She struck us between Nos. 2 and 3 hatches on the water-tight bulkhead. Several moorings parted with the impact and the gangway fell off, but fortunately all the damage was above the water line. Even so, it was weeks before we were able to sail. Sheer strake and deck plates were buckled, insulation in the hatches and air trunking was damaged and other repairs were needed.

ROLL OUT THE CARPET

During one of my voyages in the GOLFITO, I had the pleasure of having as passenger H.R.H. the late Princess Alice, Duchess of Athelone. She never sat at the Master's table, but on a table with her lady-in-waiting. The lounge floor was also used for dancing, and the carpet was therefore portable. One night a film was arranged, Her Royal Highness was seated with her lady-in-waiting and around her were 80 to 90 passengers, when the vessel started rolling and the carpet and everyone on it started sliding sideways. H.R.H. was recovering from a broken wrist and we suggested that we might cancel the film show, but she would not have it so we went ahead with fingers crossed. There was a way of securing that carpet, but someone had not done it properly!

Incidentally, on our regular 100-passenger ships, trading to the West Indies in the late 40s to early 70s, passengers often made return trips over the years. They knew of a saying we had … 'Bananas were best, Passengers a pest!' Some newcomers took umbrage about this, but the regulars laughed it off … but they still came back!

PROBLEMS

As a general rule, problems that arose on voyages were with crew members. However, on our passenger/cargo ships, passengers were not always exempt from this generalisation.

One lady passenger, not as young as she used to be, decided about four days in the outward passage that she would like to wear her ring, rather than leave it in safe-keeping in the Purser/Writer's office safe. On asking the Purser, he requested her receipt for this item and on checking his records it was obvious to him that neither party held a receipt. He advised the lady that it was quite clear to him that she had never lodged the ring for safe-keeping. However, she was adamant she had given him the ring. He told the lady that he would meet her in her cabin. He called the Stewardess responsible for the cabin and the Chief Steward and also advised me what was going on and added 'I'll find that bloody ring if it is the last thing I do!'

He found it alright ... stuck down the toe of her shoe! Maybe she forgot where she had put it (don't we all!). Maybe there was an ulterior motive. Who knows?

A second incident occurred on one of our smaller ships when two ladies embarked for the passage to New York. On approaching the port, deck chairs had to be stowed away ready for arrival, but the ladies asked the Second Steward to put chairs up on the boat deck in order to see the approaches to the port. He advised them that it was a bit breezy and squalls of rain were possible. However, he put them out and about twenty minutes later it poured down and the rain blew into the weather-side main deck alleyway. Access to their cabin was down one ladder and along one side or the other of the main deck. Of course, not understanding 'lee' or 'weather', they chose the latter. By now the storm door entrance was wet and on opening, the lino inside was also wet. One of the two ladies slipped and was later seen limping and, on docking, requested a Doctor and assistance to disembark.

All the details of this incident were carefully documented in the Official Log Book, especially when the other lady passenger was heard to pass a remark that she 'travels on claims'.

About two months later, I had a letter from the Company solicitor asking if there were any other details we could add, as she was claiming $100,000 injury. Apparently, the end result was she did not get it!

THE CRIME

Those who knew Kingston Harbour, Jamaica, in the early 70s would know the compulsory pilotage area was Plumb Point light-house to Port Royal. Again, on the GOLFITO, I made a 0500 arrival at Plumb Point to find a pilots' strike in progress. Normally, one of our two Company-appointed pilots would board at this point, but he was unable to do so as both pilots were also Kingston pool pilots.

I waited a while ... thought to hell with it, I'm going in! On arrival at the Port Royal area I was met by a Kingston pool pilot in his boat shouting abuse at me that I had committed an offence by breaking the rules, when I entered the harbour through a compulsory pilotage area. I kept my head down in the wheelhouse!

On the other side of the vessel, our Company Pilot was boarding through the oil flat door and came to the Bridge saying that he could take no part in piloting our ship, if he did he could be dismissed from the pool, so he remained at the back of the wheelhouse. There were no further problems on this trip.

GUILTY, MY LORD

The following voyage my wife was with me and we docked at Kingston as normal, the pilots' strike being settled. Our Agent boarded as usual, conducted the ship's business and then advised me that he had a warrant from the police for my arrest concerning the previous voyage, when I passed through the compulsory pilotage area with no pilot as they were on strike. My wife looked very alarmed!

Our Agent took us to the Court House which was very hot and sweaty, plus an assortment of others awaiting trial for various offences. Our Agent remained with us during the case. The offence was read out. The Judge said 'Guilty or not guilty'. I replied 'Guilty, My Lord'. A fine was imposed and we left the Court ... I with a clean bill of health!

GUN CARRYING

In the early 70s, I was appointed to one of the smaller ships, at that time on a regular schedule, Tampa to Turbo, for bananas. This was a notorious trip for narcotics. One ship was under arrest in Tampa, apparently having been warned by the U.S. Narcotics Department on more than one occasion. I was soon aware of some of our Honduran crew being involved in this practise, as large amounts of money had been seen exchanging hands in a bar toilet close to the ship.

The narcotics squad was watching the ship twenty-four hours a day on the quayside. The problem was that the labourers loading the banana boxes were planting the dope in certain marked boxes. Our Agent in Tampa had been made aware of an incident whereby another ship's Master on a ship on a regular schedule from Turbo to Florida, who was trying to stop the smuggling, had been carefully watched at Turbo and his movements had been noted. Apparently, in the evening he would have a couple of drinks, then go on deck before turning in, but on one occasion he changed his routine and, the report had it, it was just as well he did. The plan was to shoot him from a boat!

All the loading was done from an anchorage. I was advised to carry a gun by our Agent and our Superintendent in Southampton. British ships do not carry guns, but I was loaned one by our Agent and shown how to use it. When anchored in Turbo, my door was always locked at night and the gun near at hand. When I eventually left the ship, I handed the gun to my relief.

MAN OVERBOARD

An incident occurred after I joined one of the 'M' class ships in Rotterdam. We sailed the same evening. Night time in the Dover Straits and then into the English Channel. The visibility was not good, so I remained around the wheelhouse area. Some of the crew I knew from previous ships, some were unknown to me. Around the Western Approaches the weather improved and I turned in around midnight.

At about 0130 hours, my phone woke me up with the Second Officer advising me that a crew member was missing and could not be found. I carried out the usual procedure and reversed course, meanwhile trying to pinpoint what time he had been last seen. Some thought that he had gone to his cabin about midnight. It was all very haphazard, so we steamed on the reverse course for one a half hours. We started a ship search to no avail. I sent out an alarm and a couple of ships responded. I soon found out that there had been a bit of a party in the crew recreation room and a fight had broken out involving the missing man. It was thought that when he went to his cabin, he had not liked the look of his face and had decided to go overboard. Blood was later found in the stowed gangway area, photos of which I took later. As there was now a Force 5 wind and a moderate sea running, I discussed the possibilities on the V.H.F. with the two ships that had responded about the possibility of finding him. We agreed that it was hopeless and we proceeded on our way. One or two statements that I took suggested that he was a bit effeminate.

Around two or three months later, it came to light that the man's mother was not satisfied that her son had committed suicide, but that it was more likely that he had been pushed overboard. Scotland Yard was called in to investigate.

I was home when the phone rang and my wife turned white when I said it was Scotland Yard! The Detective Inspector I spoke to had been to sea as an Engineer. He and a Chief Inspector wanted to arrange to meet me at home and take statements. They duly arrived in an unmarked police car with a local Inspector driving them. When the business was finished,

I suggested that they might care for an aperitif before returning to London. They did admit that as a rule it was the done thing when on duty not to imbibe, however as they had a long way to go, they would have one. I pulled the cork out and later on threw it away as I didn't need it any more!

After my leave, I and my wife joined another 'M' class in Genoa. The two Inspectors were visiting all the ships where the crew members had by now been dispersed and they brought a present with them that was opened on the spot! The Chief Inspector said if we were ever around the London area to give him a ring at Scotland Yard and he would show us around.

A few months later, we were in London and he met us at the door and showed us round, including the narcotics investigation department. He also took us to lunch in their restaurant … it was very enjoyable. The outcome of the investigation was suicide.

Early in 1984, I received my final redundancy cheque and worked in the Coastguard Station at Crosby for eighteen months. Then it was a case of 'last in first out' as the staff were being reduced.

Here ends the Epistle of Captain T.C. Mullings seagoing days!

That was most enjoyable … thank you, Cliff.

Ted Morris
Manchester Pilot

Ted Morris takes us back to the start of his career and to life at sea as it was 'long ago' when bridges were exposed to the elements and life was cheap in the rigours of war. He was only a lad. This is about life in tramp ships. The year is 1943 in the middle of the war. This is fun in a strange sort of way.

WHAT SHIP? - HARDSHIP!

'Thou shall not enter ale-houses or houses of ill repute, unless upon your master's lawful business'

So stated a clause of the Indenture that was to bind and apprentice me to Messrs. Evan Thomas Radcliffe and Co., Steamship Owners, Cardiff, South Wales, for a period of four years to 'learn the business of a seaman'. This was not the only restrictive discipline imposed by the document by a long way, but the one that intrigued and puzzled me most as I advanced into my 'time' and became more senior as an apprentice ... or 'Junior Officer', our posh title!

It was occasionally my experience to be sent ashore by the Mate to find the Old Man, who was supposedly ashore on ship's business, and the true interpretation of the clause was soon brought home to me!

Tramp-ship-style management and operation had apparently changed very little since the introduction of steam and certainly not at all between the wars. Their fortunes had been dictated and affected greatly by years of world depression in the late 20s and early 30s, but Cardiff 'tramps' in particular, with their basic trades of 'coal out' (Welsh) and 'grain home' (River Plate and S. America generally, Black Sea etc) seemed to have fared better than most.

It was never my intention to follow the sea in such a manner, but at the time, being desperate to 'get into the war' (obviously some mental deficiency!) and too young for the Royal Navy, which was really my preference, I had applied without success to more than twenty different shipping companies for a cadet appointment or apprenticeship. Ever increasing shipping losses at the time were making it very difficult to find a berth. My only pre-sea training had been gained as a devoted Sea Cadet. However, a chance meeting with a neighbour, who was a Master Mariner in command and on survivors leave at that time, produced a promise that he would 'get me away'. He warned that I would probably never forgive him for the rest of my life. I did eventually forgive him ... reluctantly! That was a challenge that I could not at the time refuse! It seemed that this gentleman, of Welsh birthright and determination, was a first cousin to a director of the 'said mentioned' company and in very short time my father received an offer of an apprenticeship for me.

I remember well to this day the major comment that my father made regarding my aspirations ... "I hope you know what you are doing." I thought I did, but in reality didn't! But, I did learn in a very short time that I shouldn't have done it!!!

The days of medical examinations, sight tests and interviews and the gathering together of ... 1 uniform with cap and badge,

4 white uniform shirts, six pairs of black socks, 4 blue working shirts, 2 pairs dungarees, 4 pairs underpants, etcetera, were all too long in my excitement to get on with it. Then, suddenly, early one morning, I was in the car with my father, approaching a wharf alongside which were moored 3 grey-painted vessels, all bristling with guns, the outer two being handsome ships and the ugly and dilapidated 'sister' in the middle being mine.

Proceeding to the lower-bridge deck we entered the Captain's cabin, which was most impressive with its dark wood panelling and beautifully ornate brass oil lights, suspended from the deck head ... oil lighting was always used when in port or at anchor.

Here we met Captain Davy Jenkins, Master of the vessel and a very Welsh Welsh-man from Llangranog, Cardigan Bay. Of small stature and unkempt style, he was dressed in the blue, pin-striped trousers of his suit, a matching waistcoat and a collarless off-white shirt with rolled up sleeves. After greeting my father and a brief discourse, he turned to me and shaking my hand in limp style remarked, "Whilst aboard my ship and from now on, I will be your father." My first impressions of the man were not electrifying, but as time wore on and experience followed experience, he gained my greatest respect as a seaman, mentor, friend and Master of my chosen calling.

The Chief Officer was summoned to the cabin. A Welshman, also, of almost giant proportions! He was a man whom I never did quite take to throughout our enforced relationship. Very little conversation passed between us as he took me down to the half-deck to introduce me to my shipmates-to-be ... three lusty lads, all with at least two years service behind them and the Senior Apprentice just about finishing his time. It happened to be 'smoko' and they were in working gear ... weren't we always ... apart from uniform to go ashore. They were covered in white-lead or red-lead or oil or tar or some such, but at that moment were enjoying their mugs of tea and the inevitable cigarette and gossip. It was somewhat frightening to be confronted by such an awesome and seasoned trio. As the new boy, I feared that I should be well tested before being accepted. How right I was!

We all sat around the mess-room, which can't have been more than eight to ten feet square. It was at the forward end of the Apprentice's accommodation in the half-deck on the starboard side, and on your left as you entered from an inside alleyway through a single weather door. You firstly stepped into a very small reception area between the mess-room and main cabin (which was on the right); food and store lockers were situated on the outside bulkhead and there was also a centre porthole. The mess-room table, the length of the room, ran fore and aft down the centre and was fixed at the forward end to the outer bulkhead. Hardwood benches, resembling shaped and slatted garden seats, backed onto the bulkheads on either side of the table and provided the only seating that we could ever enjoy. There were no washing facilities whatsoever.

Food was brought from the galley in kits … metal trays, bowls and any such containers. After the meal, all washing up was done in buckets of water that had to be heated by steam jets in the galley and placed on the table or bench seat. All other forms of sanitation, including the washing of clothes and the necessary attentions to acts of personal hygiene were likewise performed from a bucket on the bench (or out on deck) because there just wasn't a bathroom or shower. Imagine the scene when four hulky youths, usually having spent many days or even weeks at sea, were all desperately trying to prepare themselves for a run ashore, at the same time!

We each acted as 'peggy' for one week at a time, although on that first horrendous voyage my 'turn' seemed to come around more frequently than others! 'Peggy' (like 'mother') meant that you were responsible for all domestic chores, including all the cleaning of the accommodation. In particular,

I was responsible for the victualing of it's hungry inhabitants … including the little treats that could be begged, bought or more likely stolen from the Chief Steward's or Cook's store. There was great rivalry amongst us and we were very competitive in our efforts to be the best, consequently we lived in scrubbed, polished and shining splendour and woe betide any visitor who left their mark!

The main cabin had three double tiers of bunks on the outboard bulkhead and a bench settee about four feet long and three double tier wardrobe lockers on the inboard bulkhead. That was where all your best uniforms and civilian clothes gathered mildew constantly. At the top of the cabin there was a 'bright-works' … so known because it had fancy brass handles and highly polished woodwork and provided one drawer each for six occupants.

The only form of heating was a massive and ugly 'bogey', a coal burning stove which could only be used in port because of the obvious dangers that it would create if rolling heavily when at sea. Thus, we spent our days and nights in winter, North Atlantic, invariably half frozen, always sleeping fully clothed. Apart from the extreme cold, in those days you could be required to vacate the premises in a hurry. Our oilskins were over our other bunk coverings and we usually woke up with everything frozen to the bulkhead.

On my first voyage we carried the Vice-Commodore of the convoy and his staff, which included two Royal Navy signallers, who were billeted with us for lack of any other accommodation. With six human beings confined in such a limited space, turns had to be takenwhen performing such simple acts as changing clothes or whatever, and 'privacy' was just a word in the dictionary. The only exception to this, as I remember that first voyage, was a time during one particular 'middle watch' when a loud explosion and shudder through the vessel caused us to believe that we had been hit. The four of us, who were off watch, leapt from our bunks in unison and seemed to pass through the limited door space as one! It turned out to be, on that occasion, an over-enthusiastic rogue escort who had dropped off a pattern of depth charges and landed one almost under our stern.

There was no domestic refrigeration as such, only iceboxes, which were insulated walk-in lockers. This limited the amount of fresh foods that could be carried and consumed to the length of time it took the ice to melt. Salt meat and salt fish were the standard alternatives and, when in the tropics, a glass of limejuice often replaced fresh fruit or vegetables. The iceboxes were scrupulously cleaned and sanitised before the beginning of every passage and made ready to receive new ice blocks as they came aboard. Sadly, with unavoidable deposits of dried animal blood and other wilting and rotting materials soon accumulating, they quickly became unhygienic and decidedly unpleasant. Like many other seafarers with similar experiences to mine, I am sure, I often muse when confronted by modern 'use by' and 'best before' dates now printed on food packaging, and I marvel that we ever survived.

Deck crew consisted of Bosun, Carpenter, 6 Able Seamen, 2 Ordinary Seaman and 4 apprentices. As such we were general factotums ... watch keepers, with one Apprentice in each watch and one on day work and, in addition to our normal watch-keeping, we did all the steering whenever a Pilot was on board. We were responsible for, and jealously guarded, everything forward of the bridge including all fixed and running gear, masts, derricks, beams and hatches, anchors and cables ... you name it ... there was not a wrinkle that we didn't know. Woe betide any sailor who put a foot anywhere near our domain unless invited to do so.

Seamanship had to be our forte, for the tramp-man's adage was always, 'Never order anyone to do anything that you cannot do yourself'. In addition, of course, we were always turned out

166

in weather emergencies at sea because we did not incur the expense of overtime as did other crew members. At this time, we also had our 'action stations' and were responsible to the Chief Petty Officer, D.E.M.S, Gunner, and were at his beck and call, as required. The essential academic knowledge of our profession, the understanding of navigational mathematics, spherical trigonometry, physics, hydrostatics, meteorology etcetera, which had to be mastered for our future examinations and qualifications, had to be accomplished in our spare time.

A hard life, where 'four on and stay on' was often a reality and the clock was only there to tell you the time and not the end of your labours. We worked 'Field Days' when required, which graciously allowed us to put in an extra four hours' labour in addition to the normal eight, and days of arrival and departure could be endless. We complained that we were ill-fed, but always managed to supplement our diet by thieving as much of the goodies as we could when storing ship. The Chief Steward and his suppliers were always at loggerheads as to the amount of items that had supposedly been delivered on board, but were just not always in evidence. They never seemed to realise that the supply line directly passed our cabin door! I well remember a very large and beautifully iced Xmas cake disappearing whole when in New York one festive season … down our throats! Even amateur gardeners' allotments ashore were not sacrosanct and, when lying at anchor off some attractive coastline, the jolly boat often did nocturnal trips to return resembling a greengrocer's delivery.

The Indenture also guaranteed the privilege of free laundry when in foreign places and all necessary medical attention whilst away from home, but only advised that 'time off' under any circumstances, would be granted only at the discretion of the Master or his representative. On my ultimate voyage as apprentice (Acting Third Officer) and after a lengthy period of over two years absence and well out of my 'time', upon arrival back in London I requested home leave and was asked, by the Marine Superintendent (the same one!) 'What do you want to go home for ... one egg a month?' He was referring, of course, to the food ration of the time. But, we were handsomely remunerated at the rate of:-

> £10 for the 1st year
> £12 for the 2nd year
> £18 for the 3rd year
> £20 for the 4th year

At the time, of course, a subsidy existed in the form of a 'war bonus' which valued your life less during your first year of service by only paying you £5 per month, but thereafter increasing to £10 per month, and then you were really 'in the money'. Not forgetting, of course, that all forms of emolument ceased from the moment that you were sunk, should you be so unlucky. Mind you, it was still always necessary to make a 'phone call home upon arriving back at any other port of destination in the country to ask, 'If you'd like to see me, Mum, could you possibly send me the fare?'

On completion of your Indenture and providing you had been diligent in your work and dedication and had made the necessary sacrifices to the benefit of the Company, and that reports by your Master were favourable, then you were awarded a special ex-gratis bonus of £50 ... which just happened to be the amount of premium that was necessarily deposited by your father when first you joined!

Upon qualifying as Second Mate, I was offered employment by Canadian Pacific Steamships Limited and went on to serve throughout the rest of my seafaring career in practically all their vessels of the day, both passenger and cargo. I consider myself so fortunate to have experienced the immediate 'post war era' of the last of the great Atlantic liners.

My first appointment was Fifth Navigating Officer, R.M.S. EMPRESS OF FRANCE, and my new workplace was a gigantic maze, awe-inspiring after what I had become accustomed to. My single cabin was bigger than the one that I had previously lived in along with six other lads ... and the washing facilities, of course, were 'en suite'.

To eat at a table in the elegant First Class Dining Room, dressed in one's finery and without restriction, and to be waited upon by an immaculately turned-out Steward was something. To be confronted with the intricacies of the incredibly extensive menus (for the first few times, anyway!) was something else.

But one quickly began to enjoy meeting people outside the normal scope of one's existence and savour the very special atmosphere that in those days was the hallmark of First Class travel by sea. A way of life so easy to succumb to, and one that could not possibly be other than interesting, satisfying, acceptable and in some respects unreal!

'Chalk and cheese', 'cheese and chalk', 'ridiculous to the sublime' ... or vice versa! Comparisons are odious, it is said, and although the choice of lifestyle between my early beginnings and that of the liners in which I now served was never in doubt, I remained forever grateful for the grounding in my profession that I had received in the rough and tumble of tramp-ship training and existence. I believed that it taught me well ... the business of a seaman!

Thank you, Ted Morris, that was an interesting account about 'learning the hard way'. Ted was to sail as Chief Officer before becoming a Manchester Pilot.

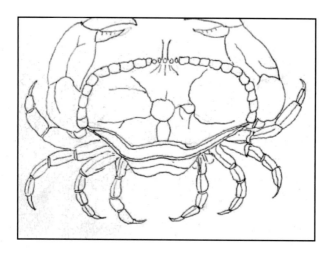

Doug Rosser
Chief Engineer

Doug Rosser joined his first ship the day war started. He had served his apprenticeship as a fitter and turner, and he signed on as the Second Refrigerating Engineer. In 1940, he moved to Harrison', obtained his First Class Engineer Certificate and then transferred to Blue Star Line to obtain diesel experience. Eventually, Doug came ashore in 1949 and joined Insurance Engineers Ltd. as Engine Surveyor and was promoted to District Superintendent of the Norwich Office. He retired in 1981. Let's get to his story ... read on.

The date is late August 1939. I had served 4 years and 9 months apprenticeship as a fitter and turner at J.W. Pickering & Sons on the corner of Sefton Street and Hill Street, Liverpool. As I wanted to go to sea as a Junior Engineer, I thought it was about time I applied to a shipping company as jobs were not easy to acquire. I wrote to the New Zealand Shipping Co & Federal Line with not much hope of receiving a reply

But, lo and behold, I received one within the week asking me to report to their office in the Liver Buildings for an interview. I reported for the interview and after a few enquiries from the Engineer Superintendent, he advised me that there was a position on the S.S. CUMBERLAND as Second Refrigerating Engineer and would I like to accept it. If so, I would have to travel up to Glasgow on Friday 1st September, 1939 to join her in Govan dry dock as she was sailing to Australia on the Monday. I could not believe my luck! I dashed home and told my parents who were very helpful in getting what kit was necessary. I missed the morning train to Glasgow and had to get the late afternoon one, which didn't arrive in Glasgow until approximately 8 p.m. and it was dark. I had not been to Glasgow before and had no idea where Govan Dry Dock was so I got a taxi to take me there. When we arrived to my amazement the ship had been painted completely grey. I staggered up the gangway with my two cases and found the Third Engineer in his cabin. I told him who I was and he said I wanted the Chief Refrigerating Engineer and he took me along to his cabin and introduced me to him. He gave me the key to my cabin and when I had unpacked, I wrote a letter home to let them know I had arrived safely. Saturday morning, 2nd September, 1939, I reported to the Chief Engineer. He said the Second Engineer would take me ashore with a new Junior Engineer and get us signed on the Articles of the ship. Incidentally, the Second Engineer was a Liverpool man so I had something in common with him. The rest of the crew were Geordies with the exception of the new Junior, who was from London. Sunday morning I went ashore for the paper and on the front page was WAR DECLARED ON GERMANY. The ATHENIA was laying across the dock to us and she sailed out later that morning and was torpedoed ... the first casualty of the war.

We were supposed to sail on the Monday, but it was postponed until Wednesday when we sailed down to Milford Haven and joined dozens of ships anchored there waiting for further orders. That weekend, we joined fifty ships in the first convoy to leave Britain and we were escorted for three days and then told to scatter. I was on deck at the time. It was just getting dusk when the flags went up to scatter. My heart sank as I thought that in this old tub we will be left behind and get torpedoed, but to my surprise I heard the engines speed up and the whine of the turbines cutting in and we left all the other ships behind.

Having an enquiring mind, I found out that this ship was an ex-German vessel, a prize from the 1914 War. She was 10,000 tons, twin screw, quadruple reciprocating engines with Borwack exhaust turbines ... and could do 16 knots, which was fast for ships then. We called in at Dakar and anchored in the bay to get a supply of oil, as she was an oil-burning ship. The Chief Engineer told me to get a clean boiler suit on as I was to go ashore to sound the oil tank before they started pumping. I would also have to go ashore when they finished to get the final soundings. It was quite a nice experience going ashore in the motor launch.

We made our way down to Cape Town, zig-zagging to avoid subs and picked up more oil. Finally, making our way to Australia we arrived at Perth. It took two months. From Perth, we went to Townsville and then worked our way back to Rockhampton, Brisbane, Sydney, Melbourne and Adelaide. Then back to Perth, Cape Town, and then Freetown where we picked up a convoy for home.

It took us approximately 5 months, but we arrived home safely with a full cargo of lambs and butter and discharged our cargo in London, having defied the German U-Boats coming up the English Channel.

I thought of a little incident that happened during the war at sea in mid-Atlantic convoy and it does keep popping into my head every now and again.

We were returning from the USA on the S.S. NOVELIST, which was a cam ship, and we were at the stern of the convoy with two other cam ships. I was off watch and was relaxing on the boat deck when I spotted a plume of smoke on the skyline.

There was a German battleship on the loose and I immediately thought this could be her. I had no need to worry as the BRIDGE had spotted her, as well as the escort vessels, and two destroyers peeled off and headed towards the plume of smoke. The whole ship was alerted on standby. As the plume of smoke got nearer, we could make out that she was a large ship and then suddenly the word came through the ship … "It's the PRINCE OF WALES". As she came nearer, the destroyers escorted her through the centre line of the convoy and as we were astern of the centre line we had a good view of her.

As she passed us, there was a placard and on it was "Churchill Aboard" and there he was, waving to us. It was a most exhilarating moment.

Thank you, Doug Rosser. I am sure that there could have been much more!

Captain Eric Gowland
Master Mariner

Captain Eric Gowland chats about his time at sea.

My sea-going service covered the period 1944 to 1985, first as a cadet, then through the various ranks until I was appointed to command in May, 1961 at the young age of thirty three. I was probably the youngest appointed to Command in my memory and it was unusual in the history of the Pacific Steam Navigation Company.

The short period at the end of Second World War was uneventful, although I did have the experience of convoy duties. My early years were in general cargo ships, but in the late 40s, I was appointed to the passenger ship REINA DEL PACIFICO in the P.S.N.C. service to Bermuda, Nassau, the Caribbean and the West Coast of South America. My next appointment was to the troopship ORDUNA, which was built in 1914. She had served through both World Wars. I made the last six voyages of this ship trooping between Liverpool and the Far East, until she was withdrawn from service early in 1951 and taken to the Clyde for breaking up. It was for my service in ORDUNA that I was recently awarded a Veteran's medal.

For the next 25 years, I served in various units of the

P.S.N.C. cargo ship fleet, mainly on the West Coast of South America route. Following this, I was given a complete change, being appointed Captain of the tanker, WILLIAM WHEELWRIGHT which was on permanent charter to Shell, trading to oil terminals throughout many parts of the world which I had never seen before.

The highlight of my sea-going career came approximately three years before I retired. Early in 1982, I was informed that I was being appointed to command a new Panamax bulk carrier being built at Govan on the Clyde, named PACIFIC PATRIOT. By this time the Furness Group, of which P.S.N.C. was a part, had been taken over by Mr. Tung, the Hong Kong ship-owner, and he had ordered two of these ships on the Clyde. As you may not know, the Chinese way of naming a ship is completely different to the way we are accustomed. The shipyard carry out the launch without any ceremony and when all fitting out has been completed and the ship ready for sea, they then have a naming ceremony.

When the allocated day for the launch arrived, weather conditions were uncertain, but eventually it was decided to 'go for it'. During the period of launching, the wind increased considerably, but once the procedure has started, it is not possible to cancel. The ship went down into the water. The tugs were not able to get hold of her before the wind had its effect. The stern swung across to the opposite bank, making heavy contact which caused the stern frame to fracture! As this was a complete casting, a new stern frame had to be ordered from the manufacturers in N.E. England. To make matters worse, a dry dock was not available on the Clyde at this time. So the ship was towed to Belfast for dry docking. There the new stern frame was fitted and the final fitting-out was done after several months.

When ready for sea, the ship returned to the lower reaches of the Clyde and two days of trials were carried out off the Isle of Arran. Subsequently we returned to the Govan Shipyard, where a further delay of over two months was incurred in waiting for a suitable date for the sponsor, Queen Elizabeth, the Queen Mother, to carry out the naming ceremony.

Of course, the day before the naming took place, a dinner was held at an hotel near Erskine Bridge. Then the next day, following the naming ceremony, a lunch was held at the same hotel. It was at the latter occasion that Mr. Tung, the ship's owner, presented a valuable piece of carving to Her Majesty in honour of the event.

I had the honour and pleasure of conducting the Queen Mother around the ship. Twenty-four hours later, we were at sea en route to the U.S.A., but, at least she had seen the ship in its finished condition, rather than in the normal condition of an unfinished steel hulk.

Due to the extended period of delays, the ship did not fit into the charterer's schedules and on the maiden voyage we were assigned a full cargo of grain from Mississsippi to Hamburg. The charter obtained was to the Aluminium Company of Canada, ALCAN. However, whilst on that first run to Hamburg, a cable was received advising that our sister ship, which had entered service six months earlier, was in trouble. She had suffered an extensive crack in her deck welding, whilst on passage across the Pacific in heavy weather. This, of course, meant a diversion to Hawaii where temporary repairs were carried out in order that the ship might reach Japan. As a result of this, there was some concern for the welding on PACIFIC PATRIOT. Immediately on our arrival in Hamburg, the shipyard commenced X-ray examination of our welding which proved to be in a similar condition to that of the sister ship. On completion of discharge, a dry dock was obtained so that the defect could be put right. In the end that took over two months ... not a good advert for that Govan shipyard.

Afterwards we carried approximately 75,000 tons of bauxite per voyage from Trombetas, one thousand miles up the Amazon to the ALCAN terminal of Port Alfred up the Saguannay river, a tributary of the St. Lawrence. This trip took a month to complete.

I took early retirement in 1985.

As a landlubber, I never cease to wonder at the skills of a Master Mariner who tackles any ship, any cargo and travels safely to places completely unknown to him with apparent confidence. On second thought, we did the same in our aircraft during the War ... we had problems too!

Thank you Captain Eric Gowland.

Peter Gannicliffe
Chief Engineer

Peter Gannicliffe is full of humour and friendship ... a peep at his sea career will explain the smiles. He has suggested a title for his opening tale

A COASTER IS A SHIP, TOO!

Having finished my leave after a fourteen month trip in one of the Hains vessels, the TREVAYLOR, the family suggested that I might elect for a shorter run. Off I went to the Pool on Mann Island, Liverpool and they thought that I might consider some time in a coaster. They sent me to join the CORAL QUEEN, a Queen ship and by then part of Coast Lines. She certainly had never seen coral and the Queen never even saw

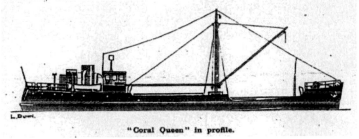

"Coral Queen" in profile.

179

her ... I almost missed her! In Canada Dock, I asked a docker of her whereabouts. "Down there, mate." He was right. She seemed to fit below the quayside ... a funny little ship of some 300 tons.

I went on board and introduced myself to the Skipper and the Chief Engineer. It is worth explaining that, having been the Fourth Engineer in the TREVAYLOR, I was now promoted to Second. That was a big jump in rank, but not in cash. After all there were only two of us!

Eventually, I went on watch. The Chief stated that we did five on and five off, as did the two Mates. So we sailed with grain heading for Bristol and I went down into the engine room to tackle the first five. A matter of minutes later as we just got into the river, the Chief came to the top grating and asked "What are you doing?" I replied that I was on watch.

"No, no, no! Get up here and help the Second Mate with the steering. There's no need to be in the engine room as long as the water is coming out and the engine is running." So, up I went and gave a hand on the wheel.

On watch were the Mate and a Seaman, both on five on and five off. There were actually three Seamen on board and one of them was the Acting Cook. He came to me and asked for my seaman's ration book (double that of civilians) and added "It will cost you eighteen bob for the food for a week." I readily complied with his request. Incidentally, every week one man got his book back and another man had his eighteen bob back. I thought that this was a very reasonable system! The galley was a tiny little thing, next to an equally small saloon where the two Engineers, the two Mates and the Skipper sat. The Skipper was a man in his late fifties and very much a coasting man. He knew every inch of the route and held a Pilot's Certificate for the Clyde and the Mersey.

Off we sailed, cutting through the Rock Channel, skirting New Brighton and heading for Anglesey. The actual course was towards Point Lynas, but in fact we seemed to be aiming rather south of this and I asked the Second Mate why this was. In reply, he said that he was the only non-Liverpudlian aboard and he lived in Moelfre, Anglesey, and that we would pass reasonably close. Sure enough, we did. His wife and daughter came out of a little bungalow and started waving a table cloth. We all waved back and blew the whistle and then off we toddled to Point Lynas.

Going round Middle Mouse, I thought that we would head for the Skerries, but in fact we went inside, passed the West Mouse and were very close to a rock called Harry Furlong Bank. That was typical of the Skipper, getting very close to the land, as he knew every inch of it. Then we headed for the North Stack and southwards to the Bristol Channel.

The vessel had a six-cylinder Crossley, and two small generators that were extremely difficult to start because they were cranked by hand and space was limited. I noticed that every cabin, in addition to the 110 volts lighting, contained two small bulbs on a wooden board. One was an ordinary 12 volts car bulb and the other was a little bigger, 48 volts. I asked what it was all about and was told that a previous Engineer, when the battery levels were low, instead of putting water in, he had added acid and had created damage, Then, once we got into port and had shut the generators down, we relied on the batteries for light. We started off with the full 110 volts. After about six hours, we would shout round "To 48 volts" and we switched off the main light. After a few more hours it was "Over to the 12 volts". So we managed some sixteen hours of light in the cabins. It worked.

Up the river we went, under the Clifton Suspension Bridge and into Bristol Docks to discharge our cargo of grain. Then we loaded drums of acetylene for the Mond Works in Northwich on the River Weaver and set out on the reverse journey.

When we entered the Mersey, we went alongside the

knuckle near the old Pilot House at Pierhead. Half the crew were on the fo'c'stle. They jumped ashore and went home. The rest went on to Northwich.

Entering the Weaver was done by entering a small lock almost exactly underneath the railway bridge at Runcorn. It has been filled now, but it had been built for barges carrying coal to the Pilkington's St. Helens Glass Works. In this way, we avoided taking on board a Manchester Ship Canal Pilot.

You are not allowed to navigate the Weaver at night, so as we often arrived in the evening, we would tie up to the bank. A number of us would look in the fields and find cabbages, potatoes or carrots and present them to the cook. He would then deduct a few shillings!

In Northwich, we would unload the drums and, in the meantime, those who had gone ashore would catch the train from Lime Street, Liverpool to Northwich the following morning. We would, I'm afraid, pocket the 48 volt British Rail bulbs for the ship ... all very convenient!

I noticed that coming up-river, we were hard pressed to do nine knots and were making much smoke. I suggested to the Chief that we opened up some scavenger valves when we arrived in Northwich. We did and found that most of them were broken. So we rang Crossleys in Manchester and they were kind enough to send a man in a car with a supply of valves. When we fitted them, it cleared up the problem. Coast Lines told us that we should have done it through the Office!

THERE ARE TANKERS AND OTHER TANKERS

I decided after a few months that I was not building up any sea-time towards my Second ticket and that I wanted deep sea again. I saw an advert by Esso for a ship in America called ESSO MONTEVIDEO, one of their latest tankers. They were building up a crew in Liverpool to go to Norfolk, Virginia, where the ship was.

Incidentally, after the War, Heathrow was only a collection of Nissen huts. I had been taken in 1935 as a child by my father to see the opening of Speke Airport in Liverpool. It was magnificent ... art déco, hangars and a stately control tower and a restaurant ... very up-market.

The plane was a propeller-driven Constellation and because of head winds we flew to Gander in Newfoundland and thence to Norfolk. It was a beautiful ship, but after a short while on it, we were told that the American unions objected to a British crew. As a result of this we were transferred to a very old tanker, called the JOHN D. ARCHIBALD. She was built in 1921.

Incidentally, I heard that shortly after I had left CORAL QUEEN, she was sold to the Gambian Government and she went out to Africa ... so possibly in the end she did see some coral and maybe even an African Queen..

The JOHN D. had had a hard life over the years. She flew a Panamanian flag. We did a number of runs from the Gulf ports of Mexico to New York and Montreal. In Montreal we had a riot. The Fifth Engineer was from Northern Ireland and tended to wind up the greasers and firemen who were all from Upper Parliament Street in Liverpool. A fight broke out and while I was trying to drag one of the firemen off the engineer, someone hit me with a hammer shaft and broke my front teeth. I was never handsome again! Two men were given a week in jail in Montreal and we sailed without them.

Finally, we did a trip to the Middle East, to Rastanura. This was the first time that we had been fully loaded, with full cargo and bunkers. Then we sailed from Rastanura.

Just after we sailed one of the greasers came up to me and said "There's water pouring in!" This vessel had Isherwood framing ... ordinary ships have vertical framing. Isherwood framing, in order to balance uneven loads, is horizontal, so one could easily climb up it like a ladder. I climbed up the horizontal framing and you could see out. All along the waterline she was like lace and you could see the sea. Being fully loaded, as we rolled slightly, the water poured in.

I rang for the Chief and he came down with the Mate and the Bosun. The Mate next went into the saloon to tell the Old Man who was just finishing his dinner. He came back shortly and said, "You won't believe it! When I told the Old Man, he said 'Do what we did in the old days. Stuff the holes up with fatty pork'." The Bosun used more modern materials ... and off we toddled.

When we got into the Bitter Lakes in the Canal and stopped to wait for the convoy, the Lake around us was filling with oil. So the Canal authorities sent some divers down in the hope that there were some rivets loose and that they could plug them. They came up and said, "She's rotten from one end to the other!" They allowed us to carry on, but added, "Don't come back!"

We went through the Mediterranean bound for America. Then one of the stern glands literally blew in. The water was shooting into the engine room hitting the engine cranks and was flung all over the room. Every pump that we could find was put on and we just about held our own. We managed to wedge the gland back in and told Head Office, New York. They thought it a bit risky to cross the Atlantic and told us to go to Falmouth and await orders.

One of the greasers had been evacuated during the Second World War to Wigan, and we were one day handing over the watch when this man came down to the engine room naked apart from boots and a little short vest down to his navel. We all stared at him and I said, "What are you doing?" He replied, "You work me like a horse so I intend to walk round like one!" He was sent off sharply to put his gear on.

On the way north to Falmouth we had another breakdown. The whole crankcase of one of the refrigeration compressors burst and filled the engine room with CO_2 gas. We cleared the room until we could get masks and go back down to shut it all off. Finally, we arrived in Southampton and handed over to the next crew. I would like to think that she went from there to the breakers because that was all that she was fit for. It could be described as an exciting nine month voyage.

Thank you, Peter Ganncliffe. That was a rare insight into life at sea as it really is … keep smiling.

Captain Brian McAree
Master Mariner

Captain Brian McAree started his career in H.M.S. CONWAY and in October 1944 went to sea with Brocklebanks. After some years in command, he came ashore in 1960 and was a Surveyor and Examiner with the Board of Trade for thirty three years... the last six as Principal in North east England. Here are two memories of past times.

A VISION

We were eastbound in the North Atlantic in the winter of 1944. I was an apprentice in S.S. SAMDEE and was on watch with the Third Mate, 2000 – 2400 hours. As far as the War was concerned it was a quiet night, although as usual and necessary, we were on full alert.

The moon was up and there was much broken cloud. I was trying to identify as many stars as possible in the clear gaps. Suddenly, there was a very well-defined picture in the clouds. The picture was that of a 'Mother and Child' ... so well known and on the walls of many homes in Britain. It was not imagination as the Third Mate could also see it.

No doubt it was caused by moonlight beams on the clouds,

but why was it shown to us? Later I related the incident to my mother and she said that it was the Good Lord guarding us from U-boats. All my life I have never doubted anything that my mother told me!

The picture was very clear and lasted for some time ... so much so, the Third Mate sent down for the Master to come to the Bridge. We thought that the Master was a Roman Catholic and should see it. Unfortunately, by the time that Captain Penston got to the Bridge, the clouds had moved and the picture was gone.

OLD CONWAYS

We all came ashore to sit for our certificates. While tackling my Second and First Mate's exams, it became the custom for a group of us, who had a few pennies in our pockets, to walk to the bottom of Hanover Street and take lunch at the Flying Angel Club. We were Old Conways and we joined others who came there when they could. Often it was Captain Douthwaite, the examiner of Masters and Mates, or it might be Doug Bottomley, a Stevedore Superintendent, and some local Marine Superintendents, whose names I cannot recall. They were good times and happened despite the rationing of food! It is worth remembering that Old Conways were gathering even then ... 1947 -1949. And, of course, the Padre was always there.

Thank you, Brian. That Padre would have been Canon Bill Evans, M.B.E., predecessor but one in the Mersey Mission to Seamen. The Apprentices Club had been established in the Mission just before the outbreak of the War and proved of great value to the young men as they established their maritime careers.

Captain Bob Taylor
Master Mariner

We are all expert 'lamp swingers' and they are swung no better than when we assemble to dine and disappear into our memories. Captain Bob Taylor was on good form, sitting at table for a recent Christmas Lunch in the Marina Restaurant, he looked across Brunswick Dock and homed in on Christmas 1950.

CHRISTMAS 1950

In those days the dock looked very different from the way it is now. There were no yachts moored there and no Marina. Where the dock is today, surrounded by houses and apartments with H.M.S. EAGLET in the corner, there were transit sheds and a small grain silo. In the background, there was still the overhead railway whose trains rattled along from the Dingle to Seaforth and the dock road. Sefton Street, was full of lorries and the occasional horse and cart taking cargo to and from the sheds. Also on the dock road were a number of busy

189

pubs ...the only one is still standing is the Seven Steps, which no longer opens as a pub and will be referred to later.

At this time, I was a Senior Apprentice on the ship M.V. PINTO and my mate had just joined to sail on his first trip. The ship had part discharged in Glasgow and was now completing discharge in Brunswick Dock to sail in ballast before Christmas for Spain. However, there were a number of problems that had to be overcome before this could take place. Firstly, there was a shortage of seamen willing to sail on Christmas Eve and having gathered up all available A.B.s, E.D.H.s, and a D.H.U. we still awaited the Bosun and six A.B.s. To cover the shortfall, the Company sent two more Apprentices whose ship was in London for the Christmas holidays to make up the manning. Needless to say, they were not at all pleased with this arrangement. They came aboard and shut themselves in their cabins until sailing time. It was also found that of the deck crew only three were able to steer ... this was in the days before every ship had an automatic pilot. So we were split into two watches, three A.B.s in one and three Apprentices in the other. Something to look forward to ...four on and four off!

It was realised on Friday that the discharge would not be completed during Saturday the 23rd so labour was ordered back to complete on Christmas Eve, the Sunday. This went according to plan. After working the normal Saturday morning, discharge was completed on Sunday afternoon and the ship was made ready for sea very reluctantly by the crew who were on board.

Some of the crew had made their own plans about how to stop the ship sailing. Although it was only a small ship, it was usual to use two tugs for docking and sailing and our crew discovered that some tugs' crews were celebrating the arrival of Christmas in that rather notorious pub, the Seven Steps ... and had gone there to help them.

About two hours before sailing time, the Chief Officer sent me as the ship's Senior Apprentice to go to the Seven Steps to get our crew back on board. Needless to say, they told me what to do. Returning back on board with their message, I was then sent straight back, but this time accompanied by the Third Officer. Very reluctantly and slowly some of the crew began to move. Suddenly things speeded up, and after a lot of shouting and abuse they moved out. What had got them moving was the fact that the crew found out that the tugs' crews they had been buying drinks for were not on the tugs standing by to take us out. They were men off duty!

We finally got sorted out and managed to sail on the night tide. What remains firmly fixed in my mind is the fact that I was at the wheel as we passed the Liver Building at midnight on Christmas Eve. What sort of day it was on Christmas Day I do not remember, but being on watch there would not have been much time for celebrations.

The thing that remains in my memory is the fact that the Master, I presume with the Company's agreement, paid us three watch-keeping Apprentices at A.B.'s rates until we got back home ... £24 a month and 2/6d an hour overtime. It seemed like a fortune, but like all good things it did not last for long.

We ended up in Seville, in fact, spending a very quiet New Year there, loading bitter oranges. We sailed early in the first week of January and arrived back in London.

The last thing that remains in my memory is the relevant phrase in my Indentures which covered my being sent to the Seven Steps ... 'said Apprentice shall not frequent Taverns or Alehouses unless upon his Master's business.'

Thank you, Bob Taylor. Most seafarers during a lifetime at sea managed barely a handful of Christmases at home. The vessels in dock over the Festival would be there for some time as the dockers seemed to elongate the season and stretched it into the New Year. But we have not finished with Bob yet ... here is another tale.

CYCLONE DAISY AND ONIONS

At the time of these happenings, I was serving as Second Officer on the M.V. FACTOR and we had sailed early in the December on a voyage to South Africa. I cannot recall where we spent Christmas and the New Year, but this had no relevance to what I am about to relate. The title may seem a little strange, but both items are outstanding on this particular voyage.

As often happened on this run, the agents cabled the Master with queries about the homeward cargo before we even reached the Cape outward bound, never mind starting the discharge. On this voyage, one of the questions was would he accept 100 tons of onions as deck cargo from Cape Town for Avonmouth. The Master declined to give any firm answer at this stage. This I felt could be one of the reasons that the South African run was known as the 'Bedlam Coast' at this time.

The discharging up the Coast had been going as usual except that onions appeared at every port. We finally arrived at our last port of discharge, Beira, the early part of January. As was customary, we had to anchor at the outer anchorage to await a berth. Finally, we arrived at No. 1 Berth on the 20th January to commence discharging. The port was, of course, full and alongside were a British India, a Portuguese and a Clan Line vessel. At the inner anchorage was an American ship. They always got special permission to come in because of their crew shore leave agreement.

During the night of January 21st and the morning of the 22nd, Cyclone Daisy struck Beira. All cargo work had stopped because of continuous heavy rain and the force of the wind. By now, there was a heavy swell running in the harbour and the crew was called to tend and augment the moorings. At Beira, being a tidal port, this was a continual task to try to stop the ship banging against the quay and damaging the ship's side.

Other ships had their own difficulties to deal with … the

British India ship put over large fenders, whilst the Portuguese crew had to crawl amongst their deck cargo of cattle to put out extra moorings, as some of the bollards for their mooring had been dislodged.

When daylight eventually came, it was possible to see what had happened during the dark hours. Some of the quayside cranes had blown along the quay until they came to a crane which was properly clamped and secured. A number of the lighters, including the dredger hopper barges, had broken adrift and were blowing around the harbour. At low water, it was seen that the American ship had dragged her anchor and was firmly ashore. In fact, when the storm had passed it was possible to walk under her forefoot at low water.

Some of the drifting lighters had managed to come to rest between the stern of one ship and the bow of the next ship. Fortunately, this did not happen to us, but as we were watching, one of the hopper barges banged against the quay under our bow. There were two crew boys on the barge and as soon as it hit the quay, these were very frightened boys and leaping off, were last seen running as fast as they could up the road.

The hopper was not only banging the edge of the quay, but also our bow, causing damage to it. Fortunately, we had a new coil of 4-inch rope under the foc'sle head and this was soon broken out. One end was used to lasso a post on the barge, and it was led around a bollard on the quay and back to our windlass. Being on No. 1 Berth, and by repeating the operation, we were able slowly to drag the barge around the corner of the quay and let it loose in the creek, where some of the port's mooring gang secured it.

The storm finally passed and the following day was spent in assessing damage. We had some rivets started and indents in the forepeak which were leaking, and also some indents along the port side. As regards the other ships, they had damage to their bows and sterns, and some had side damage. The British

India ship had large indents along the side where the fenders had been positioned. The port authorities were busy drying out the electrics of the quay cranes to get them back working and in position. The American ship was finally re-floated a couple of days later. We eventually finished discharge and loaded what cargo was available. We sailed for Lourenço Marques and Durban where more permanent repairs were completed. The final loading was in Cape Town.

All this time the Master was being pestered about the deck cargo of onions. Would he or wouldn't he load them? True to his nature, he would not commit himself beyond saying 'he would see' when he got to Cape Town. The Owner's representative in Durban was heard to say that he did not want to hear any more about Captain 'Blank' and his 'so and so' onions.

We finally arrived in Cape Town, loaded the main cargo and started on the onions, to load as many as possible before being down to our marks. This meant countless readings of the draft, not easy with the swell as normal in Duncan Dock. The outcome was that about 30 tons of the onions were not shipped as this would have overloaded the ship. Needless to say, the shipper and the agents were not best pleased, but the Master was adamant.

We sailed and duly arrived in Avonmouth after an uneventful voyage home. The onions were discharged in apparent good condition and must have tasted good as I can recall seeing some of the dock workers eating them like you would an apple.

Members of our Master Mariners Club might be interested to know that the brother of the M.V. FACTOR's Master on this particular voyage became the Master of the Club a couple of years later.

Many thanks to Captain Bob Taylor. I am certain that as with all our contributors there could always have been more.

Jim Howarth
Engineer

A HUMANE VOYAGE FROM MOMBASA

After being released from a Reserved Occupation during the War, as with many others, I was given the option of joining the Army, Navy or Air Force for National Service, going down the pit or joining the Merchant Navy. Only the Merchant Navy seemed attractive at the time. However, no ancestors had, to my knowledge, been seafarers.

Incidentally, I served my Indentured Apprenticeship with Joseph Lucas in the Shadow factories at Burnley, 1941 – 1948, where work was concerned with the early development of Frank Whittle's jet engine.

After interview with Mr. W. R. Wallace (Chief Examiner of Engineers, a well-known character) at the Ministry of Transport buildings in Tithebarn Street, Liverpool, I duly received grading as Engineer. I joined Union Castle Mail Steamship Company at Southampton after application in June 1948, at age 22. My first digs were about 200 yards from the Civic Centre whose clock played 'O God our help in ages past' every hour. The excitement of a new career and the tolling clock kept me awake that first night.

Next morning at eight o'clock sharp, I reported to an Engineer Superintendent on R.M.M.V. STIRLING CASTLE in No. 38 berth in the old docks. I was appointed as Junior Engineer to M.V. ROCHESTER CASTLE ... a fruit boat, no passengers, due for final unloading at Dublin.

On return from Dublin, I was appointed to R.M.M.V. WINCHESTER CASTLE as Sixth Engineer. The ship had been a workhorse during the War, carrying troops and supplies in the Mediterranean 'Torch' landings and others. She was handed back to Union Castle in very poor mechanical shape. She was then engaged in the emigrant trade.

We departed Southampton for Cape Town in August with about 1,200 hopeful emigrants participating in the Government-assisted scheme of the time. There were several working gangs of Harland & Wolf contracting engineers who were still on board when we left. They returned with the Pilot boat from Spithead.

Everything in the Engine Room leaked; exhaust gas, compressed air, fuel oil, lubricating oil, brine, ammonia ... everything. Between Southampton and Madeira, our fuelling stop, we had several field days. As we were carrying Royal Mail, severe penalties for delays were drummed into us. We arrived in Cape Town on time and discharged our emigrants in high expectation. Then we sailed round the coast, Port Elizabeth, East London and Durban.

We had been contracted to pick up Polish refugees at Mombasa for passage to U.K. We arrived in Mombasa and embarked about 2,000, men and women ... there were no children. Our ship had accommodation for about 800 passengers, so temporary arrangements were made with standing beds in the 'tween decks.

The relief on the faces of our distressed passengers-to-be was plain to see as they embarked. They had fled from Poland and had been hounded first by the Germans and then the Russians in a drive eastwards, then southwards, eventually fetching up at Bombay, before being shipped across to Mombasa.

We departed Mombasa for the Red Sea and later the Suez Canal. Our passengers gradually settled into a routine. Some of the stories of their sufferings were very harrowing.

Sadly, five of these poor souls died during the Red Sea transit, maybe as a result of too-rich ship-board food, maybe simply relief. I was a pall-bearer at three of the sea burials.

Conforming to practice, a hatch board was rigged, starboard side, promenade deck, the sewn-up corpse laid on it and the Polish flag covering all. Whilst the obsequies were being said, a congregation of refugees and many off-duty seafarers attended. The starboard engine was stopped, and the port engine reduced to half ahead. After the committal, it was full ahead both.

Next, there was an acute fresh water shortage, although full stocks had been taken at Mombasa; the poor, wretched people just wished to get themselves and their clothing clean. We had to impress temporary rationing of water, although we did evaporate some sea water in the engine room to assist.

On to Suez where the boat traders, Sandy McNab, Rifle-eye et al, came aboard, but had very slim pickings. They were very persistent and very reluctant to leave us. The First Officer and the Bosun urged them back into their boats with a little help from the deck water service. We arrived in the Med to very unseasonable weather ... cold with gales.

Thence to Southampton where our refugees were landed and were very grateful in their thanks to us. They left behind very powerful memories of an oppressed people in dire straits. These memories have lasted until the present day.

For a cultivated people to have been subjected to such barbarism for centuries is hard to believe ... Germans on one side and Russians on the other.

My only previous knowledge of the Poles was of

Paderewski, politician and Prime Minister; Frederick Chopin, pianist and composer and Arthur Rubenstein, pianist.

NEXT EXPERIENCES

The next voyage on WINCHESTER CASTLE was to South America. We embarked about one thousand Polish emigrants for resettlement in Argentina at Southampton and departed on time.

Most of the passengers were absent from the saloon due to seasickness during the Bay of Biscay transit, but emerged when we arrived at Madeira, our re-fuelling stop. It seemed that these people had taken refuge in England during the War, but had become 'spivs' living on the black market in fine style. Such a contrast to the poor souls picked up in Mombasa a month earlier!

Madeira was poverty-stricken in those days prior to air travel. Nuns came out in boats to our anchorage begging for yesterday's bread, which they took back in numerous large baskets. We completed our frantic repairs and re-fuelling and departed for Buenos Aires, via the Equator and King Neptune.

After the 'crossing the line' ceremonies, we forged on for the River Plate and Buenos Aires. We were allocated Darsena 'A' in the main dockyard and, at over 20,000 tons, our bulk settled on the mud at low tide.

We had heard that the Argentines were more pro-German than pro-British. However, I personally never experienced any evidence of this. There was talk of Nazis arriving in Argentina hiding from the War Crimes investigations. The drama of the Graf Spee scuttling and the suicide of her Captain (who is buried in a Buenos Aires cemetery) was also a hot topic.

What a revelation ashore, the residents eating large quantities of beef at one sitting... enough to feed a family of four for a month in the Britain. Severe rationing was still in place at home. Turkey took the place of red meat on Friday. The bright lights and unlimited food of Buenos, the wide avenues and magnificent buildings proved to be a big experience for me. We had had a marvellous reception in South Africa the previous voyage.

We were not 'jolly jacks' ashore, although some were. A good night out consisted of dinner at a place called 'Las Delicosas Papas Fritas' in Calle Florida in central BA. We would eat fillet steak, two eggs, red peppers, chips and a side order of salad. We would drink a red wine called Trapiche Viejo from the Mendoza area in the Andean foothills. Dinner might be followed by a film. We could not understand why the locals burst into laughter at a macho scene or a love scene. We found out the American films were dubbed in Castillian Spanish complete with lisp! This was soon rectified by dubbing in the coarser Argentinian patois.

There were many Italians in Argentina at this period. One's first taste of espresso coffee was a surprise, especially the small quantity in a small cup. For a 6 a.m. start in the engine room, it was most welcome. A taste of lasagne was another pleasure.

Another first was a visit out of town to an asado … a barbeque of heroic dimensions. A side of beef, half the cow being hung up over a wood fire. You were given a sharp knife and advised from where to take the meat. U.K. type barbeques have never held much attraction since then! Wine was not much drunk, being in short supply in 1948. During the War, I had a half-share in a bottle of British sherry in a raffle drawn at the works where I was an Apprentice!

An outstanding 'first' was a visit to a Tango Hall and it was nothing like Strictly Come Dancing recently shown on television. The music was very impressive from the guitars, violins and bandoneons (which are like large concertinas). Neither was it like Henry Hall or Carroll Gibbons.

By 1948, the Argentines were ruled repressively by the

dictator Juan Peron and his then wife, Eva. She was later instrumental in closing the Tango Halls and much else.

A minor 'first' was to witness some jolly jacks (not ours) ejected from a dockside bar and grill called 'This is My Place' for dancing on the tables without trousers. We were on our way peaceably (naturally) back to our ship.

After six weeks of dock labour strikes, we were towed out of the mud of Darsena 'A' and departed for the U.K.

Thank you, Jim Howarth. You were to spend some time with Blue Funnel and with South American Saint Line, which was based in Cardiff. Wisely, you saw the proverbial writing on the wall and came ashore in 1956. You remained with Shellmex-BP for some twenty-five years as a Consulting Engineer, before retirement.

Captain Graham Forster
Master Mariner

Life is a series of learning curves, some go up and some go down ... the real secret is to learn from them. Captain Graham Forster recalls a salutary tale.

AN EARLY LESSON LEARNED

I joined an Elder Dempster 'S' class ship, the SWEDRU, early in 1950 and stayed with her for my first three voyages under the command of Captain Alexander Michael Scobbie, who hailed from Dundee. 'Mick' Scobbie was a fine ship Master without doubt, but his reputation for both hard discipline and extreme meanness was absolutely  renowned. From my earliest days and for some unknown reason, he always referred to me as 'Hornblower' ... and I never did know why!

On one voyage as we neared Las Palmas, homeward bound, I had been directed by the Second Mate to make an inventory of various items stored in the chartroom. I should mention that there was little love between myself and the Second Mate, for some reason unknown to me. However, and to my delight, I counted a considerable surplus of sounding leads which were kept underneath the chronometer box.

Now, as many will know, lead in Las Palmas has a considerable value, or at least it did in those days, and I seized this opportunity to relieve the Second Mate of two 14-pounders! It was a perfect chance to make my fortune and certainly too good to miss an enhanced payoff.

Upon arriving at Las Palmas, I lost little time in negotiating the dirty deal with a well-known trader and bum-boat man on the quay and I was delighted at the apparent success.

With hands placed firmly in my dungaree pockets and obviously supporting the 28 lbs of lead, I carefully and slowly made a little progress down the gangway, when to my absolute horror, Old Scobbie bawled, "Hornblower!" from the boat deck above. Looking aloft I obviously replied, "Yes, sir". He beckoned me with the words, "Up here now, laddie!" ... and my heart sank as I made my way up to the boat deck.

Who can stand before the Captain with hands in pockets and, as mine were withdrawn, it coincided with my dungarees starting the downward path until they were around my ankles? The Old Man was standing with the Mate and a couple of passengers as he watched my plight and efforts to avoid such embarrassment with my skinny legs and Y-fronts. The horrible pause and silence seemed to last an age, but finally the Old Boy exploded unto laughter and said something like this ... "Look, Mr. Mate, the little bugger has been nicking the lead" ... with tears running down his face. "Go back and put them in the chartroom locker ... NOW!"

To say that the experience was humbling is inadequate. It was a lesson well learned, the hard way, indeed! As I stood there crossing and uncrossing my legs, my thoughts circled around the possibility of cancelled Indentures, general disgrace and a potential sacking.

Captain Scobbie had his own methods for imposing discipline and honesty and they later had certainly worked for me. Never again!!

Captain 'Mick' Scobbie was one of the few officers who came over to Elder Dempster Line when they took over the old Chambers Company, together with three or four ships. He certainly was from the 'old school'.

Captain Graham Forster now recalls the happy days aboard an Empress boat on winter cruises.

MISTAKEN IDENTITY

Coming off watch as a humble Second Officer at 4.00 a.m., it was a welcome habit to pop along the boat deck to the outside pool, and enjoy the luxury of a swim prior to turning in. Cruising in the Caribbean certainly had many advantages, and our winter cruises from New York were always a welcome break from the North Atlantic.

On this particular early morning, after quietly diving into the floodlit pool, coming up through the water, I observed a beautiful female figure just floating above and wearing a leopard-skin leotard-type costume … rather unusual, but very pretty. Now it should be promptly explained that one of our lovely shop-girls had such a bathing costume, and she was a good sport and always full of fun.

The temptation was too good to pass up, and so I swam up from below, clamped my hands around her bottom, and sunk my teeth playfully into her bum cheeks!! To my astonishment and absolute horror, it turned out to be a very distinguished, millionairess lady passenger, and my sincere efforts at a very profuse apology were not to be accepted, as, to say the least, she was furious.

Predictably, later that morning, I was summoned to the

Captain, and there she was sitting in his day room with a face like thunder. The Captain duly introduced me as his Second Officer, and then he told me of the sorry saga as he had been informed. On his request, my apology was repeated, ultimately accepted begrudgingly and she left. The Captain then told me to leave (or something like that), but on going out he asked me to wait.

"One moment" he said. "Just who the hell did you think it was?" he enquired. I replied with my belief that it was a particular shop-girl. "Oh I see, and just tell me does this particular young lady enjoy having her backside bitten at around 4.20 a.m.? Now just get out, and do try to be more selective and careful in future!"

The Captain did manage to contain his smile as he was an excellent person, but I certainly learned my own lesson ... the hard way!!

ORANGES

I spent some months with Ellerman Papayanni in earlier days, and enjoyed three voyages as a Third Mate in a new ship; FLAMINIAN, to various Mediterranean ports. On one such voyage, we topped up our cargo for home with 'tween decks filled with beautiful oranges from Haifa.

Rather sadly, the oranges were packed in very flimsy cases, and during loading our decks were soon strewn with loose oranges, in spite of our efforts to protect them. My special colleague and Second Mate chum quite promptly suggested that we should gather as many of these spillages as possible, and hopefully make our own fresh orange juice, which would prove to be a very healthy tonic.

Using our Cook's caliper type of potato-masher, we duly crushed many dozens of the very best oranges, and made gallons of superb juice which was carefully bottled. The sealed bottles were duly distributed amongst my mates, and we sailed for home with them secretly stowed away in our respective wardrobes. Great swag, healthy tonic!

Two or three days westbound on the homeward voyage, we were relishing a glorious moonlit and flat calm evening, as my chum came up to relieve me at midnight. Together we sipped our tea-mugs and smoked our fags, when the peace was disturbed by a totally mysterious explosive bang ... followed by another, and then another, etc., etc. Blind panic! 'What the hell was that??'

Diving down into the accommodation, I found our alleyway absolutely swimming in the orange juice, and bottles were still exploding during my best efforts to mop up. Over the side I dumped as many fermenting bottles as possible. We eventually managed to mop up rivers of flowing juice. What a sticky, smelly mess!

A couple of years later, a particular colleague told me of his appointment as Mate on the FLAMINIAN and I could not resist enquiring if the accommodation still smelled of lovely fresh orange juice. No doubt he wondered.

Here is another anecdote from Captain Graham Forster.

THINGS THAT GO BUMP IN THE NIGHT

One of Ellerman's ships had spent some time on engine repairs in Glasgow. This had included the removal of crank-cases and such activities that engineers get involved with in the nether regions of their kingdoms. Eventually, they set out for Liverpool in order to load our cargo which was destined for Calcutta.

Sitting in the river for the final topping up, the Chief Engineer had been burbling on about strange noises in the innards of his beloved machinery.

In due time, the vessel arrived at Calcutta with the Chief still muttering and burbling. At last, the diesels were stopped and allowed to cool. The Chief informed the staff that he would have his lunch and a siesta and that then they would examine the problem.

Realising that there was time, the Second Engineer removed the crank cover and to his surprise he discovered that a five-pound clump hammer was nestled in the machinery by courtesy of Glasgow. They promptly replaced the cover.

So the Chief arrived and they set about their task. Finally all was revealed as the Chief Engineer came across an oil-burning tilley-lamp sitting neatly amongst the machinery ... lit!

The language that followed proved the maxim that 'You cannot fool a Chief Engineer all the time.'

NIGERIA ... NEVER AGAIN!

Elder Dempster would reward a Senior Midshipman nearing the end of apprenticeship days with an Uncertificated Second Mate's job on one or other of their coasters. Something close akin to Bogart's AFRICAN QUEEN.

Second Mate, radio man, European cook, doctor and stores purchaser ... all the same fella. For my own last few months, I was appointed to the little WARRI, which trundled around the Nigerian creeks and enjoyed the odd couple of days in Lagos.

I held a 'Doctor's Surgery' most days and treated countless Africans for many problems, often and predictably involving the opposite sex. Otherwise malaria, constipation and certain skin complaints were quite the norm. During my months, and in spite of my pleas to our proper mail-boat Doctors in Lagos, I only had one single hypodermic needle. To say it was blunted is an understatement. I did have one in reserve ... .retained just in case it was needed by us four Europeans. Hey ho!

Once in Port Harcourt, we were discharging coal when the African chippy arrived at my cabin to breathlessly tell me that "Der for No.1 hatch, de ship he get hole, please come quick sah and lookam". To shorten the story, the Mate was ashore playing snooker, the Chief Engineer was in bed asleep (a little drunk), and the Captain was golfing at the 'Club'. I dispatched our Chippy to the 'Club', where his 6 foot 6 inches of coloured figure was spotted by our Captain, leaping from rise to rise and bunker to bunker. Puffing and blowing, he then attempted to give my message to the Captain who was just teeing up.

"Oh sah, Second Matey tell me to tell you the ship he get hole der, in No.1 hatch".

"Tell me Chippy, is the hole above or below waterline?"

"I sorry sir, I no savvy."

"Is there any water coming into the ship NOW chippy?"

"Oh no sah, no water he der now, but just de B. . . .Y sunshine!!"

"Tell the Second Matey that I come back tonight, and we put cement box tomorrow."

At some time, we had probably collided with the odd log which opened up the plating. Tomorrow will do! Happy days … or something maybe??

SEA SICKNESS, ME? NEVER!

I was Third Mate at the time, homeward bound in an Elder Dempster ship in fairly heavy weather and somewhere off, perhaps, Cape St.Vincent or thereabouts, main deck fairly wet, but good visibility. Shortly before midnight, our Doctor called me to say that he needed some help after midnight, as it was his intention to operate on a young sailor for appendicitis.

Our quite elderly Doctor was a popular and very interesting shipmate, and he had spent many years looking after trawler-men off the Grand Banks of Newfoundland … hard territory and very hard work for a truly 'hands on' medical man.

However, it was also well known that he thoroughly enjoyed more than the odd drop of Scotch, and usually during a heavy spell of cards (poker) with the Chief Steward. This particular night proved to be no exception, and it transpired that my function was to fulfil the job as his anaesthetist.

The Old Man had adjusted the speed to minimize the ship's movements and the Electrician had arranged a light cluster over the rather make-shift operating table, whilst the poor young victim was laid out in readiness as our Doctor scrubbed up.

Using some unknown stuff from a small gas cylinder, the patient was duly 'put out', and I had been instructed how to use an ether wad which had to be applied whenever his eye-lids fluttered.

The operation proceeded quite quickly, and with very small incision, the Doctor prodded around with his little finger until the offending appendix duly appeared. Clamped, removed, all done and dusted within about forty-five minutes or so! Amazing skill! Having made his patient comfy, the lovable old Doctor returned to his poker and whisky, whilst I recall making my own way to the ship's side to be as sick as a pig!

It has often crossed my mind that we just did what we had to do, and would only perhaps reflect afterwards, how the hell we were ever able to do it. If needs must!

The young sailor walked ashore in Liverpool some three or four days later, and he was carrying his bags.

The appendix indeed was most sailors' nightmare.

Captain Graham Forster's final tale:

THE COST OF BOOZE

At many of the Caribbean ports, it was necessary to anchor off and transport our 'punters' back and forth in special launches and a couple of ship's lifeboats. Such was the case in St.Thomas, Virgin Islands, and I was personally running what was then known as a class 'B' lifeboat, which was equipped with a cubic, mahogany-built radio shack amidships, measuring perhaps 8 ft square.

Prior to arrival at St.Thomas, however, our purser ladies had organised a book full of booze orders from various of the ship's departments including themselves. Gordon's Gin in St.Thomas was priced at about five shillings per bottle. Before arriving, and strictly under darkness cover, our junior radio guys stripped the radio lifeboat of all equipment, to leave an adequate 'cargo space'.

The Second Purser had negotiated the big joint purchase with a local chandler, and it was my misfortune to have to both run the boat with passengers (about 1.5 miles), as well as to load case after case of Gordon's Gin. The actual amount was almost frightening, and we were very low in the water with about forty passengers aboard. At one particular time, the Staff Captain asked me when alongside if I had checked the bilges as I was rather low in the water after delivering the passengers? I re-assured him! All lies. However, the real fun was yet to come, as we were due to sail very promptly at midnight, and now we had to somehow try our very best to raise the loaded boat back aboard. We all know that lifeboats when loaded can descend easily with gravity, but hauling them back aboard, overloaded with hidden gin-cargo, proved to be a great problem. Our Chief Electrician had his screwdriver across the fuses, and the Captain looked over very anxiously from the Bridge wing as the time ticked by for our scheduled sailing. Eventually, and again under the cover of darkness, the gin was unloaded and distributed, radio gear was re-installed, but it was a hard and sweaty lesson well learned. Next time in St. Thomas, I disappointed my shipmates by telling them to go ashore and buy their own booze, hardly surprising and quite justified.

Thank you, Captain Graham Forster. Those winter cruises were 'away to the sunshine for three months'! That was the way to miss the English winter.

Graham had followed his elder brother, Tony ... a Blue Funnel Master Mariner ... in 1950 and obtained his Master's ticket in 1961. Various companies ... Elder Dempster, Ellerman Papyanni, Canadian Pacific, serving in the Beaver vessels and the Empresses. Failing eyesight brought him ashore in the late sixties and he became involved with British Shipbuilders and was able to command a number of new ships during trial periods. This included service and delivery to Ascension Island during the Falklands crisis. He ended his career as Head of European Marketing at British Ships. Incidentally, I seem to have known him and his wife, Ann, for ever!

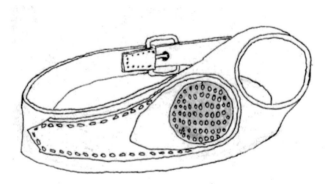

Captain Alan Bole
Master Mariner

Captain Alan Bole tells a tale that takes us back to the early fifties and it certainly takes us 'down memory lane'. No one could have believed that a 'camel coloured duffel coat' could have proved to be so important. Incidentally, Alan is a Nautical Consultant in Radar and Electronic Navigation Systems and Simulation ... this memory is somewhat in advance of such intelligence and is rather basic.

THAT DUFFEL COAT

At last, the Pilot cutter emerged from the fog and the Pilot boarded. We passed under the Golden Gate Bridge without seeing it, but a few hundred yards further on, the fog miraculously lifted. It was now dark and as we approached the berth close to Fisherman's Wharf, searchlights from somewhere in the town could be seen playing on the clouds. I asked the Pilot, what was the occasion? It was the San Francisco motor show ... the second biggest in the United States. In fact, Betty Hutton would be there that evening and would be singing hits from her movie, 'Annie get your gun'. I said that I would like to see that, to which the Pilot replied that he would be passing the show on his way home and that I was welcome to a lift if I was free to go. Without hesitation, I accepted and as soon as we were safely berthed, I cleared it with the Chief Officer. The Pilot was anxious to get home and so, just as I was ... with a duffel coat covering my uniform (no cap, mind) ... I was off. The Pilot dropped me off in the midst of all the ballyhoo outside the Exhibition Center.

When it comes to exhibitions and shows, the Americans are hard to beat. Nothing is described in anything less than superlatives, and so everything was the biggest, the best or the greatest. In recent years, they have devised new adjectives such as 'Mega' and 'Ultra' ... I wonder what will come next?

The motto, 'The Customer is Paramount' was never more in evidence as I made my way around the show. America has always been noted for its service and attention to detail, but the attention I was receiving was really something extra special. "Welcome", "Nice to see you", "Do try out the new ... ", "Could we arrange a test drive?" Invariably, there was a recitation of technical specifications. Nothing was too much trouble. It was overwhelming.

Then, with a great fanfare of trumpets, a massive car, dripping with chrome, was moved slowly on to a platform which appeared to be suspended from the ceiling. On the bonnet sat Betty Hutton, wearing a cow-girl outfit and singing, "You can't get a man with a gun". The lights went down, she disappeared and then there was a man extolling the unbelievable features of the car. A quick change and Betty Hutton was back wearing a pink soufflé of a dress and back up on the bonnet, while a baritone intoned "The Girl that I marry". I watched the proceedings along with a decreasing audience. The serious autophiles had not even stopped to look at this extravaganza which was taking place above their heads! After about forty-five minutes and a massive finale, I returned to looking at more sporting vehicles including the M.G. stand. Again, I received a great welcome, even more so when it was recognised that I was from England. At midnight, the 'circus' closed its doors, and like Cinderella, for me it was a trip on the trolley car via Chinatown and back to Fisherman's Wharf.

Life returned to its normal coasting pattern ... discharge cargo, load cargo, sail to the next port, Long Beach. I liked Long Beach as I had made friends with a skin diver while on another ship a few years earlier. He would always arrange an afternoon off and we would have a few hours exploring the prolific wildlife in the waters off the California coast. From La Jolla to Laguna, we had visited all the beaches at some time or another. He was very proud of his M.G. which at that time was regarded as 'cool'. He would pick me up shortly after I had finished my cargo watch at noon, but on this particular day, he was early and so waited for me in my cabin.

When I arrived, he was excited beyond belief. "Where did you get it?" he exclaimed. "Could you get one for me?" After I had slowed him down and I had managed to elicit a few coherent sentences, I discovered that what was causing all the excitement was the war surplus, camel-coloured duffel coat, hanging on the back of my cabin door. In the USA, this was 'de rigueur' for the trendy sports car owner ... in fact, it was worn like a badge of office or a fraternity pin. I took the duffel coat off the hook and handed it to him along with a pair of yellow string gloves (shades of Lonnie Donnegan) which I had bought from a shop alongside Aldgate East Underground Station.

In spite of it being about noon on a warm Californian day, he donned the gear, along with his sun glasses and a 'flat hat' which I had produced from a drawer. His 'street cred' must have jumped a thousand-fold. He asked how much I would take for the lot ... he had not understood that I intended it as a gift. Besides, we kept a stock of duffel coats on board in the slop chest. He was beside himself. We had a very pleasant afternoon, skin-diving and a very pleasant meal which he insisted on paying for, before dropping me off at the ship in time to go on cargo duty at 8 pm. As he drove away, still wearing the duffel coat etc, he was still thanking me and promising more afternoons underwater. So, that was why I had received all the attention in San Francisco!

Thank you, Alan Bole, for that memory. Riches are in the eye of the beholder. Alan's next tale moves us on to about 1956.

A NARROW ESCAPE

The typhoon was expected to hit the islands of Japan in the next forty-eight hours. We were in the port of Nagoya and had just finishing loading. We were anchored out in the roads and loading from lighters which were tied up alongside. Dock workers were hurrying to get the cargo from the last few lighters into the holds and then to get ashore before the first effects of the storm were felt. We were due to sail at midnight.

It was now 6 pm and the Master informed the Chief Officer that he was just 'nipping' ashore with the agent and would be back shortly. The Chief Officer informed the Second Officer that he was just 'nipping' ashore with the stevedore to make a few purchases, but would be back shortly. The Second Officer informed me ... I was on duty and supervising the loading of the last of the cargo ... that he and the Chief Engineer had a bum boat standing by and, as they were both due to be relieved on our arrival in New York, this would be their last chance to buy tea services ... they would be back shortly.

As I walked along the Main Deck, I heard the sound of giggling coming from the accommodation ladder. A group of our Malay crew were coming aboard, accompanied by an equal number of young Japanese ladies. There was little doubt as to the purpose of their visit. I gave orders for their launch to remain alongside, sent for the Bosun and told him in no uncertain terms to get rid of the ladies. A few moments later, a sheepish-looking sailor appeared, accompanied by one of the Lotus Blossoms, whom he claimed would be greatly honoured if I were to show her my cabin. During the verbal exchange, there was much bowing and tooth-sucking. To be rejected would mean a serious loss of face for the lady, but I was really far too busy to consider the niceties of the situation. I just wondered how that particular sailor had come to draw the short straw and approach me, as I considered him to be one of the wide boys.

The Bosun was not in too much of a hurry to get the girls off the ship ... perhaps he had received the same offer as I had ... but had compassion on the lady and saved her from losing face. Eventually, the girls, still giggling, descended the gangway, declaring undying love for one particular sailor or another, while the sailors, in turn, promised to remain faithful, no matter what temptations they were subjected to. The launch cleared the lee which the ship had provided and I could see it making heavy weather across the open water towards the landing stage.

The wind was steadily increasing, the loading was completed, the lighters were covered, and the little tugs set off for the shore with the empty craft bouncing around in the choppy seas astern of them. I was becoming concerned for the safety of the ship's position and while the crew lowered the derricks, battened down the hatches and fitted the locking bars, the Carpenter, the Fourth Officer and I walked back a second anchor. We then veered enough cable to feel the catenaries take the shock out of the snatches, which the ship had started to make on the cable. The engines were readied early in case they too were needed to ease the weight on the anchor cables.

Meanwhile, the various groups who had gone ashore were conscious that the weather was deteriorating faster than had been predicted, and were making their way back towards the landing stage. The Agent and the Pilot were due to return with the Master as soon as the message was received that all the cargo was aboard. The Master had returned to the stage early, in the hope that he might get an earlier lift back to the ship, but the stage was deserted and so he sheltered behind a pile of packing cases covered with tarpaulins. The rain had started and he watched the angle that the falling rain made with the horizontal, as the wind perceptibly strengthened. The eerie glow from the sodium lights and the ominous moan in the wind made him question the wisdom of going ashore in view of the weather that had been forecast. In mitigation, he did have ship's business to attend to, and in any case, the Chief Officer was more than capable of looking after matters on board. He would just wait now until the Agent arrived with his launch.

Other crew members also approached the stage hoping to make an early return to the ship, but were soon to discover that only the essential craft were out on the water that night. The Master had the most obvious place of refuge and was shortly joined by a Greaser, the Fifth Engineer and the Second Cook. The Chief Officer hurried toward the stage, but saw the Master just in time and sought shelter behind a cargo shed a little way off, near enough to make a dash for a launch if one should appear. The fat would be in the fire, but at least the ship was safe in the hands of the Second Officer.

The Chief Engineer and Second Officer scurried along the ill-lit dockside, heads bowed to the wind and rain, both wishing they had stayed aboard in the warmth of their cabins. Their tea services seemed to have increased in weight with each step and they were no longer sure that they really wanted them anyway. They saw the Master in the shelter of his packing case and so decided to avoid awkward questions and shelter in the lee of the cargo shed. Much to their surprise, as they scuttled around the corner, they came face-to-face with the Chief Officer. Who the hell was on board the ship? There was a tangible chill between the Chief and the Second Officers, and there was still the Master to face.

They could see the lighters leave the ship and the launch with the cargo workers proceed to some other area of the port to put them ashore. A launch from the ship deposited a group of wet and rather subdued young ladies, who hastily disappeared into the night. The owner of the launch was not interested in any more fares that night and rapidly headed for the safety of the typhoon dock. A taxi drew up and switched off its lights and the Agent emerged. The taxi would wait for the Agent to return from the ship. The slight figure of the Japanese Pilot emerged from another set of shadows and greeted the Agent with a bow ... both then joined the Master and his little band of refugees from the storm. Shortly, a small tug approached the landing stage ... it was probably safer than a launch as the waves were starting to take on a chaotic appearance as the wind continued to increase. The group from behind the packing case made their way out on to the wind-swept stage. There was nothing for it, but for the others to emerge and face the consequences. A couple of other crew members appeared from other sheltered spots and clambered aboard the tug. All the Senior Officers were there ... who on earth was aboard the ship? With the Pilot and the Agent there as well, what would the court of enquiry say if the tug capsized. There was going to be trouble ... big trouble ... but first, there was the typhoon to be avoided.

As the tug came alongside, the Master was first on to the accommodation ladder and I was there to meet him at the top. I reported the action I had taken, that the gear had been tested both on deck and in the engine room, and that the ship was altogether ready for sea. The Master went off with the Agent to complete the formalities while I took the Pilot to the Bridge and prepared for departure.

We were soon under way. Just inside the breakwater ...

a quick lee, some deft seamanship by the Pilot launch and the Pilot was away. Full Away!! We passed safely through the mine-swept channel across Nagoya Bay and out into the open sea. The storm was not far away and the torrents of rain and sheets of spray from the wave tops reduced visibility to little more than the ship's bow. Once clear of the land, we were able to turn away and run before the oncoming storm. We set course for San Francisco.

I was not privy to the repercussions in the upper echelons of the ship's hierarchy, but the strained relations were evident for the remainder of the voyage all the way to New York, when some of the participants left the ship for home leave. An interesting by-product of the incident in Nagoya occurred a few days out into the Pacific. The queue outside the Doctor's morning surgery was headed by the sailor whose 'young lady' was so anxious to visit my cabin. The Doctor could not divulge the reason for the sailor's visit, but there was little doubt in my mind that I could also have found myself in that queue, had temptation got the better of me.

KIDS' PLAY

I had recently qualified as First Mate and marriage was also on my mind. Unfortunately, the bank account was pretty low after three months ashore studying. Even with good management and a lot of luck the final qualification was three years hence.

I requested a long voyage of the powers that be at the Shipping Company I was working for. This was music to their ears, as most young Officers were either courting or newly married and were clamouring for short scheduled voyages, which could mean home leave every three months. My request was granted and I was appointed Third Officer to a vessel running between Fremantle in Western Australia and Singapore. Cargoes were in most cases 'general', but the specialty item was livestock. The service, with two other ships had been well established over many years. I travelled out to Singapore as a supernumerary on one of the Company's other ships and on arrival in Singapore, was transferred to the ship which was to be my home for the next two years.

It seemed to be assumed that as a South African I was a natural farm boy, and so was 'naturally' given responsibility for the livestock. I had spent a number of holidays on farms in my youth and would probably have taken up farming if I had not embarked on a career at sea. I was quite happy with the arrangements and soon made friends among the stock men in Fremantle. They were a tough, hard-drinking lot, but their expertise was invaluable. Life soon settled into a regular pattern ... a monthly round-trip carrying general cargo and livestock on the passage north ... cleaning and disinfecting ... then general cargo southbound, usually with a call in Indonesia. We soon made friends in Fremantle, played badminton at the University in Perth and attended weddings. The Engineers seemed particularly susceptible to the charms of the Australian ladies ... first was the Chief Engineer, then the Second followed by the Third. The Fifth Engineer was an Australian from Perth and his was a big Catholic wedding. I had been working cargo all night, leaving directly I finished work for the nuptial mass where I promptly fell asleep. A new Master took over, the Officers formed a skiffle group, the weather was kind with the willy-willies leaving us alone ... life was very acceptable. At this rate, two years would soon pass and I could return to England with enough leave to study and marry.

It was normal to proceed directly from Fremantle to Singapore, once the livestock had been loaded, but now came the order to proceed overnight to Geraldton to load some general cargo and a consignment of one hundred goats. Goats? Who knew anything about goats? I asked for a quick meeting with the ship's Agent who knew nothing about the carriage of goats, but he would make some enquiries. The stock loaders in Fremantle were also ignorant, but did not foresee any problems in loading them. The general consensus was that they were just like sheep, but with bigger horns.

A lot of sheep!

We kept the after deck clear. We would load the cargo into hatches four and five and then rig the pens on the deck ready to receive the goats. The area was sufficient for the expected one hundred goats. Their pens were constructed from four gate-like panels which were lashed together with rope yarns at the corners and then to the ship's bulwarks, which formed the fourth side. Straw was spread on the steel decks to reduce the chances of slipping and also to provide something to chew on ... or at least, that was how we prepared for sheep or to be more precise, wethers, of which we were already carrying two thousand in the 'tween decks and on the fore deck. In addition, there were one hundred and ten steers in pens in the centre-castle.

Unlike in Fremantle where the livestock all arrived by train in cattle wagons, in Geraldton the goats were already tethered at the rear of the cargo sheds. The Chinese Bosun and I took a stroll over to look at what we were due to carry. These were not our usual docile wethers. There were some big brutes with horns to match and what was more, they had come from the outback where they were virtually wild. They had never seen a farmyard, let alone the open decks of a ship on the ocean. The Bosun was becoming apprehensive about the crew's ability or preparedness to handle these beasts. The 'Billies', with their beady eyes and beards, looked like sinister old men. They exuded evil and an offensive smell to boot.

When the time came to load them, a small group of aboriginal children appeared and led them aboard in groups of two or three. The child would slip the thongs by which the goats were led and release them into the pens assigned by the Bosun. They were counted aboard ... ninety six head with no distinction between male and female. The loading ramp was hauled aboard and the ship was prepared for sea. We had to sail by 5 p.m. and the Pilot was ordered accordingly.

There was a buzz on the quayside. An aborigine and his family were on their way down the main street with fourteen more goats. We would need to ship them. Hold everything.

Whilst in Geraldton, we had learned a lot more about the goats we were to carry. They were wild goats which could be caught by anyone who could be bothered to go out into the bush and catch them. For some young Australian males, this was becoming a sport. They would go out with a Landrover-type vehicle and when they saw a herd, they would drive them until near exhaustion and then jump from the vehicle at the last moment and chase them through the bush until they caught one. Mostly, they were caught by the aborigines, who it was said could run the goats down without the aid of a vehicle. In any event, it was they who would build up a stock of goats and when necessary, eat or sell them. There was a sliding scale of payment, the least being for goats collected from the aborigines in the bush, gradually increasing if the goats were delivered to a rail head, with the highest price being paid at the ship's side. Hence, the family which was now approaching.

By now, the goats were in sight but the circus was in no hurry. We decided to stow the loading ramp and single up the mooring lines. The goats would be passed manually over the ship's side. The aboriginal family finally arrived, passed their goats aboard and were paid by the Agent. Before the Agent finished paying them, the ship was swung off the berth and heading for the open sea. We were soon clear of the dangerous entrance channel through the reefs and bound for Singapore.

As I supervised the feeding at sunset, it was very apparent that the goats were not just sheep with big horns. The big billies monopolized the food and only when they were satisfied, did the nannies get a look in. The make-up of the group in each pen would have to be changed before the next feed in the morning. After dinner, I relaxed for an hour before going on watch at 8 p.m. It was good to be back at sea again and the swell had a most soporific effect.

When I came on the Bridge, all was well. A perfect night … stars everywhere and a gentle breeze. The cattle decks were quiet. The watch routine progressed steadily. I checked the errors of the compass and the Quartermasters changed on the hour and reported the courses. The look-outs were on the fo'c'sle, and on the hour I watched the new look-out go forward and then the one who had been relieved, come aft. The usual creaks and groans of a ship working in a gentle swell were audible and signalled that all was well. No ships were sighted, but the track we were following was rarely used in those days.

It was all so peaceful that at first I did not realize that something was amiss. Then the bell on the fo'c'sle sounded four strokes. I checked the time … twenty minutes past midnight … the look-out had not been relieved. Neither had I for that matter. I checked with the Quartermaster and he too was still waiting. Something was radically wrong with the routine. Had the stand-by man whose duty it was to call the next watch just fallen asleep?

The Master had heard the four bells and, taking just enough time to don a dressing gown, had made his way to the Bridge. After the Master had formally taken over the watch, I was sent to investigate. I found the Second Officer … my relief … with his cabin in darkness and still fast asleep. He had not been called. Where was the stand-by man, whose duty it was to make tea before calling the next watch to go on duty? Not a sign of him. Then I caught a brief glimpse of it. A goat on the boat deck? No, it couldn't be. Yes, it was … and there was another, and another. They were everywhere and eating whatever they could find. The canvas boat cover was flapping in the gentle breeze … the rope lashing had been eaten away.

As I hurried aft to the crew's quarters, I met more goats who turned and scampered away before me. A big billy intended to stand his ground, but by now I was armed with a deck scrubber, which I waved in his direction. He thought better of it and so he turned and trotted along to join the others.

The after deck was a scene of desolation. Apparently, the goats had tasted the salt in the rope lashings which they had then eaten. The pens just collapsed. The goats now had access to the hay piled high on the hatch tops. The more adventurous had wandered further afield … some on to the centre castle and boat deck, while a couple of families had taken up residence in the Officers' smoke room. Others had wandered into the crew accommodation where a sleepy sailor on his way to the toilet had come face to face with a very large pair of horns. The sailor had grabbed a squeegee mop and with it at arms length had slowly backed into a toilet cubicle. Once inside, and with the door locked securely, he was less terrified. The toilet doors were only half height and the frightened man was standing on the toilet seat and leaning over the top of the door while brandishing the squeegee in the goat's direction. As the biggest goat approached, it was lunged at with the squeegee. It lost its footing as its hooves skidded on the mosaic tiles and it landed in a heap in the scuppers. As time passed the act was repeated, both goats and man became more and more terrified.

Meanwhile, the Master kept the watch and sent my relief to join me. The new watch keepers came on duty, and those who had been relieved retreated to their cabins and locked themselves in. The Bosun appeared on deck, but while attempting to show willing, he kept a respectable distance from the action. It was now up to the two Officers to reconstruct the pens using bailing wire instead of rope yarns. Then came the job of rounding up the goats who had by now started eating the canvas boat covers. This was slow work because one first had to find the goats which had managed to get into the most inaccessible places. Some were even outboard of the life boats and, as we approached the first of these, it took fright and leapt straight into the ocean. This was going to be a long and delicate job if we were not to lose more goats in this way. Getting goats to climb steps was easy, but getting them to descend was far more difficult. By sunrise, the goats were again penned. I had been on the go for twenty-four hours and was exhausted.

As they would say today … 'it was a steep learning curve' … but never again did we make the mistake of regarding goats as merely sheep with horns.

Many thanks to Captain Alan Bole. There are many strange stories in this anthology, but that last one must beat them all.

Captain Michael Taylor
Master Mariner

Captain Michael Taylor, ex Master of the Club, is a notable raconteur. He suggested that his 'odd notes and reflections' might well be placed in Davey Jones' Locker ... as if I would dare be so foolish! This is his contribution to this saga.

ODD NOTES AND REFLECTIONS

In September 1951, I was Third Mate of M.V. GAMBIA PALM. Whilst in Lagos the Chief Officer purchased a cine camera of which he was very proud. Proceeding up the creeks to Sapele, the Master was piloting the ship and made a bit of a mess in negotiating a nasty bend in the river. The bow became embedded in the banks and soon dozens of monkeys and other creatures were swarming over the decks ... all caught on film! This clearly offended the Master, but we eventually came clear and resumed our voyage.

In Sapele, loading heavy-lift logs, work ceased for the day and the aft jumbo derrick was secured with the purchase block that was secured to a stout deck eye pad.

Unfortunately, a crew boy inadvertently operated the jumbo winch. The topping lift wire parted. Down came the jumbo, striking the bulwarks and it resembled a banana with a great bend in the middle. No more heavy-lift logs could be loaded on the aft deck.

The Master, on hearing the commotion on the aft deck shouted to the Chief Officer, "Go and get your cine camera out and take pictures of the aft jumbo derrick, letting me have a copy for the Head Office." After that, the cine camera had limited use on board.

From 1957 to 1959, I was Chief Officer on a very old Brocklebank Liner, MATHURA, built in 1918, whose Master left his Chief Officer to attend to the running of the ship and all cargo matters. He concentrated his time and efforts on how he could accumulate wealth on the voyage with little or no risk to himself, but the Chief Officer featured in all his dubious dealings.

In the North East Monsoon season, the Master offered to take as deck cargo 2,000 goats from Tuticorin to Aden without the benefit or blessing of Bills of Lading, etc.

The Contractor built bamboo stockades around the decks, put bales of food on board and water troughs for the goats and two shepherds to look after the animals. The shepherds were to be landed with the goats in Aden.

An uneventful voyage … although fresh water became a bit of a problem and the smell was not enjoyed! However, on discharging the goats I found all the tarpaulins from 6 hatch covers had been devoured, also the derrick guy ropes and blocks. The deck winches had been stripped of all their paint and the decks looked as though a swarm of locusts had descended. Worse to come, the six cargo hatches were fully loaded with chests of tea, cases of tobacco and bags of dessicated coconut, all tainted and stained on the top tiers by goat droppings.

Whilst I had several spare hatch tarpaulins, I did not have the required three per hatch. Eighteen tarpaulins were needed. In Aden, the Agent was despatched to every ship in port armed with cases of whisky to negotiate the bartering of tarpaulins for us. He managed to get enough to see us home, but at great expense. Hence there was little or no profit from the deck cargo.

The vessel proceeded to the United States of America prior to loading for U.K. On passage, hatches were opened and the crew put to work using teepol and soda to scrub the stained cases of tea and tobacco and they stripped off carefully the outer paper from the desiccated coconut. Luckily, in the States we had our de-rat certificate renewed after fumigation, so the vessel arrived in U.K. smelling sweetly. I did not hear of any tainted cargo claims from the U.S.A. We were very fortunate.

On the same vessel and same voyage, but on the U.S.A. leg, the Master decided that we had to recoup our losses on the great goat fiasco!

He was advised that good timber was at a premium in the Azores, so we decided we would proceed well south and, as it was winter in the North Atlantic, we would need to bunker in the Azores. Being built in 1918, the vessel had very large cross bunker holds which could be used for cargo, but were invariably left empty as she could be loaded to her marks without the cross bunker being used.

Two cases of whisky went to the foreman stevedore, a Mr. Spanelli, and the cross bunker was filled to capacity with new soft-wood dunnage planks. Whilst we were a little overloaded, we knew we would be alright on our arrival at U.K.

It was a shocking voyage from Norfolk to the Azores and two oil fuel double bottom tanks took in sea water. We limped into the Azores on the very day that India marched into Goa and took the Portuguese Possession back into Indian ownership. This rather naturally upset the Portuguese Authorities and, when they found that we had an Indian crew on board, no one was allowed ashore, nor were any 'businessmen' or contractors allowed on board. We sailed with our cross bunkers still full of prime American dunnage and obviously it had to be got rid of as the ship was being sold to foreign buyers.

It was necessary to lift No. 3 hatch derricks and jettison the dunnage. On leaving the Azores you could have walked on the dunnage from the Azores to Gibraltar. A worried deck Serang could not understand the folly of dumping good dunnage over the side, but being a good Serang he just gave the Chief Officer a salaam and put it down to the odd ways of the Sahib.

On arrival in our Indian terminal port, Calcutta, I was greatly impressed when the Stevedore, who was also the Mayor of Calcutta, a Narrish Nath Moorkerjee, boarded with two bearers carrying enormous bouquets of overpoweringly, sweet scented flowers. These flowers completely filled the Chief Officer's accommodation and, of course, wee beasties crawled out from them. This generosity proved to be a liability, as I had to have the flowers on display. Half-way through our stay in Calcutta, another delivery of flowers, and on sailing yet another display arrived. What a generous Stevedore, I thought … until he produced all his invoices for signing. Tucked away in the middle of one invoice was an account for fresh flowers and bouquets for the Chief Officer's wife … 4,000 rupees. I was incensed at this. I gathered up all the invoices and threw them out of the day room port-hole into Kidderpore dock. I told the Stevedore, in no uncertain terms, that he had insulted both me and my wife. He was rather put out because I had dumped all his invoices, including his copies.

Subsequently, labour in a dinghy appeared to salvage all his invoices which were then presented to the Master as the Chief Officer for some reason had declined to sign them.

Old Indian Proverb says 'Beware of a stevedore bearing gifts'.

Captain Michael Taylor continues his odd recollections and puts forward a theory explaining 'How we lost the Indian Sub-Continent Empire without bloodshed' ... or something like that. Read on, if you can! You might even learn something.

OH DEAR!

Whilst Third Officer of S.S. MATHURA, loading in Calcutta at the height of the tea season, the ship was shifted into the River Hooghly to the Garden Reach moorings, so that at the deadline of 1800 hours the ship would proceed seaward ... otherwise she would be delayed by the neap tide for ten days in Calcutta and the tea would be too late for the U.K. auctions.

In the river, twelve gangs were employed, two at each of the six hatches, loading from lighters at each side of the vessel.

About noon two dhow-type barges, laden to the gunnels with bags of Indian chillies, drifted alongside the vessel with their dhoti-clad merchant owner asking to see the Master or Chief Officer. The chillies had to get to Colombo as soon as possible, if not sooner.

Our elderly and Senior Chief Officer informed the chilli merchant that he had to load the precious chests of tea and there was no way that his chillies were to be shipped in the MATURA. He bellowed, "Show this gentleman off the ship, Third Officer" and he added (aside) "He hasn't wished me a Merry Christmas". I thought this rather odd because it was the middle of June.

Half way to the accommodation ladder the penny dropped ... "I need to wish the Chief Officer Sahib a Merry Christmas!" We returned to the ship's office and five minutes later the Chief Officer appeared and bellowed "Stop Number Six hatch, cover it up and load this gentleman's chillies on to the hatchway, cover them up on completion with tarpaulins and secure with

229

rope lashings to prevent prying eyes seeing the chillies."

We sailed as planned at 1800 hours, an uneventful voyage to Calcutta. The chillies were discharged overside to lighters and tea was resumed loading into Number Six 'tween deck. The chillies were shipped without the blessing of a Bill of Loading or any other documentation. Christmas came early to MATHURA, but only to the favoured two!

In 1957, T & J Harrison ceased activity and our MATHURA was the first ship to load for the U.K. using the new title of Harrison Line Agency. They were a breath of fresh air.

I, as Chief Officer, fairly newly married, had persuaded a contractor to make me a blanket box. It proved to be a real dry dock job, so big that it came aboard using a quayside crane and it only just fitted into the ship's office.

The Harrison Agent was a young ex-Etonian and we thought him a bit 'foppish'. But when he gave us a list of cargo booked, sure enough the cargo arrived ... a rare feat for Calcutta.

Fresh water was always at a premium in Calcutta. This was the drill. You ordered fresh water and hung a bottle of gin over the side to entice the Pani Walla to favour your ship. Once the water barge was alongside the gin disappeared! Our Etonian Agent assured us that getting fresh water was no problem for him and off he went.

No water barge appeared, so next day when he visited we let him know how disappointed we were with his efforts and I told him that he would be punished. Our Second and Third Officers were hefty lads, so I said, "Put the Agent in the blanket box". "You cannot do this to me. I am your Agent". He was put in the box, its lid closed and hammered down. Eventually he was released and advised to clear off and get us our promised water! Very funny, we thought and had a good laugh. We would not have dared do that to our own staid and elderly Puckah Sahib Agent. Lo and behold, the fresh water arrived and all subsequent deliveries.

Several years later, I was employed as a Marine Surveyor in Manchester and visited every Harrison ship on a daily basis. The Master said to me one morning, "Our Vice Chairman is hosting a Shippers' lunch today and he has insisted that you be invited. So we will see you at lunchtime."

As I entered the Officers' Lounge, I was somewhat shocked to see the old Etonian Agent, now Harrisons' Vice Chairman. "Hello, Michael, welcome aboard and how nice to see you again. Do you remember putting me in your blanket box and hammering me down, just because you thought that I had failed you as your Agent and had not come forth with the fresh water?" I should have realised that Mr. Harrison-Rosselli, whilst in a junior position in Calcutta, was destined to have accelerated promotion in his family's Company. "Mr. Rosselli, sir, the blanket box incident was a terrible mistake, an error of judgement on my part." I squirmed. He replied, "As a young man in Calcutta, perhaps I was a little overbearing, and I realised that I was not received in the same awe as I was on our Harrison ships. Anyway, it did me no great harm."

Only last year was the blanket box disposed of, having been used as a toy box for children and grand children.

Possibly one of my worst days at sea happened in August 1957 ... my first permanent berth as Chief Officer. I joined MATHURA on sailing day in Victoria Docks, London. Her Master had particularly requested me as his Chief Officer.

As I staggered aboard with all my gear, the first thing to greet me was a flood of fuel oil pouring down the inboard alleyways. It was an overflow from the bunkering barge alongside. Luckily, the deck scuppers had been cemented so there was no spillage into the Albert Dock, but there was a mess to clean up before we sailed.

I glanced down Number Two 'tween deck and could see the refrigerated chambers. Seeping out from the bottom of one of the doors, I could see a little cream coloured liquid oozing out. The cargo of ice-cream in that chamber had obviously thawed before it could be hard frozen. We hadn't even started the voyage!

Worse was to come as we entered the Royal Albert Dock lock entrance, the Lock Master shouted up to me on the fo'c'sle, "Mate, you are eighteen inches overloaded. I'll not report it, but you could have trouble in the Suez Canal."

Thank you, Captain Michael Taylor.

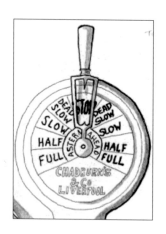

Doug Makinson
Engineer

I first met Doug Makinson in Riversdale College where he was a lecturer in the Engineering Department. The welcome I received in that College was ever warm and it was a great opportunity to meet the deck and engineering trainees. Here are some of Doug's thoughts.

A SOUTH ATLANTIC TOW

The Royal Mail Lines Limited Motor Vessel, PARIMA, headed out of the Mersey on a grey Saturday afternoon in November 1951, passing New Brighton at 5 o'clock. The PARIMA was sailing south to the Brazilian ports of Bahia, Rio de Janeiro, Santos, Rio Grande de Sul, and Porto Alegre with general cargo.

The Master was Captain Grant, the Chief Engineer was Andrew Robbie, and I was Second Engineer. Although the PARIMA normally re-fuelled at Las Palmas in the Canary Isles, on this voyage we by-passed Las Palmas on instruction from Head Office and re-fuelled at Cape Verde Islands. Here some 630 tons of fuel were pumped aboard.

About a day after leaving Cape Verde Islands, on my second

watch of that day at 6.30 p.m., the Chief Engineer telephoned me to say that we would be stopping at approximately 8 p.m. Instructions had been received to go to the aid of an ocean-going trawler, which was apparently stopped and adrift. Shortly after 8 p.m., the trawler was located and the PARIMA stopped and stood by the vessel during the night. The trawler was the MONTE ALEGRE. I was surprised to hear from the Chief Engineer that the Captain had told him that the trawler had been adrift for a few days and that although several vessels had passed by in the distance, none had responded.

I learned later that evening that the trawler had unfortunately suffered a major machinery failure by way of a fractured propeller shaft. The trawler was of Spanish origin and had been sold to Brazil and was in the process of being delivered.

The following morning, our crew set to work early at 4 a.m. to get a tow line aboard the trawler. This took some time to achieve. Eventually, we got under way and the PARIMA proceeded to tow the MONTE ALEGRE at the reduced speed of 65 revolutions per minute. The PARIMA's normal 'Full Ahead' speed was 98 revolutions per minute. Seven days elapsed to tow the trawler to Recife. The tow line parted on two occasions during the following days. On the first occasion, it took several hours to reconnect. On the second occasion, the tow line had parted aboard the trawler and its crew repaired the tow line connection.

Finally, we arrived at Recife and the MONTE ALEGRE was anchored safely in the inner harbour. Then the PARIMA anchored. The Master then went ashore to submit a salvage claim to the authorities and the PARIMA proceeded to Bahia on the same day.

Some three years later I received a letter from Royal Mail Lines stating that, as Second Engineer of the PARIMA I was to receive a salvage award of £83. This award proved to be a timely contribution towards my wife's engagement ring.

Well done, Doug ... £83 was a good sum of money in 1951. I have asked him to explain to landlubbers the training schedule for engineers in the Mercantile Marine.

ENGINEER TRAINING

There are various ways in which young men became sea-going engineers. The ultimate responsibility of running a modern Merchant Ship is in the hands of the Captain and the Chief Engineer. Although there are considerable differences in the skills and knowledge required for these jobs, the career structure for each has many similarities. In 1952, a scheme was introduced by the Ministry of Transport together with various shipping companies and it was used at Riversdale College, Liverpool. Vocational works training in the industry was followed by eighteen months at sea and twelve months in the College.

New entrants could join from school, either at sixteen with GCE 'O' Level passes or at eighteen with passes at GCE 'A' Level. Examination passes equivalent to GCE were also perfectly acceptable.

The career structure was based on the Business and Technician Education Council (BTEC) National Diploma and Higher Diploma schemes, together with periods of planned training at sea. New entrants started as Cadets and became Junior Officers after three or four years. Qualifications were completed by the mid-twenties and thereafter promotion prospects were dependent on many factors.

Training for Deck Officers followed a pattern of induction, followed by a number of College and sea-phases. For engineers, the route through followed a flexible pattern, allowing the prospective student to choose according to his entry qualifications and his career options.

Thank you, Doug Makinson.

Captain David Nutman
Master Mariner

Captain David Nutman's career stretches across time … his seagoing was in two parts. A Conway cadet, 1950 – 1951, David was to become the President of the CONWAY Club, 2003 – 2005, and is Chairman of The Friends of H.M.S. CONWAY which is responsible for the refurbishment and maintenance of the CONWAY Chapel at Birkenhead Priory. He sailed in Bibby Line from 1952 to 1959 and in Elders and Fyffes from 1959 to 1960. Then he started another career in the world of 'Finance for Plant and Equipment, Commercial Transport and Marine Mortgages, etc.', becoming Industrial Manager for his company. In 1978, he returned to sea with Canadian Pacific, sailing as an extra Second Officer on a V.L.C.C. David obtained his Masters

Certificate at Warsash and sailed as Master on Bulkers, Container ships and specialised Ro-Ro ships until 1990. For the following four years he was Nautical Surveyor with the Department of Transport covering the coast from Barmouth to Silloth, the Lake District and the Canals from Skipton to Birmingham. Incidentally, David has a long connection with the Mersey Mission to

Seafarers. He is a long serving Trustee and Honorary Secretary, but above all, has been much involved in the coming together of the two Liverpool nautical charities ... the Apostleship of the Sea and the Mersey Mission to Seafarers in Colonsay House.

But, let's start at the beginning.

SHARK

My first trip to sea, as a Cadet, was in January 1952 ... from London to the East Coast of Africa. The ship was a passenger cargo liner of 8,908 gross tons, built in 1949, carrying 90 passengers. We were on charter to the British India Steam Navigation Company.

On arrival at Mombasa, we had to anchor for nearly nine weeks awaiting a berth at Kilindi Harbour. The ship had a swimming pool and the Chief Officer was in the habit of going for a swim at 0700 every day. One night some of the crew caught a young shark, about three feet long. The other cadet, an Old Worcester, and I carried it, wrapped in canvas, up to the main deck and put it into the swimming pool.

The joke back-fired, however, when we turned to at 0700 the following morning and were instructed by the Mate that our first job was to 'get rid of that bloody thing in the pool'.

It was a lot more difficult than we thought. It necessitated draining the pool first and then having to clean it out after removing the shark.

It was returned to the crew who ate it!

David continues.

THE BANANA TALE

Early in the 1960s, I was Third Officer on a banana boat running between West Africa and Garston.

One of my duties was to keep a record of the fruit temperatures ... Air Delivery 52° F., Return 56° F. ... figures are imprinted indelibly on my mind. I also had to keep a daily record of the pulp temperatures by going down all the holds and sticking a thermometer into a few selected bananas.

These were all faithfully recorded, but there was one newly-appointed Master who regularly accused me of fabricating these temperatures in the log. At the time he was quite nasty about it.

Now, forty-six years later, that Master and I meet regularly at the Merseyside Master Mariners Club and he is 'as nice as pie' to my wife and I.

We all mellow with age and thank you, David, for bringing bananas into Garston. I regularly visited the ships there in the sixties and we never bought any bananas for years. Captain David Nutman continues.

THE SHIP THAT DIDN'T RISE

The year was 1989 and I was in command of a Ro-Ro ship that had been converted to carry paper from Newcastle, New Brunswick, to Beaufort, South Carolina and kaolin clay back to Canada. Ro-Ro ships are designed for vehicles to 'Roll on' and 'Roll off', but in this case the side door had been constructed so that rolls of paper could be loaded by fork lift trucks for the voyage south and Kaolin Clay could be loaded into specially-built tanks for the northbound voyage.

In common with most ship-owners, keeping costs down was always paramount. When dry docking became due, I was instructed to take the ship up a creek near Charleston to a small, cheap shipyard with a floating dock.

The floating dock was unusual in that it was a former U.S. Navy six-section wooden dock that had been built in the 1940s.

In 1989, it still had five sections and was reported as having a lifting capacity of 10,000 tons. At that time our displacement from draft readings was 6,929 tons so, in theory, there should have been no problem.

When the time came however we put the ship in the floating dock and they pumped and pumped and pumped. The dock only rose a couple of feet which, we calculated, meant that only 2,550 tons of the ship's weight was being supported.

To make matters worse, the ship was too long for the dock with a 39 feet overhang aft and about 80 feet forward.

Eventually, the attempt to 'dry-dock' the ship was abandoned, and after all the work that could be done alongside was completed, I was instructed to take her to Jacksonville, Florida, where we successfully lifted the ship out of the water.

This next tale was written in the house magazine of C.P.R. ... 'SEANEWS'. David was sailing as Chief Officer.

REFUGEES

Thirteen refugees, including a 14 day-old infant, were saved in December, 1984 by the crew of FORT KAMLOOPS.

The men, women and children were picked up from an open boat 150 miles off the coast of Sabah, in North Borneo, having left the Philippines 14 days earlier. They had not eaten for several days.

The Filipino families left their Zamboanga home on the very day that a baby was born to one of the women. When found, the mother and child were close to death. The other four men, four women, and four children were also weak from their ordeal.

The refugees had left the Philippines in an outrigger canoe only 18 ft. long by 18 inches wide. When the propeller dropped off their small engine, they had no alternative but to row the 500 miles to Sabah.

When spotted by the FORT KAMLOOPS' radar the refugees had travelled 350 miles under their own steam, and were 50 miles from the nearest land. Currents were taking them away from their destination.

The families were seeking a better life in North Borneo, and were hoping that the Government there would allow them to stay and find jobs and homes.

Chief Officer David Nutman told 'SEANEWS': "We were lucky to pick them up on the radar at all. We had just come out of a rain-storm. As we approached them one of the men in the canoe held the young baby aloft.

"Most of them were so weak we couldn't get them up the ship's side. In the end, we lowered a lifeboat for the women and children. Luke Fisher, the Third Officer, even went down into the canoe to help them.

"We couldn't believe it when we saw the baby. It was 14 days old and they had been at sea for 14 days. The mother had no milk and I really do not think she or the baby would have survived much longer."

David went on: "We put all of them in the ship's hospital, and watched the weakest among them very carefully. Most of the children recovered very quickly with some food inside them.

"We decided to give the baby nothing but boiled water, fed through the end of a hypodermic syringe … minus needle."

Within 24 hours the FORT KAMLOOPS had arrived at Sabah. Immigration officials came on board and the refugees were taken ashore. Some went into hospital.

David said: "The last I heard the authorities were going to allow them to stay. I hope so. They were certainly lucky to be found alive."

Thank you, David. That story is fairly common these days, but often it all ends in tragedy.

There have even been ladies at sea and Brenda Nutman, the wife of Captain David Nutman, has happily shared some memories with us. Naturally, it is not edited in any way!

As a wife of a seafarer, I think that I am one of the privileged. David was at sea when we were married, but not long after, he came ashore. He was at home for eighteen years and he saw our sons, Andrew and Anthony, grow up. He returned to sea, having been at home for a very long time, and things had changed very much during that period. We discovered that wives were able to travel with their husbands.

It became a very exciting time for me. I travelled up the St. Lawrence to Montreal, across to Rotterdam and Amsterdam countless times, through the Panama and Suez Canals ... both ways, and even as far as Japan, Africa and Australia.

A memorable time for me was when David was working along the East Coast of Canada and America. It was a charter where we made regular calls at different ports and I am no different from any other wife, I love to shop!

I was given a fistful of dollars and a shopping list and went off, with the ship's cook, to the local supermarket, called the 'Piggly Wiggly'. I purchased all the goods on the list and the supermarket manager was delighted ... he had made a very good sale! On the way back to the ship, I called at the local fish market and remember buying a great quantity of herrings at 5 cents a pound.

I would return to the ship and the Captain (my husband) and the crew were very pleased with the quality of the food. The ship's chandler didn't take kindly to this as his services hadn't been needed. This regime carried on for many months and the Officers and Crew were very contented.

Not long after this, the Company's Catering Superintendent flew out to the ship from London. Perhaps I had better explain, every ship had a 'feeding rate' set by Management and, because of my efforts, the feeding rate on this ship had dropped. The Catering Superintendent wanted to know what the Captain was up to, was he starving the men? Needless to say, when he came on board, it was all too evident that they were not going hungry.

As the Captain's wife on these trips, I had a wonderful time … no housework, no cooking, just the laundry for the two of us. I was able to knit, sew, crochet and read many books from the library. It was quite a hardship when we returned home at the end of our many trips.

There is more! Another missive from Brenda.

In the early 1980s, David was Chief Officer of a 130,000 ton DW Bulk Carrier carrying grain from the Mississippi to Europe. The Company (Canadian Pacific Bulkships) had decided that the vessel was to be dry-docked at Schiedam, near Rotterdam. The Captain at that time thought that, as the ship was ten years old, it was time the furnishings in his accommodation should be renewed. The Engineering Superintendent thought otherwise but didn't rule out an update on furnishings entirely.

It was at this time that I volunteered to give the Captain's cabin a 'makeover' and the Superintendent agreed that there were sufficient funds for materials. The Captain and I went ashore and bought all the necessary fabrics and a new sewing machine. Over the period of the dry-docking, I re-covered all the chairs and made new curtains. I probably completed some of the work during the voyage to New Orleans but twenty-five years later one's memory is a little rusty.

Thank you, Brenda.

Captain John Turner, O.B.E.
Master Mariner

Captain J. R. Turner, O.B.E., gives us a vivid picture of his first voyage at sea. John has had a full career after his days in H.M.S. WORCESTER. The list of his achievements and awards is really too long to quote in full, but includes being General Manager of the Aberdeen Harbour Board and receiving the Freedom of the City of London.

The great day came on January 5th, 1949 when I joined the CLAN MACKINNON in Vittoria Dock, Birkenhead. The first voyage deep sea is always exciting and, perhaps, I can be forgiven for describing it in some detail.

I quickly went on board to report to the Senior Officer, one 'Barney' McGill, a relief Chief Officer who then sent for my new colleague, another Cadet named John Bedford. He had already completed one voyage in the ship and was an Old Conway. John was very efficient ... and has remained a good friend to this day.

John sent for the Burra Tindal (the Senior Boatswain's Mate), and ordered him to have my gear brought up to our cabin. The cabin was located on the main deck on the starboard side. There were three bunks, wardrobes, wash basin (cold water only) and a chest of drawers, as well as a study area.

After being shown over the ship, we had lunch which seemed fantastic after WORCESTER, since there was no food rationing aboard ship. In the afternoon I had to don working gear and help the Third Officer, Bill Richardson, another Old Worcester, together with John Bedford, to check lifeboat rations up in the former gunner's quarters. The evening meal also seemed pretty good, and I met the Ship's Carpenter, who chided me for the immense amount of butter I put on my bread … due to long exposure to rationing. I'm afraid that I made a bit of a pig of myself!

Next day I was awoken at 6.50 a.m. with a cup of tea brought by our 'boy', an Indian steward, whose sole job was to look after our cabin, make the beds, and wait on us at table.

All Clan Line ships had Indian Lascar crews, mostly recruited around Chittagong and Noakhali in what is now Bangladesh. Their native tongue was Bengali although all could speak Urdu, and a few spoke a little English. The deck crew were headed by the Serang (Boatswain), two Tindals, a Cassab (storekeeper), and we had about 20 Kalassis (seamen) plus a Topass (deck sweeper).

The first morning was spent with the Third Officer on cargo watch, supervising the loading of general cargo. I was of no use to him whatsoever at that stage and could do no more than act as messenger, but I was learning the layout of the cargo holds of which the CLAN MACKINNON had six.

Later, on that first afternoon, my parents came down and I proudly showed them over the ship. My mother had been very concerned as to my future welfare, but was much relieved to see my cabin, to meet John Bedford, and to hear how relatively good the food was.

The next day, the regular ship's Officers joined. By this time, I had become part of the watering system, a duty shared by the two Cadets. It involved asking the Engineers to start up the water pumps, then by means of valves to fill the fresh and salt water tanks above the Bridge, amidships and aft. The sea water was used for toilets and the fresh water for washing and drinking. The only way we had to tell if a tank was full was to watch if it overflowed, and when it had, instantly shut it off. I, of course, learnt the hard way, and managed to flood the Bridge deck by not shutting off in time. Tanks were filled every morning and evening, and we did this for all of the two years spent on that ship.

On Thursday January 8th, 1949, we sailed for the Malabar Coast of India with a full cargo. During the morning, we had loaded six top racehorses belonging to the Maharajah of Baroda. It was the Cadets' job to look after them until we reached Bombay. Each day at 7 a.m. we had to muck out, shovelling it all over the side into the sea, then hose down the horse boxes and when they were dry, put in fresh straw. Horses were fed twice a day, and in between times had to be groomed. It was quite a responsibility for some extremely valuable horseflesh. No one knew if we had had any experience ... we did not ... but eventually they were delivered in very good condition, despite our lack of equine skills. Some of the horses were quite docile, but one named Hemlatta was a vicious brute and brushing that one was a very risky business.

At 1830 hours we let go our moorings, and with a tug at each end began to move away from the quay out into the dock, then into the locks where the ship was lowered down to sea level. As I look back, it was quite an emotional feeling leaving U.K. for the first time, literally out into the unknown.

I was stationed on the forecastle head with the Chief Officer, George Spiller, another Old Worcester, because after only three and half days I was not sufficiently familiar with the ship to take any part in the Bridge team. At 1930 we moved slowly out into the Mersey and let go of the tugs and felt the throb of the engine as we headed out to sea under our own steam. It was strange to see the lights of Liverpool slowly drop astern and finally disappear altogether.

I was allocated to the 12 to 4 watch with the Second Officer, George Rowlands. On that ship, Bridge watches had to be kept outside and not in the wheel house. Nowadays most ships have the bridge fully enclosed and air-conditioned. Such luxury was not to be ours, however, and as a Cadet I was put out on the weather wing which was extremely cold and draughty.

Slowly the lights of the North Wales coast faded, and we set our course, navigating purely by compass bearings of lighthouses. As we only had a magnetic compass, this had to be corrected for variation (the earth's magnetism), and for deviation (the ship's own inherent magnetism which varied according to the heading). Once every watch, bearings were taken of a known star, or the sun by day, and from the time on the chronometer, the true bearing of the star could be calculated in order to check the total compass magnet error. The CLAN MACKINNON was the only ship I ever sailed in which did not have a gyro-compass and, of course, we had no radar, only a very weak and unreliable radio-direction-finder. We dropped the Pilot off Point Lynas in Anglesey at 0330, then headed for India via the Suez Canal.

Each day started and ended with the racehorses and a greyhound, which we were also taking out to Bombay. In between times we had to fill the water tanks, and check the temperature of each hold to ensure that we had no fire, and that the holds were not heating up. I was not seasick either then or indeed ever, and for that I was thankful because many people are tortured by this affliction for which, in those days, there was no cure or palliative. Passing Ushant, the N.W. tip of France, we experienced our first gale with waves larger than I had ever seen ... as high as the boat-deck (about thirty feet), but little did I know I was to see very much worse over the years ahead. Because we had livestock, we worked all day Saturday and

Sunday just like a weekday, and my diary for that first weekend records ... "I wish the horses were dead".

Routine continued each day starting at 0700, an hour for breakfast, an hour for lunch, then finish at 1700, if we were lucky. There was a 'smoke-o' break of ten minutes morning and afternoon when our boy provided a cup of tea or coffee.

We passed a bare three miles off Cape St. Vincent, the S.W. extremity of Portugal at 1300 on the 13th and this was the first foreign land I had ever seen. The weather became calmer and much warmer. On reflection this was incredibly close, even for a slow ship such as ours, but the Captain, Roy Linsley, was a fine navigator and a good seaman, and in those days there was not as much heavy or fast traffic as there is today.

Part of the daily routine, when clear of land, was to go on the Bridge for an hour from 1400 to 1500 where we received instruction from the Second Officer. In addition, in our spare time, we had to work on a correspondence course of tuition.

We had our first boat drill and fire practice on the Thursday, and this drill was repeated sporadically throughout the voyage. The boats were turned out on the davits, but were never lowered. The fire drill was taken more seriously with extensive practice using the breathing apparatus for entering smoke-filled areas.

We arrived off Port Said at the entrance of the Suez Canal eleven days after leaving Liverpool. Now more conversant with procedures, I was stationed on the Bridge where I manned telephones, relaying orders to the mooring parties on the forecastle and poop, in addition to other duties. As we entered the port at midnight, I caught my first glimpse of Africa as we moored stern first to a quay, ready to unload cargo into lighters the next day. In addition to looking after our horses, we had cargo duties, and I recall being stationed in the special cargo locker in No. 1 'tween deck valiantly trying to ensure that the dockers did not steal any of the cargo of whisky ... quite a responsibility, aged seventeen and a half, alone with about ten dockers.

We moved into the Suez Canal the next morning after a searchlight had been rigged over the bows. We were glad to leave Port Said where we had been surrounded by bumboats trying to sell anything from leather handbags to hard pornographic literature ... one very furtive character wanted to take us ashore where he purported to have an exhibition in which a donkey had sex with a lady. We were not tempted, but in any event we were too busy to go ashore. Clan Line had their own approved bumboatman who, unlike the others, was allowed on board. He rejoiced in the name of 'Jock Mackay' (real name Ibrahim Waffa), and he would get you anything that you wanted. He also kept a record of each Clan Liner passing through and the names of the Cadets ... we always perused this to see who was on which ship.

In those days, there were no passing places and ships moved in convoy. When a north-bound convoy was reached, the south-bound convoy passed ropes ashore which were tied to moorings by Egyptian boatmen. We carried them along with their boat for just this purpose. Whenever a ship passed, we had to heave alongside the Canal bank. Another feature of the Canal, no longer used, was to empty the forecastle and poop stores on to the deck secured by tarpaulin, leaving all the forecastle space empty so no Canal dues could be levied on this space. Charges were according to space and Clan Line claimed that they saved a good deal of money by this trick, but they failed to take account of all the stores stolen by Egyptian dockers.

The next day we left the Canal and entered the Gulf of Suez. More cargo was unloaded into lighters, and in the afternoon we moved out toward the Red Sea where the weather was unseasonably wet and windy. On Sunday, we were ordered to take sun-sights. It was the outdated Clan Line practice for all Officers to go to the Bridge just before 12 noon to 'shoot the sun' with their sextants. This meant bringing the reflected image of the sun down to the horizon, then measuring the angle of altitude, checking the time, then calculating the latitude. In this my first attempt, I concluded that the ship was in the Persian Gulf, but eventually got it right on the third attempt.

We arrived in Aden on January 27th, some 19 days out of Liverpool. Here more cargo was unloaded and we took on oil bunkers and later in the day headed across the Indian Ocean for Bombay. On January 30th, we heard that Mahatma Gandhi had been assassinated and that there were riots and strikes in India … we were concerned as to the problems that might await us.

We arrived in Bombay two days later, but had to anchor as there was a crane drivers' strike, there were riots, and the city was under a thirteen-day curfew. Three days later, we went alongside to unload the horses and, in the evening, I went ashore with Bill and John … a tremendous culture shock if ever there was.

This was the first time that I had set foot on foreign soil and I was amazed to see the filth and squalor, people sleeping on the pavements, old ladies searching for bugs in each other's hair, 'holy' cows wandering around the streets, and the most appalling poverty everywhere. There were innumerable beggars, often badly maimed or mutilated, thrusting their handless arms in your face. Some had no feet, some had their faces mutilated and they cried out for alms in the most heart-rending manner. So commonplace were these beggars, that one quickly learned to ignore them and to say 'Jow', which means 'Go away!'

Against strict Clan Line rules we had a few drinks at Green's Hotel, then returned to the ship. The next morning we moved out to the anchorage with a scratch 'relief' crew … our own having gone home by train to Bengal. The relief crew became the Cadets' responsibility and we put them to washing out the vacated crew's quarters aft which, over the next few days, were completely painted. The Chief Officer, George Spiller, very carefully examined each part of the completed paintwork. Woe betide us if he found any 'holidays' ... unpainted corners difficult to access ... or drips, it had to be good! The relief crew were pretty dreadful and not up to the standard of our regular crews. As they spoke no English whatever, we greatly improved our own command of Hindustani (Urdu) in double quick time! The work continued every day including weekends until complete, and then we started our temporary crew painting the 'tween decks with red lead. In the evenings, we had to go to the Bridge for an hour to be taught the names of the stars used for navigational purposes.

We were much relieved when eventually we moved into Victoria Dock in the oldest part of the port to discharge our cargo. This dock was virtually an open sewer and the stink was unbelievable, with rats scuttling around the quay in broad daylight. After working through a public holiday, I had the next day off and went into Bombay alone despite sporadic rioting, which was quite scary when you found your way blocked by a lynch mob.

In the afternoon, I went to see friends of my father who took me to Breach Kandy, the 'European only' swimming club which was heavenly after the stinking Victoria Dock. There were two large swimming pools and tea was served on the terrace. Taking tea was tricky because if you had a cake in your hand, the kites would dive down and snatch it out of your hand. Their talons and beaks were very sharp so any wound had to be disinfected, failing which it would quickly become septic. I had dinner with these friends, then took a taxi back in the evening. Next day, it was John Bedford's turn to have a day off and he also went to Breach Kandy where he managed to hurt his wrist whilst attempting some acrobatics on the grass. The next day, being Sunday, we were allowed off ... the first free

Sunday since leaving home ... and again we went to Breach Kandy, which we thought was quite the best place in Bombay.

Two days later, John Bedford went into hospital to have attention to his wrist which was now very painful. After a further two days later he was still in hospital and they had diagnosed a fractured wrist, but could not set it as they had no plaster! I took some plaster from the ship so it could be set the next day. In the evening, I went up to the hospital where, sure enough, the wrist was set. We embarked upon some horse play in which John got on a trolley, I purloined a white coat, and with his body and face covered by a sheet, we pretended that we were pushing a corpse around! This puerile humour was not appreciated and I was duly kicked out and he was confined to bed to be discharged the next day.

The next crew having arrived, the ship sailed a day later for Bhavnagar in the Gulf of Kutch. Everything seemed to go wrong from the moment the native Pilot came aboard. The Pilot spoke little English and he appeared never to have been on board such a large ship. Given his volatile nature, he ended up in such a state of uncontrolled panic that Captain Linsley with his own bare hands picked him up by the scruff of his neck and the seat of his dhoti and physically threw him off the Bridge. It spoke volumes for Linsley's seamanship and ship-handling skills that he brought the ship alongside the quay unaided.

Once alongside, we began to unload a cargo of railway locomotives, using our own 50-ton capacity heavy lift derrick. Predictably, the dockers panicked and we had to put our own crew to winch-driving, as the local workers were a danger to themselves and to the ship. About mid-morning, the Chief Engineer came running upon deck to say that the condenser sea water intake was out of the water, and sure enough we were aground with the tide rapidly ebbing, thus leaving us sitting on the mud ... not high and dry, but very nearly!

We put out extra moorings so the ship would not fall

away from the quay and somehow managed to get by with no damage. We stayed there about three days whilst the cargo was slowly unloaded, but we could not go ashore as the quay was up a muddy creek, situated in an isolated spot amongst marshland and a very long way from town. Everyone was relieved to be away and free of the prolific swarms of mosquitoes that ate one alive every evening. Because we were all ordered to take mepachrin tablets nobody caught malaria, but most of us developed a yellowish hue on our faces.

Our next port of call was Calicut, now known as Khozikode. This was an anchorage port where we unloaded cargo overside into dhows and we worked round the clock. Yes, you have guessed it, I was on night cargo watch duties, with Bill Richardson, the Third Officer.

We now began loading some cargo for home. This was tea and the Cadets had to work with the Carpenter to erect wooden shoring to stop the chests of tea moving in rough weather. I managed to get sunstroke and heat exhaustion.

Our next port was Cochin which, in those days, was the most pleasant port on the coast ... this long before it became a tourist resort. The main quays were only a short walk from the Malabar Hotel where, for a very small charge, we could have the use of the hotel's swimming pool or play snooker. We went up there whenever we could, but one evening John and I decided to go into the native town, hiring a boat for the purpose and after agreeing a price, with much haggling, we duly set off. On arrival we were 'mugged' by a crowd of natives, aided and abetted by our boatman, and to cut a long story short we were forced to hand over all our money. Speaking quickly in English, so they could not understand, we assessed our chances of fighting our way out. There were about six or seven of them and only two of us, one of whom had a wrist in plaster. We might have taken them on if the odds were four to two or less, but with the handicap of a broken wrist, we were forced to pay up at knife point. How we got back to the ship I cannot recall, but one of us must somehow have retained enough money to pay another boatman.

Our next port was Koilthottam which, like Calicut, was an anchorage port with the cargo brought out in dhows ... all that we could see of the shore was a line of palm trees. We were at anchor for four or five days whilst loading illmenite sand, which was brought out in bags which were then slit, and the loose sand spread evenly over the hold. The big difficulty was trimming the cargo out to the edges so as to leave a completely flat surface on top of which we could load tea. We spent most of our time down below supervising and trying to ensure that the dockers did not steal the tea loaded previously. As we could not speak a word of their Tamil language and they spoke no word of English, we had a difficult task. The worst part was when their foreman suspended a 10 rupee note into the hold so that the dockers stopped trimming and tried to build up to a peak from which the money could be snatched. Instead I yelled at the foreman and temporarily impounded the money until they started trimming the cargo properly, but I ran quite a risk in doing so. I was severely reprimanded by the Second Officer for manhandling the foreman, but it did the trick!

Eventually, we finished and sailed for Tuticorin where we unloaded the last of the outward cargo, again into dhows since we anchored three or four miles offshore. Our next port was Galle, a delightful place in Ceylon, now Sri Lanka, and situated at the extreme south end of the island. Here we entered a big lagoon and turned the ship to face the sea so that we could easily get out if storms arose. We put down both anchors forward and secured aft to two huge coconut fibre ropes, which had lain in the sea, were covered in seaweed, and posed serious difficulties in securing because of continual slippage on the winch drum. Eventually we had to use two winches in line and in tandem ... something I never saw before or since. That first evening we went ashore by boat and found a delightful town with wide clean streets, no beggars and very friendly natives. Galle had been fortified by the Portuguese and many interesting old forts and battlemented walls remained. Shopping was also both interesting and cheap, and we all bought ivories and ebony ornaments. Some bought opals and moonstones which were produced locally and were very cheap. I could not afford jewellery since Clan Line paid Cadets the princely sum of £7.10s (now £7.50) a month and that did not go very far!

Next day, after preparing holds for loading, we lowered the ship's one motor lifeboat, and a dozen of us crossed to an isolated beach of pure white sand surrounded by jungle, with really warm water for bathing and no fear of sharks. We had had very little relaxation and never before had the opportunity for the Officers to go ashore or engage in any kind of recreation all together. Here I bathed and swam under ideal conditions, I never experienced better ... even in the West Indies. We swam and larked about in warm, crystal-clear water. That day must go down as the most enjoyable of all my time with Clan Line and I certainly never bathed in a more idyllic location. Even Captain Linsley came along and, at his suggestion, we had a WORCESTER v CONWAY piggy-back-tussle with him (an Old Conway) carrying John Bedford. I never sailed with another Captain who would have so unbent himself, and yet he was still respected and addressed as 'Sir'.

Next day we began loading, but each day we managed to go swimming at our idyllic private beach until our loading was complete and we sailed for Cochin. We were now loading cargo for home. Stowage of cargo needed great care and attention to detail to ensure that the stow for each destination port was easily accessible and that no damage occurred. Since we did not know the order of our destinations, the cargo had to be loaded so that it was accessible whatever the order of ports apart from the first port, London.

It was particularly important that none of the cargo touched any of the steelwork within the ship's holds and 'tween decks because when we reached colder climes, moisture would condense on the cold steel, and this would in turn cause 'sweat' damage to the cargo. To prevent damage, thousands of cargo mats made from coconut leaves were used, and the Indian dockers had to be constantly nagged to make sure the mats were properly positioned. The illmenite sand also had to be covered with gunny (hessian) and overlaid with wood dunnage, in order to give a level ground to load the chests of tea and to prevent any moisture in the sand contaminating the tea. Our homeward cargo comprised largely tea, illmenite sand, bales of coconut mats, bales of coconut fibre and Palmyra fibre as well as coconut yarn. On deck we had drums of citronella oil, lemon grass oil and tobacco seed oil.

We enjoyed our second stay at Cochin with most evenings spent swimming at the Malabar Hotel, and after drinking copious amounts of fresh orange squash we would adjourn to the Merchant Navy club to play snooker. From Cochin we went to Allepey, a short distance down the coast where we anchored off-shore. The cargo was again brought out by dhows, and after a day or two topping up the holds, we finally sailed for home.

One never forgets leaving the Indian coast for home. We could again have our portholes and doors wide open, they had been closed all the time in port as the Indian dockers were potential thieves and we had to take careful precautions to prevent loss. It was wonderful to be away from the overwhelming heat of the coast, and to have a cooling sea breeze circulating through the ship. It was also good sleeping weather with no mosquitoes or flies!

We settled down to routine work on deck. George Spiller, the Chief Officer, was a firm believer in WORCESTER doctrine that a good Officer should know every job in the ship, and he should never tell a sailor to do a job which he cannot do better himself! We therefore found ourselves caulking seams in the wooden deck, stripping varnish and re-varnishing, and above all, chipping, scraping and red-leading any rusty patches. In port, we had painted draught marks and plimsoll marks, and at sea we painted nearly everything that did not move, ranging from lifeboats to life buoys. Each voyage we would check the lifeboat stores of biscuits and barley sugar, and would change the water in the tanks as well as checking that all the other equipment was present and in working order. In the Tropics, we sometimes filled the bottom of the wooden boats with seawater to swell the seams which would otherwise dry out and become less tight.

There were few jobs on the ship which we did not tackle at some time or other. Always we worked apart from the Lascar crew, unless we were actually supervising them. In port, we had to rig harbour lights every night, and it was the practice to only put two bulbs in each cluster, because if they were stolen then there would be no light ... put six bulbs in, however, and four would be always stolen. It was a different story in subsequent voyages to the U.S.A. and Australia where inadequate light would cause an immediate strike! At sea the lamp connections on the masts, etc. had to be greased with 'crabfat' (mercurial ointment) which was normally given to any crew member who was infected with crab lice, but as a grease it was highly effective against sea water corrosion.

I never sailed with a Chief Officer more skilled in cargo stowage or at keeping the ship in pristine condition. From time to time, we found ourselves in port with sister ships of similar vintage, but always CLAN MACKINNON was the smartest and best kept. Sadly, many years later I saw the MACKINNON in Manchester Docks, and she was nothing like as smart as she had been under George Spiller.

Crossing the Indian Ocean and sailing up the Red Sea we were kept very busy on a number of tasks, including making a new pilot ladder. There was great excitement when we turned to at 0700 on Tuesday 6th April and found the empty horse boxes stowed on the poop were ablaze. Fire at sea is a very serious matter, there are no fire brigades, and we had to put the fire out without help and quickly too.

On this occasion, the importance of speaking Hindustani was emphasised when stressed crew members, who spoke very little English, reverted to their own tongue, and orders had to be given in their language to be effective. There is a lesson here for modern ships where the Indian crews have to speak English because the Officers do not know their language, and in an emergency they will revert to their own language. Our fire was put out after some difficulty and both crew and Officers were calm, cool and collected. Hindustani was the only language used. The Cassab (store-keeper) was noteworthy for his bravery in entering a blazing horse-box to retrieve some burning gear, but everyone did well and, eventually, we put the fire out, albeit after much damage had been done.

We arrived at Suez at noon, entering the Canal at 1630, and reaching the Bitter Lakes about 1900 where the south-bound convoy passed us. John and I were on 'watch-and-watch', four hours on then four hours off, rather tiring after a while as one never had more than three hours continuous sleep. We had a quick passage and reached Port Said at 0330 and, after landing the searchlight and unloading some cargo, we commenced the final passage home to London, Tilbury at 1330.

Through the Mediterranean we were put to hard work sprucing the ship for arrival in London, where the keen eyes of the Marine Superintendent would be inspecting the ship with particular reference to the condition of the vessel and its equipment. Two days were spent cleaning out the water tanks which were first drained, then one of us went inside in a space about 6 feet by 4 feet by 4 feet. This was not ideal for anyone of a claustrophobic disposition such as me. Each tank was scraped, wire-brushed, and then cement washed ... a tricky job when one was inside the tank and had to get out in such a way that it was possible to lean down and paint the last spot in which you had been kneeling.

Some days later the weather blew up and at 1900 we were turned out to cover all the ventilators and batten everything down. The gale only lasted a couple of days, and by the time that we had passed Gibraltar it had blown itself out and we could resume normal work.

Next day, we passed Cape St. Vincent and headed north. This spelt the onset of 'the channels', otherwise known as Channel Fever, when one began to think of home and the possibility of leave. Each evening in the Mediterranean and northward we had a poker school for which I had very little enthusiasm as we were playing for cigarettes. In fact, as a non-smoker, I ended up with several hundred cigarettes which I later used as currency.

The day before we passed Cape Finisterre, we stopped working on deck and were put on Bridge watches. On April 19th, we sighted St. Catherine's Point in the Isle of Wight, our first sight of home for three months. Later we sailed along the south coast, then up through the Goodwins and so into the Thames, arriving off the lock entrance to Tilbury Docks at about 2100.

Next morning, H. M. Customs sent for me, and somewhat concerned, I duly met with an elderly customs officer who started off by asking me what I had to declare ... and then he gave me a long lecture on the perils of smuggling. He had discovered that I was on my first voyage and thought it wise to give me some avuncular advice, pointing out that no matter what smuggling device I tried, they had seen it all before. To demonstrate, he folded down the top of his sock, then folded it up again, leaving a handy place to conceal gems! He also pointed out the efficiency of customs' spies on the ship and overseas. I later found the truth of this as the Chief Steward had smuggled in a special Masonic ring made in Galle and only three of us knew about this ... John Bedford, myself and the Carpenter, and as John and I had not informed H. M. Customs, there are no prizes for guessing who had informed them..

Shortly afterwards, I was sent up to the Clan Line Offices with the ship's papers and, after lunch, was given leave and made my way north where the family awaited me on Macclesfield Station. In India and Ceylon, I had bought presents for my parents and grandparents as well as for my brother, but perhaps more important was the food I brought. In those days of food rationing, we were allowed to bring in 25 lbs weight of food with no more that 5 lbs of any one commodity. I had bought my full quota in Bombay ... mostly tinned goods and sugar.

My leave lasted for a week and, then, I was back to sea and we sailed two days later for Rotterdam, Antwerp, Middlesbrough, Dundee and Glasgow, our home port.

Thank you, John. That was an excellent account of your opening voyage. Over many years I had the privilege of meeting young men before their first trip to sea. I was never quite sure of their thoughts as they set out on their chosen careers, but one thing I am certain of is that when they returned they were men.

Captain John Turner has given us the rare privilege of sharing his thoughts about training, but does stress that they are personal to him. There are endless tales told about the fearsome examiners, most were naturally exaggerated and many were apocryphal. Not one ship's Officer forgets his examinations for the various Certificates of Competency. John Turner tells a tale that will be near to many an Officer's heart.

In Liverpool, one examiner, named Keatings, was supposed to have above his door an advertisement which was said to read

... 'Keatings kills bugs, fleas and cockroaches' ... and he was supposed to have added the words ... 'and you, too, if you do not know your Articles'. It should be noted that 'Articles' meant the collision regulations.

In London, there was supposed to have been an examiner, Captain Saul, who repeatedly failed one candidate who finally stood at the door saying 'Saul, Saul, why persecutest thou me?' Upon this, Saul is supposed to have called the man back, gave him another chance and passed him! This really sounds like an imaginary tale as Captain Saul was later met and he seemed to be a nice and perfect gentleman. The tales are endless and the examiners never appear in a good light.

Liverpool was the examination centre for North West England, and although there was a nautical School in Fleetwood, all candidates had to be examined for their Certificates of Competency in Liverpool. The Liverpool Nautical College has since become John Moores University, and from at least 1950 to 1957 the buildings also housed the local bricklayers school to the disadvantage of the latter it has to be said! At 'school' as the college was affectionately known to the students, the staff were both long-suffering and patient. Generally, they were very good, mostly they held Extra Master's Certificates.

The students were a very mixed bunch. Some, to their credit, had done over four years as seamen before the mast, some had been Cadets as per normal, but a few had also served as Uncertificated Third and Fourth Officers. However, at school all were treated the same. Occasionally, if they had done something silly, they would be shouted at, but always they were treated with some respect as 'Mr ....'. To those who had been lucky enough to have been at a Training Ship, it really was very easy for Second Mate, especially if one had been given the opportunities to learn aboard ship. All that was required was some thorough revision. For others it was very hard.

Except for Blue Funnel who paid their Midshipmen in full,

the rest were paid an amount less 26 shillings a week which
had to be claimed from the 'dole office' … the 'twenty-six
club' as it was named by candidates. This office was located
in Renshaw Street, and the staff there well understood the
situation. Thus, when one claimed 'dole' they never ordered
anyone to other work. In local country offices, however, it
was a different matter during holidays and one experienced the
greatest difficulty explaining why one should not become, say,
a dustman! Ship-owners, at that time, had a legal obligation to
pay two months for Second Mates and First Mates Certificates,
and three months for Masters. Having said this, the course
lasted two months for the Mates Certificates. There would then
be two unpaid weeks of revision and two unpaid weeks for the

Liverpool Nautical College   1960

Top Row   L to R

Tom Maddox. George Singleton. Tom Ferryman.
Keith Jones. Gordon Salisbury.
Ossie Stewart. Rob Screech. Ray Morton.
Frank Holland. Geoff Nelson. Ron brittlebank.
Safda Azad. Cliff Steer.

Bottom L to R: Manhire. Lewthwaite. Commander Coffey
Twntyman. Webb.

actual examinations. In short, one either had wealthy parents or had to get it finished whilst on pay! Luckily, I did the latter.

Liverpool was unusual in that candidates were all expected to have Lifeboat Certificates, although this was not a statutory requirement like the First Aid Certificate. It first required attendance at the Lifeboat School, under the tutelage of one Captain Taylor, a uniformed ex-Master in the Blue Star Line. He was an amazing character much given to yelling and bawling. Occasionally, he would be on his knees praying for the class, and at other times, he would be shouting, "You bloody murderer", to anyone who did something stupid! For those used to boatwork, it was child's play, but to others such as Stewards it was a terrible ordeal. Part of the time was spent in the classroom and some was spent in a filthy lifeboat. Captain Taylor would sometimes drop a lifejacket over the side, yelling, "Man overboard!" That required whoever was acting as helmsman to react quickly. The examination itself was conducted by a Captain Vincent who was very fair and came as a breath of fresh air to all.

The First Aid Class was also very amusing and, it has to be said, the examination was very easy. Candidates were supposed to learn the name of all the bones as part of the course. For this purpose there was a skeleton christened 'Horace' by the class. Inevitably, at the beginning of each session poor old 'Horace' was suspended by a noose from the neck by a rope thrown over a beam, or he would be put into some impossible contortion, or into some rather rude situation! The poor old instructor was nearly reduced to tears at times. Halfway through the afternoon, a rather naive young lady brought tea for which there was a charge. The class sometimes paid by dropping coins down her front, or she was accidentally on purpose pushed with vociferous apologies and a straying hand clutching at her ample bosom. Nowadays, there would be accusations of sexual harassment, and what was then thought of as really harmless fun would now be taken very seriously indeed.

The actual examinations were then taken in three parts ... signalling, written papers and an oral session. For the signalling, the Second Mates examination was carried out by a Chief Yeoman of Signals at the Admiralty Signal School, and it was widely rumoured that for a ten shilling note (50p today) anything not understood should be left blank, and he would fill in the blanks! Everyone attended the Signal School for a short time and all duly handed over their money at the end and all passed their exam ... or so it was said. In fact, if candidates had been to a pre-sea Training Ship, the speeds were not fast and this was by far the easiest part of the exam ... a fifty-word message by semaphore, a twenty-five-word message by morse lamp and a block of maybe one hundred jumbled letters and numbers by morse key.

The written examinations for all Certificates took place over three days or so, and they were very strictly invigilated. Each desk was separated from the neighbours by six feet ... front, back and to each side. Slide rules were banned and calculators had not been invented. Beforehand, the candidates were severely warned about cheating. There was always someone prowling round the room and nobody was allowed to go to the toilets, but in an emergency the clerk is said to have accompanied the candidate and the doors had to be left open! For certain examinations nautical almanacs and nautical tables were provided, but if you wanted to use your own books, they had to be submitted the day before for a very thorough inspection and they were retained overnight.

Overall in the written examinations, the aggregate percentage marks had to be very high, and for navigation all candidates had to obtain at least three quarters of all marks ... navigation is a very exact science, in which only slight mathematical errors were permitted and all errors in principle resulted in failure.

Oral examinations were always considered to be the hardest and to some extent they depended on the individual examiner. You were taught in the school that for one examiner one answer should be given, but for another it should be phrased differently.

I had two amusing incidents (in hindsight!) in the orals and one resulted in failure, although every other examination was passed right up to and including Master's.

It so happened that for Second Mate, Captain Vincent conducted this particular examination, which commenced with a table full of buoys. I was given a model ship and had to navigate through a very twisty channel. Grabbing the model, there was so much hand shaking due to nervousness that several buoys ended up on the floor, whilst all the others were moved far out of position. Captain Vincent, then considered to be the toughest examiner, pointed out that he was there to pass candidates and not to fail them, unless they did not know the answers. He asked me to turn away from the table whilst he rearranged the buoys. Before grasping the ship, Vincent asked that my hands be firmly placed on the table palms down, applying downward pressure, then to take the ship ... this cured the shakes and the exercise was carried out without fault. All nervousness had disappeared.

For First Mate, it was different and the examiner was the Principal Examiner, Captain Douthwaite. The examination was initially perfectly fair, and all questions were answered correctly, until he posed a hypothetical case. My ship was in heavy weather with seas coming over the fo'c'sle head, and No. 1 hatch was stove in. The question was then asked ... "What action would you take?" The obvious reply was that the ship should immediately heave to until the seas stopped coming over the bow and then the damage had to be made good. Douthwaite rolled his eyes and said "No! Try again". The same reply was given ... and I was told to come back in two weeks.

The tutorial staff at the school were told and all were flummoxed. They all argued that the question had been answered correctly. Anyone faced with such a situation just had to stop heavy seas breaking over the bow by heaving to or by slowing down the ship and the damage just had to be repaired.

Now for a first failure, if it were very small, there could be a re-sit in two weeks. Thereafter two months at sea had to elapse before re-examination and the whole exam had to be re-taken! In the case of a really serious error, say leading to a potential loss of life, six months sea time could be prescribed. Thus it was with great fear and trepidation that re-appearance took place before the orals were re-taken!

In the event, Captain Douthwaite was busy, so it was Captain Vincent who opened with the self same question. He was given the same answer and he heaved a sigh of relief saying, "Why could you not give that answer before?" It was very tempting to say, "I did!" but that temptation was resisted. There were no further questions and those magical words 'passed' were quickly written on the form.

For Master, the examiner was the dreaded Captain Fletcher, who had failed all the candidates the previous week! He had the most fearsome reputation. In actual fact, he was very fair, very very thorough, and the examination seemed to go on for ever. If in the end a pass was recorded, the candidate felt utterly exhausted as if he had been through a mangle!

Years later, Fletcher was seated opposite at a lunch of the Honourable Company of Master Mariners and he leaned across saying, "Have I not seen you before?" Replying in the affirmative, Fletcher said, "Then you have a real Master's Ticket!" How very right he was. Nevertheless, he was a very interesting table companion. He had very bad wartime experiences and had little or no sense of humour. But, he was a very straight and honest man and, although he did not suffer fools gladly and was intolerant of inefficiency, he was a fine seaman indeed.

There cannot be any ship's Officer who does not remember these examinations for the various Certificates of Competency, this despite enormous changes in format as modern technology develops. In the early fifties, Britain had the biggest Merchant Navy in the world and top shipping companies could pick and choose their Officers. That is no longer the case and we now have one of the smallest numbers of ships sailing under the Red Ensign. There is already a shortage of trained personnel and the problem will worsen as demand grows for Pilots, Harbour Masters and other qualified Master Mariners.

Thank you, Captain John Turner, O.B.E., for all your thoughts and especially for the notes on training. John is an OLD WORCESTER and admits being biased in their favour, but states that he will always give his many OLD CONWAY friends a fair hearing! He did offer me a footnote.

Writing notes brings back happy memories, but the most nostalgic of all in WORCESTER were the evening prayers at which we sang "Eternal Father, strong to save ... " every Saturday night and often on a Sunday evening we had "The day thou gavest Lord is ended ... " Our Padre, known as 'Holy Joe' (the Reverend G.P. Jodrell-Day) tried very hard to give us religious instruction, but we regarded it as almost relaxation, if not comic relief!

Thank you, again, John. There was so much more that you had written in your books and private memoirs ... sadly space controls all.

The stories continue in
Volume Two